SO-AYE-904

ANTHROPOLOGY
OF SPACE

ANTHROPOLOGY OF SPACE

Explorations into
the Natural Philosophy
and Semantics
of the Navajo

Rik
Pinxten

Ingrid
van Dooren

Frank
Harvey

University of Pennsylvania Press
Philadelphia   1983

Library of Congress Cataloging in Publication Data

Pinxten, Rik.
  Anthropology of space.

  Bibliography: p.
  Includes index.
  1. Navaho Indians—Philosophy.   2. Navaho language—
Semantics.   3. Space perception—Case studies.   4. Cog-
nition and culture—Southwest, New—Case studies.
5. Indians of North America—Southwest, New—Philosophy.
I. Van Dooren, Ingrid.   II. Harvey, Frank.   III. Series.
E99.N3P56   1983   306'.08997   82-23703
ISBN 0-8122-7879-8

Printed in the United States of America

Designed by Tracy Baldwin

To Leo Apostel,
the inspiring and challenging friend

Contents

Figures

Foreword

Rik Pinxten has done a yeoman job collecting, analyzing, and synthesizing very complex Navajo data. With his background, unencumbered by American traditions of Navajo ethnography, he brings a new and fresh outlook on Navajo world view. More focally to this book, he attacks successfully the unbelievably extensive and elegantly complex Navajo spatial terminology.

Pinxten's semantic analysis is synthetic rather than analytic. Whether he is actually more synthetic (descriptive) than analytic (universalist) is an interesting question that need not be resolved in this brief preface. However, this book should lead to an intensive discussion of these notions that will benefit all concerned.

A great strength of this volume is that Pinxten takes a very clear, explicit position. He does not hedge his point of view and honestly tells his readers exactly where he stands. Such a book is bound to be controversial. But the controversy will illuminate the difficult problem of indigenous spatial terminologies and their description.

Pinxten's careful fieldwork, with the competent assistance of Ingrid Van Dooren and the able collaboration of Frank Harvey, make his Navajo materials his greatest strength. The introductory Chapter I (The Natural Philosophy of Navajo Language and World View) sets the stage by exploring the general principles of Navajo world view. This fresh look at the Navajo will be of particular interest to specialists. For some the Navajo materials may be confusing because Pinxten's view breaks clearly with the past and the "Harmony" dogma of Clyde Kluckhohn and his successors. The best advice one can give anyone who reads about the Navajo world view for the first time is to look at both views and let the evidence, especially the evidence backed up by the Navajo's own philosophical statements, determine his or her final judgment.

Perhaps the most controversial aspect of Pinxten's work is his Universal Frame of Reference (UFOR). The attempt is heroic: to present the spatial terminology available in any human language by a single standard, a maximally complete set of spatial discriminations that human beings are capable of making. That is, Pinxten's UFOR is intended to do for the conceptualization of space what Munsell color chips do for the conceptualization of color. The modern view of the color solid (or its Mercator projection represented by the Munsell color chips) has been around for about a century. The creation of an analogous set of universal categories of space (UFOR) is a grand, new undertaking which Pinxten first tried out a few years ago by deriving an earlier draft of the UFOR from the spatial terminology of the Dogon of Africa.

It is well to remember what the introduction of the Munsell scales did for the ethnographic research into color terminologies: First, it allowed for the identification of focal colors that are almost identical in all cultures and thus paved the way for the work by Berlin and Kay (1969), establishing a set of perceptual/physiological universals. Second, it permitted a quasi-evolutionary statement of the development of color terminologies from simple cultures to more complex social forms. The development of the UFOR, by providing a uniform standard against which to "measure" the spatial terminological system of any people, will certainly encourage interesting research in the social and cognitive sciences and may lead to the recognition of perceptual universals as well.

It is unreasonable to hope that the UFOR and its application to cross-cultural research into physical, social, and ideological spaces will solve all problems. However, if its application to the Navajo data contributes, first, to a better formulation of the UFOR, and second, to a universally valid description of spatial terminologies in other parts of the world, then this book will have done more than its share to push this important frontier forward.

Pinxten's work has already inspired applied research projects designed to improve the mathematical/geometrical education of Navajo children. The book literally cries out for such applications and Pinxten himself makes several valuable suggestions within this book about the implementation of such didactic goals (chap. V). A volume that combines the highest standards of philosophical and epistemological research coupled with theoretical innovation into the semantics of spatial terminologies, and one that offers practical solutions to burning problems of Navajo education at the same time, is a rare book indeed.

Rik Pinxten started this work as a Fulbright-Hays postdoctoral fellow at Northwestern University. This book is a new departure and a continuation of work undertaken by some of my students, particularly Edward Garrison (1974), James McNeley (1977 and 1981), John Farella (1980), Judith Remington (1981); of unpublished work by Kenneth Begishe, G. Mark Schoepfle, Norris Minick, Joel Fagan, and Judith Abbott; and of some of my work (especially Werner, 1968, and Werner and Begishe, 1970). This places Rik Pinxten's book in a Northwestern University context. Perhaps more important is the fact that, coming from a European philosophical tradition with his own theoretical framework, Pinxten has created a volume that is new and unique.

Oswald Werner

Evanston, Illinois
December 1, 1981

Acknowledgments

It is my greatest honor to thank numerous people who helped us in various ways during and since the stay on the Navajo reservation. I thank the Wenner Gren Foundation for a grant-in-aid I was awarded,[1] and the Council on Education (U.S. Department of Health, Education and Welfare) for a similar grant. I acknowledge the warm and often lasting interest and advice of L. Apostel and F. Vandamme in Belgium, and D. Campbell, John Farella, Clifford Geertz, Edward Garrison, Paul Kay, D. Lancy, Oswald Werner, W. Willink, and Gary Witherspoon in the United States. I am grateful to Lars Mogensen and Padmini Sankaran, who kindly corrected my English. It is perhaps my lack of openness with respect to critiques that will be responsible for the mistakes and shortcomings that may be found in this work. A special word of gratitude goes to Robert W. Young, who kindly corrected the Navajo texts. And last but not least, to Kathleen and Erik Soberon for preparation of the manuscript.

Most of all I thank the Navajo consultants, my landlord, and the members of the Tribal Council who made it possible and really enjoyable to work and live among them for a while. Not only that, but they also convinced me of the irreplaceable value of fieldwork as an endeavor of human beings in search of a better understanding of oneself and of others.

1. Wenner Gren Foundation grant 322-64-7826 for fieldwork 1976–77, with the Navajo Indians of Arizona, U.S.A. I also acknowledge a Fulbright-Hays grant which allowed me to spend some time in the United States as Appointed Researcher of the Belgian National Science Foundation (N.F.W.O.).

Introduction

I did fieldwork among Navajo Indians for ten months (1976–77). The complexity and beauty of Navajo thought and culture often fascinated me, during and after the actual fieldwork. My combined philosophical and anthropological background may have helped me in some instances to grasp the Navajo perspective on the problems talked about; it may have been a mere hindrance in other instances. In this study I present a complex analysis of Navajo spatial semantics and natural philosophy, with some pretensions to depth in analysis. The treatise may, in places, appear rather unusual for the anthropologist, and it is certainly quite uncommon to philosophers. I hope that the gap between armchair and fieldwork research is what strikes both, and the present work offers at least an attempt to bridge the traditional separation between the two "kinds" of work. In particular, I concentrate on the concepts of "space" and "nature" in the Navajo knowledge system, because I believe these concepts (and others) to be of importance in both disciplines.

In this Introduction I will give a point-by-point survey of several theoretical views we share. This is done in order to enable the reader to understand clearly the theoretical context in which the work grew and from which the discussions arose. At the end of the Introduction I will very briefly outline the structure of the content of the book.

Anthropological Position

I explicitly claim to work within cognitive anthropology proper. But, while this kind of study tends to concentrate on applications of sophisticated methodological principles and models on pretty well-defined subjects, the present work takes a different position.

I share the general interest of cognitive anthropologists (ethnoscientists, ethnosemanticists, and others) in knowledge. I agree also that the study of community can sensibly and profitably focus on its system of knowledge. Indeed, I believe that knowledge systems are of a central concern to man as an agent, a knower, and a perceiver; the study of the cultural knowledge system consequently gives important insights into the behavioral, linguistic, and mythological scope of a community and its individual members of the world and man's place in the world.

In contrast to "classical" cognitive anthropologists (most of all the ethnoscientists), I believe it is possible and indeed important to investigate comprehensive categories of knowledge, rather than to concentrate on readily definable, but sometimes peripheral, subsystems of knowledge, e.g., timber-wood classifications or, maybe, kinship. Thus, I think that the study of categories such as "space," "time," "universe," "man," etc., is overdue in cognitive anthropology. One cannot do the comprehensive job at once, and I choose to concentrate on "space" for the present study. However, I aimed at thoroughly analyzing spatial behavior and statements about spatial differentiations in Navajo cultural knowledge. In order to study a category as broad as "space," I developed a device for semantic analysis, called the "Universal Frame of Reference" for spatial analysis (UFOR). It is meant to have universal validity, that is, it presumably transcends any individual or cultural bias and, at the same time it effects deep and sensible analyses of spatial representations and differentiations within any particular cultural knowledge system. Detailed information on the device is given in Appendix B.

A second contrast to "classical" cognitive anthropologists is in the emphasis on the relevance of a people's natural philosophy. While this aspect of knowledge is usually disregarded altogether by anthropologists (with few exceptions), I favor a strong emphasis on natural philosophical insights for the understanding of broader categories such as "space."

A third point of divergence from the "mainstream" cognitive anthropologists is more technical in nature. I attempt to offer a nonaprioristic and indeed purely synthetic semantic analysis (cf. "semantics" below). One of the more striking effects of this position is the absence of taxonomic and (ethnoscientific) paradigmatic models.

Finally, I claim no logical primacy or other superstatus for my sort of study within anthropological studies, but I emphasize that this and similar (cognitive anthropological) studies give important insights into the system and range of a culture. Symbolic, social, economic, or other anthropological investigations may accomplish the same. But, let it simply be said that the present kind of study aims to give information about Navajo culture that was entirely lacking or unavailable in any consistent way for a deeper understanding of that particular culture.

Anthropology and Philosophy

I think that the philosophical (epistemological and methodological) views of a fieldworker matter a great deal in his actual observations and in his way of reporting, since, of course, his subject matter is a group of people who think on their own. One way this surfaces is through the selection of some aspects of a culture rather than others. In this study we claim that the Navajo's fundamental conception of "nature" is important: Navajos seem to stress both process rather than substance and cohesion rather than segmentability of reality. Taking into account such insights from consultants puts considerable constraints on the method and the models that may be appropriate for an adequate description of Navajo space. This was how the regard for Navajo philosophical insights had an effect on this research.

At the most general level, however, the interference of philosophical insights of both researcher and consultant shows in the orientation of research. The insights function there as a heuristic means in the actual fieldwork. Indeed, not only broad categories like time, space, and universe, but also process, state, thing, system, part, and whole are not universally and uniformly given in any particular culture in the world. Even partial recognition of differences in these respects between the researcher's and the native's opinions can yield most important results. These broad categories serve as "vehicles" for less englobing concepts and subsystems of thought, and thus offer the necessary heuristic devices for description and interpretation to the fieldworker. This can be illustrated most strikingly with an example from Navajo studies: two eminent researchers of Navajo thought and social life speak on the one hand about "amorality" (Berard Haile) and, on the other, of "magic practices" (Gladys Reichard) concerning Navajo morals. An insight into their own biases and into the opinions of the relationships between man and nature in the Navajo knowledge system would have offered the opportunity of questioning and discussing the topic of morality consistent with the native (Navajo) opinions on the structure of the world. It would have avoided recurrence of either "amorality" or "magic practices" as explanations for that which was not understood properly (cf. Pinxten, 1979b).

It is in this context that I decided to investigate and make an exposition of Navajo natural philosophy (chap. I).

It is probably incomplete, but it serves the purpose of presenting a concise survey of some points that appear to be of central concern to anyone who wants to deal with Navajo spatial knowledge.

Although it cannot be said that all people are eager (neither among the Navajos, nor in our own culture) to discuss such matters, some really were. I have met some eminent thinkers among Navajos. Moreover, even with native nonthinkers (nonphilosophers) the relevance of the philosophical insights to other aspects of the cultural knowledge was recognized. Philosophical insights cannot be considered outlandish or totally separated from common knowledge in Navajo opinion. In general, the native philosopher seemed to focus on the more general relationships between convictions and opinions. This did not lead to extravagant ideas on his part, since totally idiosyncratic outlooks showed themselves extremely rarely. It is obvious that the status of thought and thinkers in the Navajo context eased the identification of thinkers for us. It did not make it any easier to get the information, however, since knowledge is a part of the world the Navajos live in and, consequently, cannot be traded or given away carelessly.

Navajo and Western Outlooks

There is no systematic comparison of Navajo and Western outlooks in this book. Any differences that were deemed relevant to the study are presented by means of detailed ethnographic and ethnolinguistic material. Thus differences with respect to spatial semantics are dealt with in the analysis of linguistic material (chap. III) and in the presentation of a model of Navajo space (chap. IV). Differences with respect to training and schooling in spatial thought are dealt with in Chapter V.

Here, in this general introduction, I would like to add a very broad comparison between Navajo and Western outlooks. It should not be considered as a genuine analysis, but rather as a guiding rule for the reader.

The biologist Waddington (1977) strikes the right note in the opening of his brilliant little book, with the observation that several pressing problems in the sciences might be solved more easily, that the Western scientist shifts from a world perspective constituting "things" and "states" to a world perspective constituting "processes" and "events." In the context of Navajo studies a similar guiding rule can be spelled out for the Westerner: Navajo knowledge cannot really be understood unless one adopts a very clearly processual or dynamic view. The processual view that is apparent in Navajo knowledge is different from the one Waddington speaks of. For one thing, the Navajo view is more particular. Nevertheless, the attitude and the kind of shift that is expected from the Western observer is similar to the one referred to by Waddington.

With reference to Western outlooks another difference, I am convinced, is that Navajo knowledge is strictly action-bound in a way Western knowledge is not. That is, not only do most Navajo notions have a clear meaning in terms of action (as they do in the Western system), but moreover they are most often defined with reference to action. The subtlety of this difference is difficult to render in full. Yet it cannot be denied. The short chapter on educational payoff brings this point out clearly.

Semantics

With the employment of the UFOR goes a different view of the nature and function of semantic models. This study is not primarily concerned with philosophical semantics, but aims to work in the domain of descriptive semantics. In that domain its aim is to give a complete illustration of the power and usefulness of semantic modeling that denies any analytical or a priori elements of meaning. The present work thus constitutes an alternative to the classical Katzian semantic stand. It is an alternative that is hospitable to Quine's fierce critiques of analyticity. At the same time I believe I have been able to overcome Quine's pessimism concerning translatability to some degree. I cannot really develop these ideas here, but refer the reader to the extended presentation (chap. II).

Anthropology and Application

The mere awareness of the difference in status and appreciation of knowledge and instruction in Navajo and in Western settings points to the near impossibility of a Western type of schooling within the Navajo cultural outlook. The critique of the schooling systems can be dealt with in two ways: one can either focus on the institutional or organizational aspects, or one can take a look at contents.

The critique of the institutional aspects of Western education in the Navajo cultural context has not been taken up in this work. On the other hand, the critique of the contents of instruction is dealt with to some extent in Chapter V. It is suggested that, in view of the structure of spatial knowledge as revealed in the foregoing chapters, classical "Western" mathematics and sciences in the curriculum of any school on the reservation could lead to many misunderstandings and, eventually, to alienation from Navajo tradition. Attempts are made to reconstruct the basic presuppositions of such curricula and to introduce a "genuinely native" entry into sophisticated knowledge of the structure of the world.

Short Survey

The chain of thought that runs through this book is divided into several chapters. I can trace the line I followed through the characterization of the chapters:

Chapter I presents the "natural philosophy" of Navajos and thus makes the reader familiar with the philosophical background of the Navajos. The reader will need this background to understand the construction of "Navajo space."

Chapter II discusses several theoretical questions in semantics and prepares the reader for the use of the UFOR in descriptive semantic parts.

Chapter III is very long. It presents the bulk of empirical evidence for the book (apart from that in Chapter I) and lists statements and descriptions of

Navajo usage of spatial differentiations. The material has been elicited and ordered in the field by means of the UFOR.

Chapter IV presents the semantic model of Navajo space. It draws on the evidence of Chapters I and III and applies the principles discussed and outlined in Chapter II.

Chapter V is a reevaluation of the impact of contemporary curricula on the reservation schools. Its aim is to present alternatives for instruction in mathematics and the sciences, particularly by taking into account the information gained in all foregoing chapters.

"The Device" is in Appendix B. It gives a brief presentation of the UFOR, the main tool for descriptive semantics in the perspective I favor.

1 | The Natural Philosophy of Navajo Language and World View

Preliminary Remarks[1]

The term "natural philosophy" is used in the sense of Russell (1914) or Goodman (1968): it denotes the set of interrelated notions about or the basic characteristics of the world as perceived in the commonsense knowledge of the members of a community, which is most often implicitly presupposed in the conscious, and explicitly elicitable or debatable. It comprises the basic ontological and epistemological presuppositions inured in the way of perceiving, acting upon, or thinking and talking about the world in a particular culture. Therefore, it cannot be elicited from a random member of the community, precisely as Russell or Goodman could not, at will, elicit the "natural philosophy," that is, the contemporary scientific view of nature and the structure of the world, from any random physicist, biologist, or the like. Still, scientists could be said to work in the same kind of "world" as is characterized on the explicit level by such general features as being subject to physical, chemical, and biological laws, being alterable or controllable in certain respects, and so forth. Some researchers tend to concern themselves primarily with basic concepts, and hence to stress the implications of certain natural physical presuppositions as opposed to others. Einstein's theorizing on the basic identity of mass and energy is a famous case in point (e.g., Einstein, 1949).

I do not wish to push this argument concerning Navajo natural philosophy as it stands, but rather pursue two of its general consequences which I find particularly fruitful and convincing: a) it is obvious that one must be aware of the natural philosophy of a particular community in order to understand the statements and theories of a community in a proper, intrinsic context, and b) certain people of any society tend to concern themselves explicitly with this basic level of "dealing with the world."

I am convinced that Navajos do indeed have a distinctive world view which is embodied in their language, their actions, their social organization, in fact in the whole of their culture. The mere existence of an abundance of studies of their specific ways is sufficient evidence in this regard (cf. espe-

1. I am grateful to Oswald Werner, Willy Willink, and Fernand Vandamme for critical comments on this chapter. Most of all, the patience of our consultants in such difficult matters should be acknowledged most heartily.

cially Kluckhohn, 1964; Witherspoon, 1977; and Werner, Manning, and Be-gishe, in press). Moreover, it is our conviction that thinkers on this basic level of "Navajo natural philosophy" exist and are still active in the Navajo community, as in ours. Their social position, their relations to ordinary people might differ from those of their Western colleagues, but their preoccupations tend to be quite similar.[2] One difference we see is the one defined by the mediation of anthropologists: the researcher most probably gets an account as comprehensive and systematic as possible from a native philosopher, thus imposing some system or model in the process. Also the difficulty in attaining the explicitness demanded from the (rarely confronted) informants, on the topics concerned, might pose definite limits on the endeavor.

In conducting this particular research, I moved around and asked questions at random on specific deities, on the apparent generality of the concept of motion in the Navajo language, on specific social rules and taboos, on time and space, and on the nature of the universe. Gradually, some explicit rules were found to have a common ground in the views on nature and existence. A series of more pointed questions was constructed, as a second attempt, to attain both clarity and deeper information. Further systematic questioning and relating of the questions and answers were engaged in, by both researcher and consultants. Subsequently, a first draft of the text was written out, featuring the Navajo correlates to basic (Western) natural philosophical notions. Finally, I went through this first draft systematically, correcting it and elaborating on it with one consultant, working on the whole, and with several others on certain parts only.

The material obtained is organized under the following headings:
a) structure and general form of the universe/world;
b) dynamic nature of the world; the concepts of winds, time, and being;
c) boundedness of the world; the notion of a center;
d) closedness of the world, orderliness;
e) interrelatedness of "all things that were placed."

These labels refer to the presumably basic Navajo ontological categories, and as such serve as the Navajo correlates to the Western ontological concepts. The procedure of selecting such concepts in Navajo thought and of organizing them and segmenting them along the proposed lines certainly betrays a Western way of dealing with knowledge systems; the actual contents of the chosen labels, however, is basically Navajo. The purpose of the introduction is thus to delineate the impact of both native Navajo and basically Western concepts and biases.

On all matters discussed, Frank Harvey worked as the main interpreter and consultant. Generally, two or three of us worked together with the following consultants on the material: CM, BW, BB, M-AL, AD, LT, HT, TB, and LB, both men and women, from 26 to 104 years of age.

Since Frank Harvey had such an important role both in the position of

---

2. This idea is not new, of course. It has been advocated brilliantly by the late Paul Radin, who pointed out the presence of "thinkers" and "doers" in any society (Radin, 1957, p. 1).

consultant and that of interpreter for the present chapter, this name is never explicitly mentioned in the text, but presupposed for the complete information discussed. We corrected and reread the text together and he agreed with all the information it contains. All quotations without source are references from him, while only the affirming, declining, or modifying remarks from others are explicitly attributed to the particular speaker (the name following the particular statements, in brackets). In general then, the text can be said to report partially or fully or to multiply asserted beliefs on these matters,[3] as elicited from persons of different sex and age in an area of the present Navajo reservation roughly confined to the locations surrounding Lukachukai, Tsaile, Rock Point, Crystal, Tonalea, Sweetwater, and Round Rock.

The Structure of the World

The general belief of the universe, as conceived of in traditional Navajo belief, is illustrated in some detail in the form of the hooghan (house). This fact was stressed by several consultants on many occasions, and in literature, for example, by Berard Haile.[4] Finally, it is said to be depicted in the Navajo wedding basket as well.

The Navajo world or universe[5] consists of a shallow, flat disk in the form of a dish, topped by a similar form which covers it like a lid. The lower part is the Earth, while the upper part (the lid, so to speak) is the Sky. Neither of these forms can be conceived of as genuinely round, dishlike forms, since both are represented as human or anthropomorphic forms, lying down in an arching stretched manner, one on top of the other. The lower one is Mother Earth, nahasdzáán shimá, lying from east to west, while the upper one is Father Heaven, yá' shitaa', lying in the same direction, on top of and above the Earth.

The Navajo world is definitely bounded by the Four Sacred Moun-

---

3. This is sometimes a delicate matter: some persons only possess part of the knowledge to be had, or restrict themselves from talking freely and fully about it, or distrust white people enough to report about it in a systematically evasive way. Individual testimonies are thus sometimes difficult to compare: one person is willing to go into details on some point (because he feels like it, or because he knows this part well . . .) but not on another, while a second person displays totally different emphases and preferences.

4. Father Berard Haile was inclined to use the "hooghan" as a major introductory notion to the Navajo universe. This is apparent in his introduction to the magnificent work on Blessing Way (the "backbone" of Navajo mythology); however, this introduction was not included in the final edition of the work by Wyman (1975). The original can be consulted in manuscript form at the Library of the Museum of Northern Arizona, Flagstaff.

5. The terms "world" and "universe" are used throughout this book for creation, the totality of things, and events known in the Navajo conception. The term "earth," however, refers to the lower part exclusively, that is, the part of the earth that is inhabited by Navajos. "Earth" and "Sky" (with capitals) are terms used in the Navajo mythological vocabulary, referring to approximately the same physical instances, but restricted to their mythological (and somewhat anthropomorphic) sense.

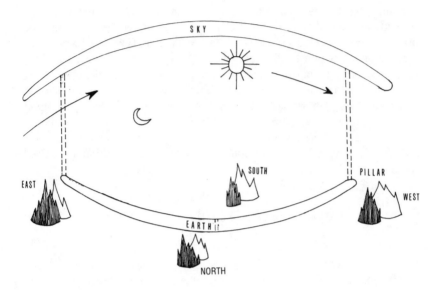

Fig. 1   The structure of the world.[6] Cross section.

tains, located roughly in the East, West, South, and North, working out a territory that approximately covers the Northern halves of the present-day states of Arizona and New Mexico. The territory defined by these mountains (for particular names and places see below) is *the* world, exclusively for the diné or people, the Navajos. The sky, with the air, moon, sun, and stars under it, arches over the earth realizing a domelike or indeed hooghanlike global form. The one opening to the East is essential. Furthermore, the sky does not really touch the earth at any place, not even at the horizon. Instead, the air between Earth and Sky continues under the earth's surface, on its backside so to speak, leaving enough space at any point for the sun and moon to pass through.

A sketch of the general form may clarify this description. It should be kept in mind, however, that a clearly three-dimensional world is depicted:

The general characteristics of the world can thus be summed up, in close similarity to the physical characteristics of the hooghan:

a) The global, domelike shape is oriented in a space dominated by the four major directions: East, South, West, and North. The sole opening of the world is directed toward the East, that is, the sunrise position (just as the opening of the hooghan is always eastward);

b) The basically correct way of moving about in a hooghan is clockwise (East, South, West, and North), that is, corresponding to the sun's movement during the day in the outside world;

6. Consultants tended to refuse or at the least to evade any actual picturing or designing of earth, sky, or universe.

c) The hooghan has a flat (even dirt) floor and a slightly spherical roof. The correspondence to the phenomenal appearance of the earth and sky is clear;

d) The center of the hooghan's ceiling is a hole, the smokehole, while the center of the floor is occupied by the fire. The corresponding points in the universe are the zenith, yá ' ałníí, conceived of as a unique hole in the Sky, and the center, ni ' ałníí, the articulated center of the Earth, considered to be the hole through which the present inhabitants of the earth emerged;

e) The hooghan's foundation is a set of four poles, sa'dii', situated one in each direction. Again, the correlates in the universe are referred to by the same expression: The Sky is held up by four pillars, one in each direction. This information was difficult to obtain, since most Navajos considered it to belong to restricted parts of medicine man talk (AD, BW).

Starting from this basic model, I can now provide more specific information on several aspects of the Navajo world.

Earth and Heaven

According to traditional beliefs, Earth and Heaven are referred to as two beings analogous to humans: they are said to have arms, legs, a head, a trunk, and so on. All consultants insisted on their relationship to the now living Navajos, as is indicated by the names that are given and are used to call upon them, bless them, or ask a blessing from them: nahasdzáán shimá (the Earth [is] my mother), and yá' shitaa' (my heavenly father, the Heaven [is] my father). The Earth is thus considered female, while the Heaven is male (BW, AD, HT, TB).[7] Moreover, the male lies on top of the female, "just the way we, Navajos, mate." Both are stretched out lengthwise; the Earth lies with the head to the East, with the eastern Sacred Mountain as a cushion, and with the feet against the western Sacred Mountain. She lies on her back, with both arms extended sideways. The male Heaven lies face down on top of her, and oriented the same way. As shall be seen, however, there is space between them at all points. In this way the Heaven must be seen rather as a shell-like cover that tops the whole space between earth surface and stars including all living beings in between, instead of this space itself. If ever Earth and Heaven would actually meet, cover each other and touch each other all around, this would mean the end of the world (BW, CM: initially, however, they had been together; cf. subdynamic view, below).

The role of the Sacred Mountains, in Navajo tradition, is well known (e.g., Kluckhohn and Leighton, 1947). They are the ultimate boundary points of the Navajo universe and serve as referents for the four major directions. Each has a different color referring to particular precious stones that are located in it (BW, TB, HT, and M-AL): in the North is the black of the jet stone, in the South is the blue-green of turquoise, in the East is the white of white

---

7. The situation is more complex, though: both Earth and Heaven have male and female aspects, but the former is predominantly female, and the latter is primarily male. BW carried the comparison over to humans as well: we have this "queer" combination within ourselves as well.

shell, and in the West is the yellow of the abalone shell. According to traditional belief, the Mountains are situated at the very edge of creation, in reality not in, but rather beyond the factual Navajo world. In that way, Mother Earth is said to rest between the Eastern and Western Mountains.

Two more Sacred Mountains are recognized besides the four already mentioned. They are Gobernador Knob and Huerfano Peak, both clearly near the center of the world and invested with specific mythological meanings (cf. section on Boundedness; Center).

Earth and Heaven are the two substantial parts of the Navajo world. Both are named and have functions, while there is no word denoting the total structure that encompasses both Heaven and Earth. The lack of conception and of naming of this totality is explained by the fact that both are distinctive and "that there is air between both at any particular place." The absence of an englobing term and concept is confirmed by all consultants.

The Earth cannot be considered as a perfectly round form, since "it should be thought of as a female person, lying down." Moreover, in every direction, beyond the four Sacred Mountains bounding the Navajo world, an ocean, tónteel (wide water) extends. I was unable to elicit definite knowledge on the global form of this lower level composition (earth and four seasons).

Apart from the two Sacred Mountains that are situated on top of the Earth (Gobernador Knob and Huerfano Peak), and the four that serve as boundaries, the earth has a large number of animals inhabiting its surface, as well as a specific set of plants growing from its soil. All these were "placed on Mother Earth for the use of the Navajo people" (BW). On top of, as well as under the surface are several resources to be found, again to be used in the proper way by the Navajo people (precious stones, coal, etc.).

Heaven includes a variety of phenomena that exist between the earth's surface and the shell (Sky) topping the whole creation. Each phenomenon has its specific place.

The air (including winds) níłch'i, spreads out on the Earth in all directions. It has no limit one can perceive, it exists parallel to the earth. It also extends upwards, but here only up to a certain distance. "You feel it gets thinner already, when going up a mountain." The air has a certain density during the daytime, in fact, such as to blur our perception of the stars. With the coming of twilight, the Dark starts pushing the air (most of it) into the West, thus making the stars visible (BW, TB).

Some way up, but below the sun, is the place of the moon. Sun and moon move through the sky in daily cycles. This explains the eclipse of the sun: the latter is positioned above and thus behind the moon at some point. Both are said to need air, and both rest under the earth when not visible.

Above the sun and moon are the stars (and planets). They are "held up by some kind of force against the sky, so they will not fall down; they hang down in different layers, forming a wavelike structure" (TB).[8] A further ex-

8. With this information goes a Coyote story: during the gathering for the placement and naming of the different stars (as part of the creation event) Coyote did not want to wait for the

planation is provided by means of "falling stars": they fall down a certain distance, and are then thrown back again into the sky so as not to fall back upon the earth (TB, who drew a map of the night sky by heart, went into great detail on these points).

Some stars are named, that is, they are "placed" by the Holy People who were present at the time of the creation. Most of the stars have no name. For example, the Big Dipper constellation has a specific meaning attached to it: the Polaris, náhookǫs biką'i (North, one above/male) and the Ursa Major, náhookǫs bi'áadii (North, one at a distance/female) are placed apart from each other. If they come together and mate, the whole universe will collapse (TB, BW).[9]

In the above descriptions places of different phenomena were pointed out. Earth and Heaven are such that in, under, and upon them there is always something. It is in no way possible to say that there would be nothing, emptiness, or open space within the universe or creation since "then creation would not have been finished." In the same sense, no things, animals, or anything else can really be added to reality and humans cannot expand the set of things that were placed by the Holy People (BW, CM).

| The Substances

The air was placed for the human beings to breathe. Through the air the fire can be lighted. Again, by means of air the water is in motion. Finally, the air (nítch'i) is a means of communication between Earth and Heaven, and between the Holy Ones and human beings.

Earth, mud is the substance of Mother Earth.

Water is important in this arid country. Clans, places, and stories are related to water (CM, BW). One consultant considered it to be part of nítch'i, namely his means of travel (HT). It is said that thunder and lightning are moved by the wind, which makes them appear "under or in the clouds." The rainbow that appears after a rainfall is considered "a blessing that extends between the earth, the air, the moisture, and the sun. It is made up of all of these."

Air and dualism: A characteristic feature of the traditional view of the world is the role of air/wind inside anything that was created. Since the notion of nítch'i is a highly complex one,[10] only data considered most relevant have been taken into account here.

---

lengthy procedure to be finished in the proper way. He took out one star, called it his star (ma'ii' bisǫ) and placed it. The stars that were not yet placed (the majority) he took hold of and threw in the air, where they are still. Through this event, however, most of the stars did not get a name, and were scattered, rather than properly named and placed.

9. The term biką'i literally means "he, above, someone," while bi'áadi stresses the fact of being somewhat separated (from another one), at a small distance from someone else. Consultants always translate the full expressions as male and female star respectively. The reference to sexual intercourse and the Navajo position during that event is again apparent from the spatial terminology used (man on top, woman under).

10. James McNeley has done the major work until now on the analysis of the Navajo

The things were placed on the Earth and in the Sky in the Holy Way, and they were intended to remain there till the end of the world.[11] Therefore, they have a certain type of níłch'i within them which "accounts for their being as they are, their actual way of existing." Two types of níłch'i can be distinguished: a) níłch'i bii'sizíinii (sometimes called bii'siléi) on the one hand, and b) níłch'i bii'gistíín on the other (M-AL, TB, CM). I understood that they constitute the distinct active frames ("the skeleton, like the foundations for a building") of the things they inhabit. Therefore, I prefer not to translate them by such terms as "spirit," "soul," or even "ghost," but will propose more neutrally descriptive terms instead.[12] The latter interpretation may account as well for the distinctness of níłch'i not only in clearly visible things that presently exist, but also on another level, being found as such, "staying around after the disappearance of these things or the death of human beings" (BW, AD, CM).

Níłch'i bii' gistíín was placed in every mountain, the Earth, the Moon, and the Heaven: "It holds them together, until the day the World will end." This aspect of níłch'i I will call "the dynamic foundation" of the instance it inhabits. It has a connotation of being dynamic, we conjecture, because a basic characteristic of anything in the Navajo world view is precisely this (BW, CM). All consultants agreed on the following types: ni' bii' gistíín is the dynamic foundation of the earth; dził bii' gistíín is the dynamic foundation of the mountain; yá bii' gistíín is the dynamic foundation of the sky; tł'éhonaa'éí bii' gistíín is the dynamic foundation of the moon; jóhanaa' éí bii' gistíín is the dynamic foundation of the sun; and yadiłhił bii'gistíín is the dynamic foundation of the (dark) sky. And this list is not exhaustive.

Níłch'i bii'sizíinii (literally: the inside standing one) is the principle underlying several other phenomena in the World. We understand it as the active, dynamic structuring principle or frame "which makes you live, walk, and think." It has a definite connotation of "living being," and of "structuring vital force." I follow McNeley's advice and translate it as "the wind within one" (1980, p. xvii). It is present within the human being, as within several other creatures. Jóhanaa'éí bii'sizíinii is then the structuring vital force of the sun, while lightning and winds have a similar "wind within one"; for example, níłch'i diłhił bii' sizíinii is the structuring wind within the black wind. The snake has a similar internal form, however, with a particular characteristic: tłiish bii' siléii (the snake's inside-lying one).[13]

---

wind theory, distinguishing between different instances of níłch'i and their respective moral and ontological connotations (1981).

11. Navajos claim to be in the fourth World, coming up through three preceding Creations. Each World has specific features and the Navajo people themselves are confined to this present World. It has an end, which evidently is bound to be that of Navajos, too.

12. Researchers used to speak of the particular instances of níłch'i in man as "soul," while those in other things were "spirits" (e.g., Haile, 1943). A lot of Western connotations are implied here, even up to the loss of the actual air/wind concept. Therefore, these and similar transliterations are abandoned in this work.

13. The snake has a lying-in-one, since it is thought that the lightning is the force that was "placed inside the snake" and "that makes the snake crawl the way it does, in zigzag." One

The difference between the two forms of nítch'i is not altogether clear. Both have the connotation of "placer of things" (McNeley, 1980, p. 11), that is, to bring order; but they differ otherwise. A general characteristic of the bii' gistíín form is its endurance. Consultants claimed that it was considered to be the stronger, since it lasts till the end of the world. The phenomena inhabited by a bii' sizíinii are seen to have a moving life (walking, circling, crawling), of a shorter endurance.[14] The nítch'i aspect of creatures of this category lasts, but the particulars it inhabits fade (e.g., man, lightning, animals). The same vital element later reappears[15] in another particular body (CM, BW, AD).

A final interesting point in the relation between the two forms of nítch'i can be stated in the following way: the several phenomena inhabited with a bii' gistíín cannot be said to have a bii' sizíinii themselves. However, as stated hypothetically by Haile (1947), it can be said that their bii' gistíín (clearly "visible" in their representations as figures of human form in sand paintings, etc.) do have or are in themselves inhabited by a bii' sizíinii.

The Dynamic Nature of the World, Time, Being

A basic characteristic of the Navajo world view, inherent in all partic-ular phenomena it distinguishes, is the fundamentally dynamic or active na-ture of the world and anything in it.[16] This feature is indeed fundamental and difficult to grasp, at least in the conceptual framework of the Westerner. It can be illustrated best through its practical, visible consequences. For example, with the static Western view it proved easy and dependable to divide space into segments, to structure the world according to types of objects, units, even atoms, all of which enjoy a certain "objective" status. The segmenting or

---

consultant (HT) used this expression with reference to a snakelike Mountain near Lukachukai as well.

14. The verb sizį designates an upright standing animate being. The verb silá refers to either a long flexible object "in place" (e.g., snake), or objects of several classes "in place" (cf. Garrison, 1973).

15. The question of the nature of bii'sizíinii arises here: in talks with John Farella (working on this topic) it became clear to us that (in or near the Sacred Mountains) the total amount of bii'sizíinii in this world is concentrated in a pool; individual human beings are inhab-ited with parts of this, while these aspects of nítch'i (from persons who died) return to these places, to be purified and "reborn" in a next generation of human beings. (Corroborated by BW, CM, AD)

The relationship between death and the Sun (the Sun is said to claim a certain number of lives each day, in compensation for the warmth and light it gives) appears here: both human beings and the Sun have a bii'sizíinii, so that the Sun can be understood to need "food" in the form of human lives (separating their vital force). I surmise that the same is true of lightning, which can also take life or take trees, etc., not touched any further by living human beings. Fi-nally, the Earth, too, takes lives from time to time (BW, HT).

16. Astrow (1950) started an investigation on this aspect, without however going to great depths. Haile (1947) and also Young and Morgan (1942, 1980) recognize this basic per-spectival difference from Western thought and language.

"slicing" of reality (or at least the continuous stream of phenomenal reality) into chunklike, static units is possible in an easy, intellectually unsophisticated way, only within a fundamentally static world; only within a world of objects, so to speak. The Navajo world, on the other hand, is essentially dynamic, and in consequence it is much less suited for the kind of segmenting required by this part/whole logic which we consider "natural," as it were.[17] To quote Witherspoon: "a cosmos composed of processes and events, as opposed to a cosmos composed of things and facts" (1977, p. 49).

The dynamic perspective is inherent in all things within the Navajo universe. Still, a second type of dynamic or active principle is operative in the Navajo world: man has a certain impact on the world order through his actions and his thoughts (cf. again McNeley, 1980, p. 49).

We recognize, then, two main and global dynamic aspects in the Navajo world view. The following information has been elicited with regard to this:

The most general characteristic of the dynamic world of Navajos was reached through the use of analogy. In order to investigate the vague notion that "everything moves in the Navajo world" systematically, I told a story relating how one man in ancient Greece claimed that everything is really moving, changing all the time; nothing can be said to be still.[18] Very much the same words were used by BB, a highly educated young Navajo, in a discussion we had on the dynamic nature of the world. The idea is illustrated in the traditional belief of the creation of the world. After things had been "placed" on Earth, it is said that First Man and First Woman pulled out a feather from Bald Eagle and blew on it, saying: "From now on everything is on the move. Nothing will be still, not even water, not even the rock."

A rock, for instance, appears to the eye to be still, unmoving and unchanging; but somehow it is moving. A mere description cannot belie this dynamic aspect: tsé si'á means "the rock is in place, it is in the process of being in place." The most striking manifestation of the rock's movement is said to be visible for man in earthquakes, but also in process of erosion. The different geological layers that are visible at several places are held to be exemplifications of the earth's essentially dynamic way of existing.

In general then, everything that was placed is moving; it is changing all the time (BW, TB). HT claimed that the verb naaldloosh (moving around) is the appropriate word to describe a lot of changes one experiences, for example, the change of season, or the change of diurnal rhythms are typical instances. There might be only one exception to the general rule of change (and activeness): "the dead body of a person is the one and only thing that is still."

17. I met with a great many difficulties while representing and then investigating the part/whole relations with our consultants, a fact which seems to sustain the advocated view.

18. The story relates the philosophical insights of Heraclitus, the pre-Socratic philosopher, who held that movement or change is the basic ontological given. The consultants were asked to react to these views, which were presented simply as those of a "very old man in our country."

Although, here again, some consultants object to this specification (BW, HT). The "soul" or active structuring force (bii'sizíinii), on the other hand, goes on living, moving: it is said to move to the Sacred Mountains for purification and to return to the body of a newborn (TB, HT), or else to stay around (without further embodiments). (BW, AD)

This general dynamic feature of created things cannot be understood as actual movement or displacement; rather it is a much less specific and more general "persisting through eventual change."[19] When it comes to human beings, for instance, it is said: "It is not the way we move. It is the way the Holy Ones want us to continue our thoughts, and our minds."[20]

Finally, the fact that things are inhabited by nítch'i is interpreted here to throw some light on the nature of this dynamic view: the mountains, the earth, and so on are said to be "held up and erect" through the bii'gistíín in them. The essentially dynamic character of wind/air (thus) helps to grasp the idea of a "(dynamic) mountain," a "(dynamic) earth," and the like. In this way, all consultants agreed that nothing could be considered static, indefinitely invariable, unmoved or unmovable. The pervasiveness of dynamism is stressed by means of the character of air/wind: "it is not only omnipotent and omniscient, it is also omnipresent" (Witherspoon, 1977, p. 61).

The second general dynamic principle designates, in fact, a type of movement: the pulsating movement of several major phenomena. Information on this was elicited from and/or checked with CM, BW, HT, BB, and M-AL.

Although the earth is believed to have no rotatory movement, it is subjected to long-term expansions and contractions on a cosmic scale. After creation, it is said, the earth (and the sky) was stretched from the center toward the periphery.[21] The same expansive movement, in a clockwise spiral, is apparent in baskets, which can be considered a scale model for the Navajo world (BW, TB, HT, LB, CM). It is likely that the end of the world will see its shrinking back into the center, thus realizing a perfectly symmetrical, pulsating movement over the whole period.

The people (Navajos) came up through a hole in the center of the earth: hajíínáídéé' ni'ałníí'déé', emergence from the center of the earth. They spread out in all directions from there. They are to come to the center and return in the end. The fact that the dead people, before final disposal (hanging in trees, eventual burial nowadays), are dressed inversely and lopsidedly is an aid to their "initiation into the other world, their belonging to another party." The expression is ałhádabikee' kéhoshch'į: shoes crossed (on wrong foot, inversely); when the shoes are put on the wrong foot, the knots are made inversely, the jacket is put on back to front, and so forth. The practice amounts

19. Again it is difficult to find a proper description in English: the use of an active mode (-ing) might bring some clarity.

20. Cf. Alexander (1953), who suggests the use of "forces" rather than objects, states, or things as the basic ontological category in Navajo (p. 230). On the other hand, Witherspoon states that the main verb in Navajo is "to go," rather than "to be" (1977, p. 49).

21. Cf. the emergence story related by Matthews (in Alexander, 1953, pp. 13–15).

to an enactment of their going "counterclockwise" and exemplifies the same pulsating movement: they are on their way back to the context of emergence.

One consultant developed a similar idea on the evolution of languages: in the beginning there was only one "word" (saad), that was diné bízaad (Navajo, the language of the people). Six other "words" are gradually developing. At the point when the expansion of languages comes to a stop, the reverse movement will set in, leading finally to one "word" again. (CM, the thinker who talked about this theory, felt that the final language would be English, and feared that Navajo language, thought, and culture would be extinguished; BW agreed).

The construction and destruction of the Sandpaintings, used in the healing ceremonies, exhibit the same basic "movement": the Sandpainting must be built up in a clockwise movement, and is then demolished or "destructed" before sunset (or perhaps sunrise) in a counterclockwise sense.

All these aspects of the Navajo world[22] thus show the same basic movement of expansion followed by contraction, of emergence followed by the return to the initial state. All cases show the movement to be very systematic, gradual, and regular in its dual form; they allow no discontinuities, and allow a uniform path for the movement and for its reversal.

Existence

The notion of "being" or "existing" is similarly a dynamic concept.[23] In contrast to the Western static and segmentable reality represented in the distinction between "being" and "becoming" or "growing," the Navajo view of "being" implies an essentially dynamic perspective. In this way, "existing" should be understood as a continuous manifestation (or "manifesting"), a series of events, rather than states or situational persistences through time. As mentioned before, the "backbone" (be it bii'gistíín or bii'sizíinii) of any phenomenon is a continuously active force that makes the phenomenon persist as it is, rather than the mere static skeleton suggested by such translations as "pillar," or "internal form."

Time

Due to the biological cycle of human life, we expect a certain temporal linearity in any community. Navajos are no exception to this rule. The difficulty with their view lies in their different method of time recognition.

22. The list of examples is not exhaustive; the same pattern can be observed in the initial state of the earth (covered by water, which is blown off in the next stage) and its final state-to-be, as in the basic movement throughout this world era of the "northstars" (from combined or mating states in the beginning, they became separated; the end of the world will be apparent from their mating again; cf. below). Other instances may be found.

23. Landar hardly treats this aspect in his analysis of the verb "to be" in Athapaskan languages (Landar, 1967).

1) In a cosmic, or for that matter, mythical conception of time Navajos hold that the time span of the present creation is limited and subject to circular movement: the concept of "pulsation" made this clear (cf. above). The span between initial creation (things coming up from the center of the Earth and being "placed" on the Earth) and the final collapse of creation (the return to the center) is finite; so the present world will come to an end within a number of human generations (TB, CM, BW, AD). Through abuse of the things and relationships that were created, the Navajos can affect this cosmic tide, to the effect of their shortening the period to be lived in this (fourth) world (HT, TB, CM, BW). So, due to the pulsating movement that is occurring during and through this period of time, a certain circularity can be seen: the beginning and end of this world exhibit the same forms, after which a similar cycle (but probably without diné), the fifth world, is to commence (HT, BW, TB).[24]

2) Although the overall time of the present reality is cyclical, the part of it to be lived by each individual Navajo (or each generation) is clearly conceived of as linear. The more common model for the course of a human lifespan is a line. Some consultants claimed it should be imagined like a zigzag line (like a snake), while others favored the model of a straight line, with occasional sidetracks (literal deviations or faulty behavior). A typical illustration of time being limited and linear is found in the expression for eternity: shá nihonít'i' bijįjįį'[25] which translates freely into: "until I die of old age, until my period has completely passed," using the same verb stem as one consultant (involved in Bible translation as a Navajo) who spoke about eternity with the expression doo'ahoonít'i' (lit., a line with no end to it; KB).

In the same way, dying of old age proves good; in fact, it is a proof of living a good and thoughtful life. This is not so because of the age itself, but because in that case "you made use of everything you had." Apart from the moral values implied in this view, there is a definite stress on the finite character of life time: each person has a certain amount of valuable potential within her or him and time is available for living only until this amount is used up (BW).

3) Finally, the Navajo view of "moment" or of particular progression through time is different from the Western correlate. In a general sense the Western time perspective can be described—at the psychological level at least—as arrowlike, a continuously progressing line of events, infinite in the past and the future (cf. e.g., Whitehead, 1919). Time exists, and progresses relatively independently of man; it even affects man. The Navajo alternative can best be approached through a rule offered by CM: Navajos continuously

24. A parallel to the four-world cycle is stated explicitly in that of the four seasons (BW).

25. shá nihonít'i bijįjįį' can be analyzed as follows: shá, for me; ni indicates termination, ho- indicates space, the verb stem anít'i is used to denote a fence or a borderline, so that the complete expression is rendered as "the end of the line"; bi-, pronoun; jį-, day, period, cycle, and jį' means till that point: in globo, one then gets: up till the very end of his/her period.

define themselves in the temporal amalgam of reality through smoking, building a hooghan, hunting, etc., and always stress the relationships between what exists, what existed, and that which they want to come into existence.

Again, I came to a better understanding of the Navajo time conception by means of lengthy analogy: I elaborated on the "Myth of the Cave" with drawings and ample explanations, in order to build a context for broad response.[26] Some reactions stated that

> If you want something, you can imagine it. For things that were yesterday, are past now; you cannot look at them anymore. But the things you imagine, you see in dreams or think about, you realize them through prayer. It will be coming to you gradually, becoming more concrete [or 'real'] and more attainable the more you are busy with it. If you want something, you take it (in thought) in the palm of your hand, then in your armpit, then on your waist, then in your kneehole, on your ankle, and then back in your head. Gradually it will become real through your care for it.[27]

Other consultants confirmed this information: you should care for everything around you in order to live in prosperity; disrespect is the worst attitude possible, since it disrupts nature and the good order (CM, BW, HT).

By analyzing these statements as descriptions of the conception of time and temporal moment, I can extract valuable information: the past of the individual is completely past (in other instances consultants reminded me of this, stressing the consequence that you should not feel guilty of past deeds, because they are completely past). The present is a very limited timespan, in fact delineated by the duration of the experience itself. The future, then, or what would amount to it from a Western perspective, is not to be understood in uniformity with either the past or the present. Rather, it appears like a stock of possibilities, of incompletely realized events and circumstances. They are

26. The Myth of the Cave by Plato served as a model (*State*, book 7). Plato formulated his ontological opinions through the use of this story: suppose you are sitting in a cave facing a wall on which all kinds of shadows or reflections appear and move about. You will think these phenomena are the real things, since it is only them you are able to see or experience. In reality, however, these shadows are but the reflections of things that are carried around behind you, which you cannot possibly see or be aware of. Even the latter things are not the "real" things, since they in turn are but representations of the only "real" world, that is the one existing outside of the cave and of which you cannot have any knowledge of either. The story was used as a heuristic device to elicit information on the relation between knowledge and reality. It was recognized by Navajo consultants as dealing with notions of time and dynamic aspects of reality: the shadows (Plato's phenomenon appearances) were located in the back of the spectator, since shadows of this sort are unreal, that is, things of the past. Instead, the objects carried around (in Plato's myth) should be in front of the spectator, since they "represent things that are becoming, that are coming into existence" for the spectator. The latter can still influence them, make them more pronouncedly manifest, while the former appearances are completely unretrievable (according to CM, BW, HT).

27. The different places on the body are mentioned in elaborate blessings and are touched or "treated" (with herbs, paint, etc.) in several ceremonies.

still most of all "becoming" (rather than being) and involved in a process of "manifesting" themselves.[28] A human being can, through his thought and desire, exert an influence on these "possibles."[29] This aspect is stressed in Witherspoon's beautiful book: he states that everything in the Navajo world with a capacity for self-animation is directed and controlled by thought. Intelligence, or the excellence to think and perceive, gains a high status because of this: "the crucial question in Navajo determinism, is who can control what or who can control whom" (1977, p. 77).

Consequently, Navajo time cannot be conceived of in the Western "spatialized" form (e.g., Reichenbach, 1958). Instead, it proves informative to consider time as just one aspect of a multifaceted reality. Similarly, some of the spatial aspects might be better understood if they were considered as distinct facets in one multifaceted Navajo world. Through the detailed semantic study of Navajo spatial terminology, this point will be elaborated considerably (cf. chaps. III and IV). At this point, it can be pointed out that the present view is very similar to that of Young and Morgan (1942 and 1980), lexicographers of Navajo, who refrain from speaking about tenses in the Navajo grammar and lexicon, but rather determine the status of different aspects in the verbal conjugations: continuative, durative, imperfective, iterative, perfective, progressive, repetitive, semelfactive, and semeliterative (1942, pp. 121–23; elaborated in 1980, pp. 103–7).

Boundedness; Center

Both the notions of "boundedness" and of "center" in their specific Navajo meanings seem to constitute basic features of, or constraints on, Navajo conceptualization of space. I therefore dwell upon this philosophical frame of the Navajo world view in some detail. The notion of "boundedness" points to limits of the world that is called THE world (or the Navajo world). It does not correspond unequivocally to any directly understandable correlate in Western spatial thought, and will therefore be dealt with second. The notion of "center" is more readily understandable.

Center

The frequency of references to centers in many contexts of Navajo knowledge and practice led me to consider "center" as a basic and ramified notion of order and organization. It seems that ordering and placing of things in everyday life as in mythological beliefs evolves around an approximate

---

28. The term is Whorf's in his description of the Hopi ontology. It seems appropriate here (1956).

29. Cf. a more thorough analysis of the moral consequences of this view of time in an article on Navajo morals (Pinxten, 1979b).

center most of the time. This notion is dominant in several instances, according to consultants:

1) First of all, in the mythological history Navajos are said to live in the center of Creation. They reside in the center of the Earth, branching out in all directions to some extent. The Earth, again, is in the center of the lower part of the universe surrounded on all sides by an ocean (TB, BW, M-AL).

A social correlate of this mythological fact (or the other way around) might be the clear, often emphatically held distinction between Navajos and non-Navajos: [30] the only phenomena of real importance are the world and the deeds of the Navajos, while anything else is non-Navajo and therefore considered potentially dangerous to the Navajo people. In this context one can point in fact to the existence of two distinguished "catalogues" of Navajo ceremonial beliefs and practices in the Navajo lore: [31] On the one hand Blessingway (Hozhǫ́ǫ́jí) dealing with the Navajo world and anything holy within it, on the other hand Enemyway (naaghé'ee hózhǫ́ǫ́jí) dealing with alien aspects and meant for the purification of any Navajo who came under their influence (warriors, etc.). These data tend to support a strong status of some notion of "centrality" in Navajo thought.

2) The "pulsation" referred to above evidently presupposes a center from which the movement originates and terminates. In the basket, the center (hole) is the main point of reference, since movement of the specified clockwise kind is said to start from there (as is illustrated in the actual construction of the spiraling basket). Also, the ultimate boundary of the world, in the basket model as well as in the verbal expressions referring to this topic, is vague or somewhat fuzzy. Varying, noninclusive information is brought forward on this matter (one piece is the development of seven languages as a sign of reaching the ultimate expansion, according to CM; but also the subsequent existence of up to four generations of Navajos—without specification of the meaning of "generation"—as emphasized by HT and TB; and again the spatial occupation of all territory between the four Sacred Mountains—on which all consultants agree—leaving the extent of Hopi territory in doubt, etc.).

In this way, the mythological notion of center turned out to be relevant to an ordering of the world. However, settlement of order is considered difficult or even irrelevant (AD). In contrast, some informants identified Gobernador Knob and Huerfano Mesa as center(s) in this particular sense (CM, corroborated by information from TB and HT): ni'ałníí', the place of emergence and center of the Earth, is located on top of or near Huerfano Mesa, while basic personalities in Navajo mythology were created on top of the nearby Gobernador Knob. [32]

30. Werner (personal communication) encountered the strict opposition between Navajo and non-Navajo worlds when trying to induce consultants to consider both as branches of an englobing tree structure. Every Navajo consultant firmly rejected the structure.

31. Cf. Wyman's edition of Blessing Way, pp. 3–5 (1975).

32. Changing Woman (asdzáán nádleehí) is said to be created here. Through her, human beings came into existence (Wyman, 1975).

3) In profane terms consultants always recognize a geographic center. Typically, each individual claims his own neighborhood to be the center of the Navajo world. HT emphasized this very peculiarity through his own experience.[33] TB, HT, M-AL, and AD, who live in the part of the reservation enclosed by Black Mountain and Lukachukai Mountain, claim that that was the genuine center of the Navajo world. BW, of Cow Springs, pointed to the nearby Navajo Mountain (to the north of the two other mountains and near the northwestern border of the reservation) as the center and heart of the Navajo world: nahasdzáán bijéí (heart of the Earth). All consultants, however, consider the peripheral territories more loosely tied with the real center of the Navajo world, because they are thought to be subjected more to foreign (and thus bad) influences from other tribes and most of all from the whites.

4) During the several healing ceremonies, Sandpaintings are constructed on the hooghan floor. They depict forces or phenomena of the world (the Holy aspects) in some way or other. Invariably the patient is put in the center of these designs, and thus in fact put in the center of a (partial) picture of the Earth. The healing is then to take place through the patient's confrontation and contacts with the "World" around him. That is, the singer imposes his will upon the nílch'i depicted in the Sandpainting and thus transfers his thought to the patient in order to cure him or her (Witherspoon, 1977, p. 61, relating on Reichard's view).

The Sandpainting is constructed in the center of the hooghan floor, on and around the place where the fire is usually situated. Also the center is considered a main point of reference in the daily activities in the hooghan: one should walk around it, sit around it, sleep around it, never cross it, and so on. I witnessed that all these rules are still obeyed when I assisted in the construction of a Shooting Way Sandpainting by X, a Lukachukai medicine man.

In conclusion, the notion of center seems to take up an important position in the Navajo way of dealing with the world, be it strictly spatial or otherwise. However, rather than pointing to a particular spatial, static point, it appears as a directional point originating, ending, or merely locating particular movements, events, or displacements.

Boundedness

The best way to characterize the "boundaries" of the Navajo world, according to the consultants, would be to consider them to be the ultimate range of influence of the powers or forces recognized in the Navajo world. Boundaries are the ultimate points, that is, the ones most distant from the center of the world and still under the influence of the particular forces that hold up, sustain existence, or regulate the Navajo world, as it was "placed" through creation and remains there now. It is clear that these boundaries can-

---

33. This attitude is reported in several cultures. Gould and White (1974) had similar data on white Americans and on British subjects as well.

not be pointed at in an unambiguous way, and they may be considered to be "fuzzy": they are unstable, since they may move continuously with expansions of population and/or territory; they are not visibly marked (boundary posts or any such things are absent), but remain at all times within the region defined by the four Sacred Mountains.[34] HT used the model of the Navajo basket to explain this point: the basket represents a continuously expanding universe, expressed through the spiraling design and the thread in it. In the same sense, the Navajo world is said to be continuously expanding and therefore cannot have fixed boundaries.

One consultant (M-AL) declared that, on her two travels away from the reservation (to Chicago and to San Francisco) she did not notice the border of the world she believed to have crossed "since it was night." Her account of the travels was interesting on this point, since she gave rather detailed information on the following stages: a) traveling through the Navajo reservation, b) having passed the Sacred Mountains, and c) being at the place of destination. Neither the actual boundaries of the Navajo world nor the vast territories covered between Navajo territory and Chicago and San Francisco, respectively, received any attention in the narrative.

Although the exact extension of the Navajo world and its precise borders cannot be known, it is stated over and over again that this world cannot extend, under any circumstance, beyond the four Sacred Mountains. Any expansion or contraction of the world must take place within the territory defined by these mountains. However, the mountains themselves are said to be located "just beyond the Navajo Earth" (since the Earth is to rest on them; BW, TB, HT, M-AL).

The names of these mountains are well known, although the location of each of them (and their actual identification in the landscape) has been debated:[35]

a) In the east is (dził) sis naajinii (mountain, black belt crossways): a white mountain with a black belt. Some recognize it as the Blanca Peak in the Sangre de Cristo Range, near Alamosa.

b) In the south is tsoo dził (coneshaped, mountain): turquoise mountain. All agree upon this being Mount Taylor near Grants, New Mexico.

c) In the west is dook'o 'oosłííd (dził) (reflects colors, up in light, mountain). The mountain is agreed upon as being the San Francisco Peaks, near Flagstaff, Arizona. Its precious material is abalone.

d) In the north is (dził) dibénitsaa (mountain, sheep on top). Its pre-

---

34. Of course, the existence of the borderlines of the present reservation area can be pointed out, but they should not be considered the boundaries of the Navajo earth, primarily because they were set by a treaty (and were redefined several times afterwards), and secondly because the actual territory is considered to be but an instantiation of the concept of "Navajo world" (for example, excluding the Hopi, who, territorially, clearly live surrounded by Navajos).

35. Haile undertook to reidentify the mountains, together with several medicine men (cf. Wyman, 1975, Intro.), but even now some people disagree with the results (e.g., CM rejected the interpretation by Haile and his group).

cious stone is jet. Some identify it as the Hesperus Peaks in the La Plata Range (BW, M-AL, RB), some as the San Juan Mountains (Franciscan Fathers, 1910).

Apart from these, of course, there are an upper and a lower limit to the Navajo world. These were discussed above.

To make clear what is actually meant by "boundedness" (and for that matter, "finiteness") in Navajo cosmological beliefs, people were questioned on how the world, or the whole of creation, could be represented from an external standpoint, that is, by somebody who would see the Navajo world from the outside. The question held no meaning for the consultants BW, AD, and HT, even after it was rephrased in several different ways. One final answer went as follows: "If you go on top of the hill, you will not reach the limit of the sky. If you go on top of the highest mountain, you will not reach it. It is impossible to really reach the ultimate border of the world, above or below." In the context of the question this answer clearly states it is impossible to have an external view of the world, to go "beyond it" in the full sense. The resulting characteristic is usually referred to as the "absoluteness" and the "finiteness" of the space of the world. It is simply not imaginable to put oneself outside of the universe and (as on this occasion) conceive of the world and of all that exists in an endless void, an infinite nothingness.

Closedness of the World; Order

Analytical Remarks

The "closedness" of a world view is understood as a degree of closedness or self-sufficiency. It is my opinion that this concept can be applied in the description of any given world view, be it that of a Westerner, an African, an Indian, or even a scientist. Only the degree of closedness may differ considerably, a fact that enabled philosophers to talk about the "breaking open of the world" in the Age of Enlightenment (contrasted to the cumbersome Middle Ages in Europe).[36] I will call a world view more closed, the more it shows a disregard for or a systematic avoidance of other worlds, or opinions other than the ones held. The more the phenomenal world is incorporated in the knowledge system of a community, the more it is regarded as being a unique world in that it is there for the purpose of the particular perceiver (or community) and his (its) particular conception of reality exclusively.[37]

36. The work of modern philosophers of science (most of all Koyré and Kuhn) inspired me to consider this concept; it is this sort of work in our tradition that comes closest to the notion involved here.

37. It should be borne in mind that one is looking for a cognitive anthropological distinction, instead of a purely psychological one. The psychological aspects (like anxiety toward others and their opinions) may be relevant, to grasp the context of the system of knowledge, but are not properly part of this research.

The more telling features looked for, in the course of this investigation into "degrees of closedness" of a world view, can be summed up under two labels:

a) intrinsic completeness of the world as perceived, and

b) special, culture-bound meaning of the natural phenomena, exclusively so for the particular community of the one who bestows meaning.

/ *Navajo Data*

Intrinsic completeness. The world was created, laid out in such a way that people might live in and with it in a beneficial way. This view can be found to a considerable degree in contemporary Navajo beliefs (although a favorable attitude toward this view might be encouraged by the uncertain position of being "between" two traditions, the old one and the one imposed by whites, neither of which are viable alternatives to the contemporary Navajo). In this sense, it is said that the world was created in the Holy Way (that is, in a particularly orderly way) for the Navajo to make use of it. In a similar way, anything from outside the Navajo world is understood to cause trouble or chaos: the alien is looked upon as a source of "noise" (bad influence, chaos) or as the one who will take away the Navajo knowledge and thus weaken the persons who possessed the knowledge (hinted at by BW, TB, and HT).

In the same way, the world as it was created is such that no genuine improvements or additions can be made by man. The role of man is believed to be essentially that of a good and thoughtful respecter and perpetuator of the world as created (CM, BW).

Specific meanings. The common natural phenomena, ranging from stars and sun to several animals and plants, have a specific meaning, which is for Navajos only. The sun, moon, earth, stars, but also animals like the bear, the spider, and the snake are said to be in a very special relationship with the Navajo people: they are either ancestors of man (the snake, the bear), or heavenly persons who had a large share in the creation of and in the subsistence of human beings (sun, earth . . .). In this way, most of the phenomena in the everyday world are claimed by Navajos to have a specific (indeed mythic) relationship with the Navajo people.[38]

Several instances of such relationships can be found:

a) The notion of order (captured in the beautiful notion of hózhóní) itself, which will be discussed below.

---

38. A very peculiar instance in this respect was a reaction recorded to the American landing on the moon: "We Navajos are not allowed to do that, but if they want to go to the moon (the white Americans), that is their affair." In this way, it seems to be understood that a celestial body like the moon is recognized as existing for anybody, for different tribes, but also as having a particular relationship with the Navajos, restricted to them and excluding all others. In the same way, the Navajos themselves have specific duties toward the moon. (Anecdotes on the patience and tolerance of Navajos with innumerable missions are understood in the same way: it is not uncommon to have a Navajo listen to some missionary, and hear him reply afterward how he sees similar problems from his point of view. It is as if the missionary came to "compare notes.")

b) The role of the sun in the death of people: as will be remembered, the sun takes lives as a reward for his daily warmth and light to people. As a consequence of this belief, people are told to stop working whenever there is an eclipse of the sun and let the eclipse pass, after which the sun will refrain from taking lives during a certain period, because "he already took too much, which led him to an eclipse, a sort of death" (HT, TB). The particular "agreement" with the sun and the fact that the sun too is called "our father," point to the exclusive connotations of this natural phenomenon in the Navajo conception.

c) In a similar way, the rainbow is said to have a particular meaning for Navajos alone: its appearance is generally a sign of good luck for the people. However, when it appears "on top of particular people" (or their house) it is feared that some calamity will happen to them (TB).[39]

d) The "figures" (níłch'i bii'gistíín) within the four Sacred Mountains are said to be of extreme importance to the Navajo people: they have a holy name that can be called upon only in extreme circumstances and by particular human beings. Secondly, they take care of the formation of "winds within one" in newborns (bii'sizíinii), and thus control the life of human beings to some degree (CM, BW, AD). I conjecture that their location in the outer boundaries of the world (the Sacred Mountains) and their considerable role in the fate of human beings (Navajos) adds to the picture of a self-sufficient world, a creation exclusively for Navajos.

e) I interpret the role of the two northernmost stars (part of the Big Dipper constellation) again as an illustration of this point: they "were placed" to be watched by human beings as signs that might tell the end of the world (HT, TB, BW).

f) In their mythological knowledge a very general belief in the ways of things points in the same direction: with creation (that is, according to the myth, after the Earth was cleared of water and of the Monsters that plagued the Holy People) all things under, upon, and above Earth were "placed" and given names and functions; the same happened with the heavenly bodies (Stars, Moon, Sun). They were placed in a Holy Way, which means that they are in the right place, are arranged in an orderly fashion, and avoid imbalance or waste in any sense (CM, BW). In this way, again, all things were related to everything else through the same principle and toward the final good use of the people, that is, the Navajos. The people themselves were part of this creation and were thus (though not as fully and definitively) "placed" in a similar way (HT, BW). The basic attitude that was placed in people was that of respect for everything "placed," that is, making use of things without spoiling or wasting them,[40] and to show consideration for anything living or existing in

39. In mythological stories the rainbow serves as a means of transportation for the Holy Ones (HT).

40. CM told a lengthy story about waste (as a Christmas present): In the old days people had been wasteful with games and crops and were consequently "punished." All game was put away in a safe place where people could not reach it. Starvation was to follow. Only upon

one or another way (including standing rocks, but also plants and animals), going about things in a thoughtful and balanced way rather than risking anything for a few benefits. So, while it was agreed that nothing could be added to creation by humans and that their basic attitude should be one of respect for anything in the world, they can, however, spoil or disrupt things, which incidentally will make them the ultimate victims of their handling (BW, CM, HT). Here, again, the "closedness" of the world is obvious.

g) The use and mere gathering of knowledge is to be understood in the same way. Knowledge is the private property of the one who has it. The expansion of one's knowledge is a slow progression through a lengthy and careful observation of the way things are and through the collection of insights and information from others who are believed to have some. It seems as if man commands a certain force through knowledge and through his "mind" in general (BW, TB, CM). He can use this force to understand the world better. He can even risk a lot and, if lucky, eventually gain more or spill parts of his knowledge-power for nothing. This is the way gambling is spoken of too: you can take risks with gain or loss, depending on your good perception and clear thought. The same applies to the knowledge one has acquired over the years: it can be spoiled or given away to someone else, thereby weakening the one who owned it in the first place (because of one's real and thorough departing from it—BW). In this way, CM told part of his knowledge to Frank Harvey (who paid him for it) "because he felt weak and knew his end was coming soon; therefore he sold parts of his knowledge before dying." Characteristically, CM was known to have kept his knowledge to himself and to have been exploring and elaborating on it continuously, only to start telling what he knew very late in his life (he died at 104 in 1977). In the same sense, BW told me to come back to him in twenty years (he was nearly 60 at that time), at which time he would be in a condition to tell a lot more: "You know I am still too young now to risk all that," he told me. The attitudes to knowledge described above reflect, again, a certain "closedness": it is as if there is only a limited amount of knowledge one can gain (varying from person to person) and it strengthens the person who has it; consequently, parting with it, especially with the more fundamental insights, weakens him. Similar information on the role of knowledge (and language) is central in Witherspoon's treatise (1977, especially chap. 3).

h) Finally, the practices of daily life show several features that corroborate this particular characteristic of the Navajo world: the clockwise movement inside the hooghan in a way delineates the world and makes it definable in a definite sense. Again, the way some modern and previously unknown things or events are treated in the language is highly illustrative: instead of taking over the English words, Navajo "translations" are introduced in the common language. Words such as chidí for car, and chidí bikee' for tire

---

promising to refrain from wasteful behavior was the game eventually discovered and turned loose again by the Crow.

are well-known examples.[41] Now, however, the language abounds with similar examples. The little book on Navajo terminology for auto parts, worked out at the Rock Point Community School, is a beautiful case in point (in press).

The mere existence of these things might at least point to a certain amount of self-sufficiency embedded in the Navajo world view.

Order

The notion of "order" or "in an orderly way" is of enormous importance in the Navajo world view. The statement that abusing means disorderly treatment, gives a hint of the significance and indeed the pervasiveness of this notion. In the Navajo language the words dzidísingo and nizhónígo and yá'át'ééhgo are used as follows:

a) dzidísingo means "holy, in a holy way." It points also to a good or respectful way of doing things. Its meaning, however, is restricted to the sacred way, to ceremonial contexts, and it is less commonly used than the others (RB, LB).

b) nizhónígo is an expression that is used very broadly, meaning "in a beautiful way, orderly" in general. It can be used to speak of the prettiness of a woman or of a man, or of the beauty of a house or a landscape, or indeed of anything else. At the same time it has to convey a sense of orderliness, of smooth and respectful treatment, of good and nondisruptive characteristics (RB, TB, BW).

c) yá'át'ééhgo is a term meaning "in a good way." It seems most of all to convey a meaning that something is (or is done) the way it is supposed to be.[42]

Upon analyzing the use of these expressions, I conclude that rather than simply denoting something good, a beautiful thing at one moment, nizhónígo and yá'át'ééhgo describe the beauty, goodness, and orderliness of things that go on, change, exist through time. The order thus is continuously realized ("manifesting itself"), rather than being a static quality.

Orderliness manifests itself in several ways in the Navajo beliefs:

1) The hooghan, the basket, and the world are all oriented in the proper way, showing their sole opening pointing to the East; the strong correspondence between their form and other specific characteristics already illustrates the notion of "order." This and all similar features of order in the world, and in the things and processes within it, are said to have been "placed" with creation (TB, HT, CM). The Holy Ones, that is, the níłch'i in the Sacred Mountains, the several Holy Beings in the universe (Black God, Haashch'-

41. chidí could be an onomatope imitating the sound of a starting engine (Young and Morgan, 1942), while bikee' literally means "his foot." One could in the same way refer to the bijáád (leg) of a car, that is, its axle.

42. yá'át'ééh is the common Navajo greeting, in fact meaning "it is good." The enclitic -go is used pretty much like the English -ing, pointing to a process taking place or giving information of "the way of, like."

ééÉzhiní; Watersprinkler: tó neinilí; Gray God: haashch'ééÉibáhí; also Talking God, the One Who Is Unable to Talk, the Dawn People, the Twilight People, etc.), all those who worked together at the time of Creation and placed and named things in the proper way, theirs is the basic idea of order, of the good way of existing and of enduring (CM).[43]

2) Human beings ought to respect and live by the order that was established. This refers first and foremost to human use of everything under, on, and above the earth's surface. They should use everything in a thoughtful way, not waste anything or disturb the ways of anything unnecessarily. If human beings do wrong in these respects they are liable to get into trouble of one kind or another; for example, individual illnesses as well as epidemics are explained in this way (BW). Only the restoration of the orderly way will make healing possible. Stargazers, handtremblers, and windlisteners are called upon to detect and diagnose the real cause of distress or sickness (what wrong did the patient do the cosmic order?) and to prescribe the appropriate ceremony to be performed (DH, BW).

The basic rule for a good and orderly life is given in the following formula: sạ'ah naagháí bik'eh hózhóón,[44] the literal meaning of which is 'old age, strong forward going, in her way/along her path, in a beautiful/good/orderly way'. The formula is in fact composed of two parts.[45] Witherspoon gives an extensive and intriguing analysis of it, which will be partly reproduced here. According to him the two parts of the expression refer to mythological beings embodying basic human capacities: sạ'ah naagháí is a holy being "representing thought" and "the second one representing the speech of holy people and called Bik'eh Hózhǫ́" (1977, p. 19). Their unison as the two basic principles of Navajo life is central to the ceremonial beliefs of Navajos to such an extent that one can say that "the entire ceremonial system is primarily designed to produce or restore conditions symbolized by the phrase sạ'ah naagháí bik'eh hózhǫ́" (1977, p. 19). Thus, the two parts of the expression refer to holy people, on the one hand, and to their combined ideal principle as it is feasible for the living Navajo, on the other hand. Witherspoon interprets this delicate relationship between both holy people/principles in terms of their structural links: speech/beautiful way (bik'eh hózhǫ́) is the

43. Types of air or smoke must have a particular meaning here: CM said that, when smoking a pipe, one is in fact dealing with kinship, with relationships between human beings; on the other hand, the practice of laying the newborn near the fire, his fontanels facing the smoke/fire, is said to give him or her a good thought in later life. However, the full meaning of these (fire/smoke) and their links with other beliefs is not entirely clear to me.

44. J. Farella works on this concept. He drew attention to its centrality during extensive and fruitful discussions. Witherspoon did major work on the expression (cf. below) in his important attempt to understand the Navajo philosophy by giving a very central ontological role to language. I am sympathetic to this approach, but I feel incapable of judging the adequacy of the insight.

45. The expression remains problematic (as was already pointed out by Haile, 1947): sạ́' means old age, while sạ'ah does not seem to have any meaning as such in Navajo. Cf. also his 1943 paper.

outer form of thought/old age (są'ah naagháí), which is the inner form. Thus, the total formula reads: by means of the way of beauty you will reach longevity, or: your thought will become real or expressed by means of speech (as in a good ceremony). Witherspoon continues to frame these and other principles in a more englobing structure (1977, pp. 25–32), but this would lead the present discussion too far. The formula is a blessing or prayer one reads to onself, while asking the Holy People for a long and good life. (It should be remembered that longevity and goodness are strongly linked.) The reasoning behind this is as follows: if you can live a long, harmonious, and rather well-to-do life, you live a good, orderly life. You live the way it should be (CM, BW). In this way, human beings fit into the grand structure of the Navajo world.

3) Coyote and níłch'i sometimes appear to bring about disorder. In several instances Coyote is believed to cause disruption in risky and thoughtless acts (the story of Coyote's messing up the stars is well known; in several children's stories he appears as a kind of rascal, always ready for jokes or tricks). In stories and in common beliefs alike, some winds of the Universe are believed to have a similar role (e.g., heavy winds are linked with witches; DH). With these phenomena goes a sense of disorder or transgression of the understanding of the order that is spelled out. The kind of action is not really disagreeable, but it is believed to be full of risks for the one who engages in it. In a similar way the thinker or philosopher is looked upon somewhat like a Coyote, since he dares go beyond the immediately spelled out and agreed upon order, to investigate greater depths by means of his quick and perceptive mind.

Interrelatedness of Everything in the Navajo World

In the preceding exposition of the findings on "order" in the Navajo world, it became apparent that all things should relate to one another. In other words, if Navajos are to know the right way to live, the general concept of "order" should convey information that is sufficiently applicable to nearly everything in the Navajo universe, which is to say, it makes people capable of treating natural phenomena (sun, moon, etc.) as well as animals, plants, and other human beings in the proper way. In order to justify the claim to general applicability of the notion of order, we shall now discuss the beliefs concerning the interrelatedness of everything in this world view.

The best way to grasp the function of this concept in the Navajo world view is to think of the cyclic character of nature for Navajos, much as it is explained in ecology:[46] all living beings, and even all things in general, are such that they serve one another to some extent. Some plants can be eaten by

46. The notion of "cycle" was proposed both by BW and Frank Harvey, since it appeared to be the best translation of the Navajo idea of explaining these things.

some animals, who in turn can be eaten by man and by other animals. Even rocks have a role in this system: they serve as referents or as homes for specific animals (bears, eagles, etc.). Consequently, everything has a place and a function in a long and mutually dependent chain, which ultimately includes the whole universe. To destroy or abuse (waste, spill, use disrespectfully) one element is, in the end, to disrupt the whole system. In this way, all phenomena in the Navajo universe are interrelated and interdependent.

As elicited from consultants, this general character is exemplified in numerous ways in the traditional Navajo knowledge. The Navajo universe seems to be structurally uniform and homogeneous throughout, that is, of all things "placed" for the use of Navajos there is none that is of an altogether different nature from the others. All those things that are believed to be of this world have one form of breath or another (BW, TB, HT). All animals and plants have a breath and a heart in the physician's clinical sense (biiéi: heart, yee'ńdídzihii: breath, that by means of which one breathes). Things that were placed in the Holy Way (that is, according to myth) are said to have or to be inhabited by a different type of breath as well, that is, a form of níłch'i (níłch'i bii'gistíín and níłch'i bii'sizíinii). Analysis of the fact that all things in the Navajo world have some form of "breath" led to the hypothesis that they are interrelated in some way. Reality as such would then amount to a "pool of winds within one," distributed and continuously recycled in the individual phenomenon in some specific way (agreed upon by BW, HT). Still, the partaking of all things created in this "pool" points to the global interrelatedness of all things in the Navajo universe.

Even more convincing instances of the interpretation advocated above are provided by the role and place of human beings (Navajos) in the world. This is made transparently clear by the role of the Navajo diagnosticians: the handtrembler, the stargazer, and the windlistener. Any of these specialists can make out, through prescribed procedures, what ails the patient and, most important, what the cause of his ailment is. The handtrembler, by using his arm as a pendulum, locates the nature of the ailment and the nature of its origin.[47] "Through quick thinking" he has the insight of the factual cause, of which the present ailment is an effect: "If the patient has eaten shash bitsį' (bear meat) he then should have a Mountain Way Chant performed over him, or if he was struck by lightning or disturbed something struck by it, he should have a Shooting Way Chant performed over him." The stargazer looks at a particular star through a crystal; through the picture in the crystal he can see what went wrong with the patient's relationship with the world. The diagnosticians thus have the following tasks: they determine the cause of the illness in the disruption of good relations with the world; then they advise on the ceremony that is

47. FH, once a handtrembler himself, explains it all as follows: the handtrembler, guided by some force, moves his arm across the patient's body and subsequently above a set of figures drawn in the sand (snake, bear, etc.). In the latter process he gradually wipes out some figures (of the universe represented there), leaving one or more as the cause.

needed in order to restore the good order, more specifically the patient's share in the universal order (the order of the outside world is restored as well as the patient's relationship with it), and finally they advise on herbs, practices, and even singers (medicine men), who would be appropriate for healing (cf. Reichard, 1950; Underhill, 1964). This fits in with the general idea of the interrelatedness of all things in the world: man does not live above, outside, or independent of the rest of the world; instead, his actions and states are clearly linked with those of the rest of the universe (CM, BW). His mistakes, the disrespectful handlings of things, and his negligence disturb the good order in the universe, and consequently his own mental and/or physical health. There is interrelatedness and interdependence between everything in the Navajo world.[48]

Several parallel pieces of information can be listed to exemplify this. The attribution of sex to a whole range of paired phenomena is a case in point: Mother Earth (nahasdzáán shimá) and Father Heaven (yádiłhił shitaa') are said to be a couple, in the physical position of lovers. The Earth, especially, is said to have many female features: she has arms, legs, a head, a vagina, and so on, but also a heart and feelings of motherliness (BW). Human beings are related in yet other ways: "We are not different from Earth and Sky, they say: we see what comes from the rainbow, our hearing is protected by the air . . . they (Earth and Sky) have five senses like we do." The Sky's characteristics are less clearly defined. Still, he is said to be male and is believed to hold his hands under Mother Earth (BW, TB).

The "figures" (cf. the famous Navajo Sandpaintings) in the Sacred Mountains are couples too, each composed of one male and one female personality. The same is true of the different Holy Ones in all directions: Dawn People, Twilight People, Cornpollen Boy (ashkii tádídíín), and Dragonfly Girl (at'ééd tániil'áí), etc.

In the same way there is male and female thunder, rain, and lightning (BW), male and female stars (TB), male and female mountains (e.g., Lukachukai Mountain and Black Mountain, respectively; TB, HT), male and female rivers (e.g., the San Juan and the Rio Grande), and so on. In daily life, male and female hooghans are distinguished (coneshaped, and round, cribbed-roof hooghans respectively; cf. also Wyman, 1975, Introduction). Some practices are directed along the same lines: left hand and arm and left side is male "because it is the side the bow is held on while shooting with the wristband." So also, in the hooghan, when sitting around the center, the men generally face Northward, while the women face the South.

A similar pairing is found with colors spread over the different directions: East is associated with white (white shell, White Shell Woman lives

48. The example of the diagnosticians is important since most of the Navajo religious and social practices have to do with "health." Werner (1979) concluded that the concepts of health and sickness should be considered the core concepts of Navajo traditional culture (the way, maybe, technology would be of traditional American society and culture).

there . . .), South is associated with turquoise, West with abalone (yellow), and North with black (jet stone). These colors are correlated with different precious stones, and with the mountains in each direction (where the particular precious stone is to be found). Again, each part of the day has the same colors associated with it (as several Holy People who inhabit dawn, daylight, twilight, and night) going in clockwise cycles: white dawn coming from the East, changing to turquoise/blue daylight in the South, going to yellow twilight from the West, and ending in the black night coming from the North (HT, BW).

The uniform way these characteristics are generalized—assigning them to englobing and pervasive aspects of the world—again points to the interrelatedness of these aspects, or, rather, to the way Navajo knowledge states and recognizes relations between phenomena and processes that are perceived in the world.

On the social level a similar analysis is possible. In mythology, of course, but also in daily life, everybody seems to be related to everybody else. This feature is very striking when one asks Navajos to explain their kin relationships. Apart from the strictly perceivable relationships of family members between one another, there are those of clan memberships, which expand sometimes to several thousand persons.[49] By retracing two or three generations, it then easily works out that practically everybody has some type of kin relation (of first, second, third degree of closeness) with somebody else.[50]

As explained by LT, clan members have easier contact with each other than with other Navajos, while of course the general taboo against "marriage within a clan" unites the members of the clan by kinship as well. Even smoking is considered a manifestation and (maybe) strengthening of kin relation (CM).[51]

For the people in general, some social rules stress their interrelatedness as Navajos. First, their cultural tradition and their language distinguish Navajos (and their world) from anyone from the outside, including other tribes. This feature is highlighted dramatically through the ceremonial practices of which any part having to do with Blessing Way can help the Navajos regarding problems in the Navajo world, while Enemy Way ceremonies can cure them of foreign influences and reintegrate them in the Navajo world (cf. Wyman, 1975, Introduction; further information was supplied during the

49. Some clans like dibé łizhíní (Black Sheep) may comprise only tens of people (LB), while others like the dích'íí'nii (Bitter Water Clan; DH) may comprise hundreds, if not thousands, of people, thus securing the "relatedness" of all of these.

50. Only 100 years ago the Navajo people counted ca. 5,000–10,000 members, growing to 175,000 today.

51. CM made his point while in fact talking about kinship. He stated that smoking (of course of tobacco only) is to be considered a highly significant phenomenon. Smoking a pipe in the proper way would then amount to being busy with your own "bedding" (tsásk'eh) and your kinship relations.

1977 Healing Ceremony Symposium at Navajo Community College, Tsaile). The performance of an Enemy Way ceremony over those Navajos who had served in foreign countries during the Second World War is a beautiful example of the social significance of this ceremony.

In the second place, the interdependence of all Navajos on the traditional world is stipulated in a general social-ethical rule: it is not good for any individual Navajo to accumulate too much wealth, to become too prosperous in comparison to others since, through his collecting and stocking, he is in fact "stealing from the others." That is, he is denying sufficient resources or livestock or whatever to the rest of the people. In a similar way, stinginess, the refusal to share or help whenever possible, is severely censured. Connecting these types of behavior with "witchcraft" is understood to be a way of enforcing obedience in a changing world.[52] Finally, the fundamental relationship between human beings and natural phenomena is explicitly demonstrated in the names of the latter: in the holy way Sun, Moon, Earth, Sky, Dawn, Twilight, Thunder, and Lightning are called "father" (shitaa') or "mother" (shimá); darkness is called chahałheeł shichó (Grandmother Darkness); these designations do not, as one might expect, indicate differences in age: "They are all the same to us, earthpeople, they are all like parents/ancestors to us." Also Changing Woman (asdzą́ą́ nádleehi) and Whiteshell Woman (yoołgaii 'asdzáán), the mythological daughters of Mother Earth and Father Sky (or the Sun), are related to the Navajo people in the same way: shimá (BW, TB, HT).

None of these stress any literal kinship, but rather a relationship of interdependence between human beings and these phenomena; this is an intrinsic part of everyday life (BW, CM).

Other natural phenomena take a similar place, though indirectly. The rainbow, a blessing sign for human beings, is formed through "investments" from sky, earth, sunbeam, and moisture. The sunbeam and the air are said to "be there to give light and warmth and something to breathe for the human beings," while darkness (that is, absence of both of the former phenomena) protects human beings against evil things, at night when you cannot see them (BW).

Thunder, lightning, and clouds are said to "belong together" by an active role of the sun and the wind in their joint performances (HT). In this way, these phenomena too are related to the ones already mentioned and eventually, to the earthpeople. Disrespect for any of these, of course, is likely to generate a penalty, such as being struck by the lightning. Again, a special ceremony will be performed over the patient to restore the order between natural phenomena and humankind.

In conclusion, it appears that relationships can be demonstrated between several (eventually *all*) things "created" in this world and human beings (Navajos). The relationships are particular and should be respected each in their good, orderly form to avoid punishment or chaos in the universe.

---

52. Detailed information on these ethical issues is to be found in Pinxten (1979b).

Summary

Five basic conceptual clusters of Navajo natural philosophy have been analyzed:

1) The structure of the world: Earth and Heaven have a slightly arched form. The structure of the hooghan is based on these forms, thereby helping to explain through comparisons not only the actual form of the hooghan, but also the forms of Earth and Heaven. There is no explicit conceptualization of a totality, encompassing both Earth and Heaven.

2) The dynamic nature of the world: in opposition to the common Western belief of segmentability of an essentially static world, Navajos systematically represent the world and every discrete entity as a dynamic or continuously changing entity. A complex time-space notion seems more applicable than clearly distinct concepts of one-dimensional time and three-dimensional space.

3) Boundedness; center: the notion of center appears to play a basic role in the organization of the Navajo world. While the Navajo mentality speaks of a finite world, its notions of boundary cannot easily be grasped within the Western perspectives; again, the essentially dynamic nature of anything existing has to be taken into account so that boundaries are recognized as extreme variations of processes, rather than static positions.

4) Closedness of the world; order: the Navajo world is closed in that nothing can be added to it (by man) and that every possible act or event can and should be interpreted within the confines of this world. The difficult and very subtle notion of order plays an essential role in this respect.

5) Interrelatedness of everything: any single aspect or entity of the Navajo world enters specifiable, often delicate relationships with something else. One of the main consequences of this opinion is that any human action involving any one particular aspect of the world has a certain impact on other aspects (eventually on the whole creation). Respect is considered the most rewarding as well as the most natural attitude.

Concluding Remarks

The information presented in this chapter has been collected by means of classical ethnographic methods (asking questions somewhat at random, going deeper into selected topics, attempting to synthesize at several points in the process, confronting the consultants with the synthesis at several subsequent moments, recycling questions several times, observing as much as possible, etc.). In the following chapters a thorough semantic analysis of spatial terminology and spatial behavior is presented. The material presented here is taken as a general context for the semantic meanings. The sophisticated, highly refined methods and techniques for semantic analysis (cf. Appendix B) are believed to be as yet inadequate for the eliciting of those very basic and genuinely "deep" beliefs about the general characteristics of the world presented in this chapter. Therefore, these methods were not used during this investigation. On the other hand, I believe that the material in this chapter must be taken into account if one is to properly understand particular terms and behaviors related to space.[53] Evidently, a certain amount of mutual control from one body of information to the other, and vice versa, is liable to be exercised. Heuristically, however, I believe that more forceful means for an adequate understanding would be found in the most fundamental and therefore generally pervasive notions, in this case the beliefs based on the general features of the world. Since these were only elicitable through classical ethnographical work (instead of sophisticated anthropological linguistic work), I hold the opinion that the more intricate semantic analyses must rest on the methodologically rather vague "classical ethnography."

Consequently, the semantic analysis of the following chapters presupposes the valid use of a general, culturally independent "frame of reference" in order to reach proper "emic" analyses (cf. Appendix B for this "frame of reference"). At the same time it takes the "natural philosophy" of Navajos into account. In this way it functions as a general auxiliary means to understand the specific range of concepts and the general context of meaning and use in which certain expressions are to have meaning.

Finally, it is my conviction that the meanings of particular terms or phrases cannot be inconsistent with the features of the world as described above. This is to be taken as a general rule: it is imaginable, indeed, that particular meanings differ considerably from, or even contradict this world view. However, a very considerable degree of consistency and coherence may be expected and warranted a priori.

53. The resulting position is similar to Quine's philosophical maxim: In order to grasp the meaning of the word, you should at least understand the theory in which it is functioning (1960). In our case we claim it is necessary (or at least advisable) to understand the general characteristics of the Navajo world in order to understand the meaning of spatial terms and behaviors.

II | Semantic Analysis of Navajo Spatial Talk

Preliminary Remarks

In the present chapter a thorough analysis of semantic modeling is proposed. A full-fledged semantic theory has been presented in Pinxten, 1977.

One general remark on the Navajo material gathered is in order. A complete exposition of all material used is found in Chapter III of this book. As stated there, the emphasis of the fieldwork program and hence of the analysis and model presented here is on the more basic, less specific, or less detailed aspects of dealing with space in a language. Therefore, it cannot be concluded from this analysis that Navajos have only certain notions of space and "unfortunately must do without some others." This may be true in some instances, marked clearly and explicitly when the occasion to draw such conclusions presented itself. However, in a general way the emphasis was on the basic distinctions and constructions in spatial matters as they became apparent through the language used. I believe I have been able to reach this basic level through my methods of field investigation, and hence I present what looks like the structure and general systematic outlook of the information encoded in these basic levels of spatial semantics. As in the elicitation work, so in the model building parts of this scientific investigation, the same UFOR (cf. Appendix B) is used to guide the researcher in his questioning and organizing of material.

Principles of Descriptive Semantics

The semantic analysis and the model proposed in this chapter amount to arguments favoring a semantics which I might call post-Quine and anti-Katz. It is important to draw the basic features of this semantics (elsewhere applied to Dogon material; Pinxten, 1975, 1977).

1 | Toward a Synthetic Semantics

In his vehement plea for the abolition of the analytic-synthetic distinction in semantics, W. V. O. Quine (1960) used the example of an ethnographer who, in his field experience, encounters an unknown people speaking an unknown language, in order to make his point more readily understandable. He describes the ethnographer whose native informant reacts with "Gavagai" to the appearance of a rabbit in his visual field. Quine elaborates on the scene (1960, chap. 2) and concludes that it is impossible for the linguist or ethnographer to choose between the various, in fact endless series of translations that may be appropriate for this specific situation: "Gavagai" can denote the rabbit, or the running of the rabbit, or the ancestor in the rabbit, or the whole scene of nature with a rabbit running freely in it, and so forth. Hence, it is impossible, Quine states, to point to aprioristic, analytic elements of meaning. The only thing you would be doing, eventually, when picking out one possibility in the series of possible meanings for the utterance, is to impose your own interpretations and your accepted meaning on your situation. So there is no point in speaking about analytic elements of meaning (or rather, reference, for Quine); instead, a learned and therefore synthetic knowledge is employed to cope with the situation at hand.

Quine's criticism has had some effect on contemporary semantics, in linguistics and in other disciplines.[1] Still, plenty of current works in these disciplines prove that his criticism is not always digested: it remains challenging for the anthropologist in particular to develop synthetic semantic models, which do away with aprioristic elements in one's model and theory of meaning. In anthropology and linguistics the basic question from this point of view, then, becomes: How can one describe the semantic structure of a word, sentence, or text in any language without assuming certain basic, kernel semantic elements to be known, a priori, as absolute and universal points of departure for any semantic analysis? With regard to spatial concepts, one must ask: how can one describe the spatial representation of an unknown or very incompletely known people without assuming or presupposing a priori, or on analytic grounds, that certain aspects of space should be primitive, should be universally or humanly basic in any person's representation of space? The question is one of methodology. The classical analytic approach is defended by Katz (1972). According to him, ultimate distinctions of any semantic description are laid down in innate concepts of a rather sophisticated kind. To escape this sort of highly debatable assertion one poses the question of an alternative methodology and several alternative methods have been devised over the years. One of them is the sociolinguistic method using techniques to detect and "fill in" "registers" in any text or set of utterances (e.g., Halliday, 1968; Vandamme, 1977). A second one, and the one which I advocate, is known in several forms; it boils down to the use of "Universal Frames of Reference," continuously refined through a historical and empirical process. A detailed presentation of the nature and use of such devices is given in "The Device" of this book; here suffice it to say that anyone working with

---

1. In a fairly recent volume on semantic models (Vandamme and Pinxten, 1977) a set of alternative, post-Quinean, synthetic models of meaning is presented by several renowned scholars.

such a Universal Frame of Reference (UFOR) explicitly and systematically avoids a priori facts of analytic pieces of meaning, but uses instead a frame to explore, question, and search the language of the natives he is investigating. The primary result of the use of a UFOR is the development of an exhaustive and rather unstructured set of utterances and glosses, all having to do, in a yet unknown way, with correlates of the scientific concepts expressed in the meta-system of the UFOR. Thus, a primary and absolutely indispensable aspect of this semantic analysis is its neutrality vis-à-vis any ontological or episte-mological (say cultural) principle or order expressed in the particular language system that is studied. Hence, it is taken as a point of departure that no semantic element whatsoever is known, prior to thorough empirical analysis and actual painstaking field procedures having been carried out. On the other hand, it is taken for granted that, in order to avoid the total intranslatability Quine in fact talks about, a finite set of terms and scientific paraphrases of terms in a metasystem (the UFOR) can be used as a guide for, or as a system of minimal constraints on the intuition of the linguist or fieldworker in the process of gathering material, asking questions, and finally recognizing structures in the set of utterances and glosses he is eliciting. This is my position, as a defender of a synthetic model of semantics in the present debate. As such, the fundamental insights on meaning in the present analysis should be understood.

In close connection with questions on analytic versus synthetic aspects of meaning, the questions of the use and status of primitives in semantic analysis are raised.

2 | Primitives

The traditional, Katzian approach to semantics postulates a finite set of unavoidable and necessarily primitive semantic elements: the linguistic rules as internalized by the speaker (Katz, 1972, p. 16) and the "semantic markers" (Katz, 1972, p. 40) that form the set of building blocks, of unalter-able elements of meaning and that are put in particular series to produce the meaning of any given utterance. It is claimed that a finite set of these primitive or "unbuilt" notions will suffice to describe any meaningful complex in any language and thus would be de facto refuting the validity of the statement of intranslatability worked out by Quine.

The factual difficulties with the Katzian system are apparent to anyone who ever worked in a language different from the Western European lan-guages. I will not dwell upon the refutation of his position and theses (cf. again Pinxten, 1977, but also Kay, 1975), but will simply outline my own interpretation of the problem of primitives in semantics, consistent with the views expressed in the previous section. I do not accept primitives in a strict sense since I refuse to accept analytic elements of meaning in semantic analy-sis. However, when trying to determine the structure and hierarchy in the par-ticular Navajo spatial glosses elicited, I came upon a complex distinction between levels of "basicness" or levels of "primitiveness" as expressed in the system of spatial references of the Navajos themselves. That is, some clearly and distinctly recognized aspects of spatial representation (say the Navajo conceptualization of what corresponds, vaguely, to the Western or the scientifically paraphrased UFOR notion of "nearness") are distinguished in the language and behavior of the natives as not being built up or structured by means of other spatial aspects in his cultural knowledge. In that sense they may be considered "given" or "basic" or "primitive" to the native spatial system. So these labels refer exclusively to their culture-specific function and the operational frame to which they are particularly restricted, in this study. Moreover, it is conceivable that the same aspects may not be basic or constituent in another approach, which stresses a different and possibly just as relevant perspective on Navajo space or world view. It is in this highly relativistic sense that the labels of "primitives" or "basic aspects" are used in this study. Not only will the particular primitives found be confined to the particular language community investigated (they may in fact be different or the same in a second language), but moreover, their validity is restricted to the given perspectives inherent in the present analysis, especially to those imbedded in the present UFOR. In keeping with Don Campbell: the sole perspective of the present UFOR is advocated in this study, but at the same time it explicitly stresses that it is but one perspective of a doubtless polyvalent reality (Campbell, 1977).

The use of "primitives" in this highly relativistic sense entails a central difference between analytic and synthetic semantics. (The status and use of the UFOR is a second crucial point in this outlook, cf. below). In this approach, there are no "natural" or "necessary" or "given" primitives for any system of meaning. Instead, by means of and only as an end result of thorough empirical investigation I have reached the conclusion that—within the confines of the approach used and in the particular group of speakers talked with—x, y, and z are semantic units that have a prominent or "primitive" status. That is, x, y, and z are irreducible to any other unit and they are components in a large set of other semantic units in that language. All this points to the highly relativistic and indeed contextualized meaning of the term "primitive" in the present volume.

3 | Universalism Versus Relativism

In relation to the standpoints just defended above, I must situate this work with regard to universalism and relativism in language and thought. A general and well-known relativistic position is found in the works of Benjamin Lee Whorf (1956), while the universalist position is often linked with the presupposition of innateness of categories, as made popular in Noam Chomsky's work (e.g., Schaff, 1976, Chomsky, 1968).

Along with several other scholars these days (e.g., Berlin and Kay,

1969; Kay and McDaniel, 1978; and Kay, 1979), I defend the view that a more subtle position is required in order to deal with the available facts in a satisfactory way (cf. e.g., Pinxten, 1976). Certain percepts and the linguistic expression of these percepts might be universal or they might be limited to a particular cultural or linguistic community; but only detailed and painstaking empirical analysis can decide this question in each case. Thus, some notion of, for example, "nearness" may well be found in every cultural knowledge over the world, but its actual content and the degree of similarity between corresponding culture-bound notions in any two cultures will be determined through empirical analysis. It is in this sense that Berlin and Kay's universals of color discrimination can be understood (again, restricted to the perspective of their analysis, which is in this case restricted to the use of the Munsell card of color representation used in that study, cf. Conklin, 1973). In short, my arguments favor what might be called an a posteriori universalism.

4 | The Relevance of Natural Philosophy

As stipulated in the first chapter of this work, I take it for granted that a people's natural philosophy is important as a basic frame for better understanding of the people's world view (a rough ethnographic sketch of the fundamental insights is important in order to understand the elaborate and peculiarly sophisticated knowledge of the above-mentioned people). As such, the information of the first chapter will be used as an ethnographic guide in the many decision and structuring processes that are to some extent dealt with explicitly in the treatment of the detailed cultural knowledge of space elicited from several consultants. The logical norm of consistency is always considered to be of primary relevance for the general system of cultural knowledge, because this norm was always stressed by the Navajo consultants themselves, during both the interviews and the informal conversations.

5 | Semantic Fields

A linguistic corpus can be structured in different ways, depending on the method of linguistic analysis. Such a structured corpus of meaningful items is called a semantic field (or a lexical/semantic field). Werner does major work in this area of complex semantic research. He defines lexical/semantic fields as follows: "lexical items (possibly also sublexical items) form an associational lexical/semantic field. The units of the fields may be simple or complex . . . which are linked by lexical/semantic relations" (1977, p. 137). In this section I will try to make clear how my approach of semantic fields relates to the different types that are now known.

Werner et al. (1974) distinguish between four models of lexical/semantic fields:

1) The thesaurus model: this model defines a linear structure between

all lexical items with a lot of intersections of synonymy lines. Werner et al. analyze the usefulness of this model and conclude that it has a very limited use for the representation of meaning in diverse cultural complexes.

2) The single-page model (developed by Bierman): the lexicographer conceives of a total corpus as one giant page covered by all lexical items and their multiple semantic interconnections.

3) The inverse of the single-page model: in this case a semantic field is built up for a whole corpus of lexical items by working through three general— presumably universal—formal semantic relations: synonymy, taxonomy, and attribution.

4) The "componential" lexical/semantic field: cognitive anthropology develops a specific model for semantics in componential analysis. Sets of lexical items are ordered in paradigmatic or taxonomic structures (cf. especially Werner and Fenton, 1973). In this model all relevant dimensions of meaning in a language are used in a consecutive way to produce order in the meaning of the set of lexical items. The combination of these dimensions results in the particular type of semantic field that can be called "componential."

Excluding the first, Werner et al. (1974) interpret these models as valid for the study of meaning. They exemplify different types of lexical/ semantic fields in the sense that they offer workable models of the use of one basic and sufficient set of semantic relations: the relations of taxonomy, synonymy, and attribution. In a later publication (Werner, 1977), the implications of this perspective on semantics are analyzed in depth.

Werner gives a formal characterization of all semantic relations. He differentiates the set of relations further in order to reach a set which represents all the relations of classical formal logic. However, the three fundamental relationships of componential analysis are dominant in Werner's new proposal. Moreover, the general procedure of semantic description remains the same as in previous papers: Werner aims at building semantic fields, which consist of lexical/semantic relations. The latter are not found by means of empirical or ethnographic analysis, but "these relations are language universals that link lexical items which are language specific" (1977, p. 154). In other words, according to this view, semantic fields are a combination of aprioristic aspects (i.e., semantic relations) and aposterioristic aspects (i.e., lexical items). It is obvious that this model of lexical/semantic fields cannot be accepted by me: earlier in this chapter (especially subsections 1 and 2) I explained why analytic semantics should be abandoned. This refusal pertains to Werner's model as well, insofar as it necessarily implies aprioristic semantic aspects.

Situating the present volume in the domain of semantic field studies, I claim that it offers yet another model of semantic fields. My approach is very similar to Werner's in many ways, but it tends to introduce a new model: that both lexical items and semantic relations ought to be language or culture specific, according to its philosophical leitmotiv. No semantic bias can be depended on in the process of semantic description: therefore, I introduce a new notion of semantic relation, namely the relation of constitution, which then refers to Navajo semantic linkages. It is a genuinely synthetic semantic relation (cf. below, the Procedure of Descriptive Semantics).

The Role and Status of the UFOR

I have claimed elsewhere that, in order to have an emically correct and dependable description of any aspect of a culture or language of a community, one has to work on a sort of common ground between researcher and native informant, preferably a neutral or strictly scientific grid representing the problem area under investigation. That "grid" was called the Universal Frame of Reference (UFOR; Pinxten, 1975, 1977). Such grids have been used in a somewhat different sense in the Munsell card of color chips in the study by Berlin and Kay (1969) and in the similar, but debatable work on kinship terminology by Goodenough (1970). Much criticism has been forwarded against both approaches, most of all against their sole concern with linguistic material (e.g., Harris, 1976). The latter criticism seems valid to me, and is taken into account in the actual gathering of material, as reflected in Chapter III.

The general concept of the use of frames in the ethnographic and ethnosemantic methodology is agreed upon and carried further in the research on spatial differentiations in the present study. The actual UFOR used is developed in a synoptic form in Appendix B. As such, the form and the particular entries of the UFOR for space research are, in this chapter, assumed to be known, or at least to be retrievable. Only the actual procedure of its use in semantic analysis remains to be discussed in greater detail in this section. The UFOR for spatial analysis covers all levels of spatial differentiation. In the text these levels will be referred to as O-space (object space), S-space (sociographical space), and C-space (cosmological space). It is taken for granted that all cultures will know this general distinction, however much variety they may display in the detailed glosses and paraphrases.

The status of the UFOR is that of a necessary, but hardly possible tool of research. Studies on world view in other cultures tend to demonstrate that universal frames cannot be defined in this field of research. My "universal" frame of reference subscribes to this fact in a particular way. All cultures have their specific way of representing the world. Yet, all of them refer to the same sun, moon, or earth "out there" and all do this by means of the same basic "tools" to gather knowledge and understanding, that is, by manipulating matter with their hands, by looking at the world through identical eyes, by moving around a uniformly structured body in an identical way (e.g., walking forward and backward, turning in a horizontal plane), and so on. Among these things, the ways of exploring nature and the way to combine information of different experiences in a specific representational system, as well as the occurrence of natural accidents (e.g., an eclipse) or of cultural interaction may account most of all for the variety in cultural knowledge systems. The anthropologist is confronted with both facts: there is, presumably, some universal basis in the physical and biological conditions of man-the-knower, while at the same time there seems to be a wide variety of world views. The UFOR is an attempt to bridge this gap to a limited extent by offering a tool that can be used by the anthropologist to probe the question: anthropologist and consultant interact and communicate about "something out there" when they confront each other in an ethnographic field situation, and this "something" is represented in the most neutral and culture-free (or "pre-culturized") way possible in the entries of the UFOR. This "something" is some physical color in the Munsell card, and communication will eventually lead to the demarcation of the particular semantic color categories referring to the physical items, which are known in their differential ways by the anthropologist's and by the consultant's color categories (Kay, 1979, stresses the lack of direct correspondence between physical and semantic color categorization). This "something" is a spatial phenomenon in the present study. The UFOR maps out all spatial differentiations with which man-the-knower has to deal and which are subject to cognition because of their physical prominence and/or because the biological constitution of people induces these spatial characteristics (e.g., the structure of the body induces the distinction between three spatial dimensions, cf. Appendix B).

In the present UFOR an attempt was made to sum up all spatial differentiations at this physiologico-physical level, which would be relevant for any knower. By making these differentiations explicit in the field situation (by means of examples, body positions, artifacts, drawings, or whatever possible), the anthropologist creates a minimal common ground of discourse between himself and the consultant. Subsequently, both can go through a delicate and painstaking process of determining the particular culture-specific form which deals with the same or similar differentiations in the cultural knowledge system of the consultant. For example, in the case of the analysis of "distance" in Navajo culture by means of this procedure, one ends up with at least three somewhat different notions: the neutral notion in the UFOR, the specific Western notion of "distance" of the anthropologist, and the notion of "distance" in the Navajo cultural knowledge system. Differences between all three can be more or less dramatic and incommensurability can be more or less apparent.

The UFOR approach thus has the advantage of controlling the intention of both ethnographer and consultant in the field situation (since both start out from an alien, neutral notion which does not capture the semantic differentiation each of them has in mind). Moreover, it offers a basis to allow both thorough emic research and comparative studies between cultural knowledge systems of varying origin. At the same time it will be clear by now why the UFOR device has an important role in the synthetic semantics approach: the UFOR does not introduce any analytic elements of meaning in the ethnographic situation, but it offers a minimal ground of common understanding (linguistic or not, but by necessity highly provisional) as a "clothes hanger" with which the actual semantic identification or refutation can then proceed. It makes clear what the question might be about, without implying an answer in any sense.

The Procedure of Descriptive Semantics in This Study

Descriptive semantics is a more hazardous enterprise than formal semantics for the very reason its name suggests; it is purely descriptive in character. One cannot, of course, be a naïve lexicologist anymore, and one is cut off from all strictly rationalistic approaches, as was pointed out in the first section of this chapter. Then what does description amount to? How much interpretation is one permitted, or maybe obliged, to include?

The semantic description comprises three stages of clearly distinct activity and emphasis. All of them appear during the ethnographic work, of course, but their delicate interplay and mutual correction in the process of investigation can only be understood through active reference to the UFOR throughout the process. That is, the researcher and the consultant agree more or less on the UFOR or "common ground" notions to be investigated and then proceed to try to identify the often very particular and sometimes widely diverging meanings of the native terms considered relevant for each UFOR notion. It is important that consultants have an idea of the contents of the UFOR notion investigated so as to have an insight into the anthropologist's initial semantic domain. Then follows a delicate play and a series of tests by anthropologist and consultant alike in order to grasp the particular set of native terms and phrases in their semantic finesse. In subsequent phases the semantics of each unit is identified more or less and related to other units. It is thus clear that the UFOR is not meant to be used as a rigid grid that would limit the consultant to any particular direction; the mere content of the conversation most certainly accounts for this general and often regrettable characteristic of the consultant-anthropologist contact (Fabian, 1978). Instead, this initial imposture of an encounter is recognized and the UFOR serves as a primary device. The ethnographer can go back and check his intuition and the range of interpretation he is opening (or, eventually, closing) in the course of subsequent conversations; it is taken for granted that the mere printed form of this set of initial and presumably universal differentiations on the subject investigated will make the ethnographer conscious of shortcomings, pitfalls, broader or narrower ranges of meaning attributed to physiologically or otherwise grounded differentiations in the potentially meaningful materials he is handling. As such, the UFOR is a supplement of a more sophisticated kind to the older, though still useful, ethnographer's notebooks or diaries.

Step 1: Data Gathering

In the first stage I gathered as much linguistic and nonverbal material as I could get on Navajo spatial differentiations. Glosses of specific terms, folk definitions, paraphrases of the words presented in the field interview, exemplifications of the use and the semantic range of particular terms queried, and so on were searched for in order to have a set of data as broad and varied as possible. Occasional observations of particular native behavior (with or without the use of the terminology elicited) complemented the mainly verbal material. The first results of this fieldwork were checked with different consultants with reference to the terms and concepts discussed. Throughout this stage the UFOR was used as heuristic device and an instrument to control the intuition displayed in the questions and the observations. The actual cross-questioning by consultants themselves (of the anthropologist and of each other) on several of the terms discussed served as a supplementary control on the adequacy of the data we gathered. Finally, a topological test of drawings was used to check and refine distinctions.

Step 2: Identification of Meanings

In this second stage of the ethnographic process, the unprocessed data were organized along the dimensions grasped in the material itself. Each tentative conclusion was subjected to the criticism of and often elaborate discussions with one or more consultants. At this stage a double identification is pursued: in the first place the meaning of each term investigated is described by the amount of information gathered on it. No definition in the strict sense is worked out, but rather a minimal characterization of the special meaning range of the term (or expression) concerned is built, taking into account the glosses and terminological distinctions between terms the consultants produce before (in the data-gathering phase) and during the identification interviews. The result of this term-by-term identification is found in Chapter III, where a selection of all verbal and nonverbal material on each of the four-hundred-odd terms or expressions investigated and a minimal characterization in the sense indicated here are given for each.

In the second place, a core identification procedure is set up within the range of meaning provided by the UFOR. That is to say, I actively try, from the investigator's point of view rather than consultant's, to formulate a Navajo correlate for each and every entry of the UFOR. Still more concretely, I search for a core of meaning (or a conglomerate of meaningful aspects) in the ethnographic description of the characteristic sought through UFOR: for example, a set of six expressions in Navajo (all of clearly distinct stems) was found to be used to render different aspects of the sole concept of "nearness, being near" in the UFOR worked with; consequently, in this second step of the semantic interpretation of Navajo "nearness" I search for similarities and eventual differences in the semantics of all six expressions in Navajo in order to eventually reach one or two basic linguistic renderings of the physically and physiologically expressible characteristic of "nearness" in space. Maybe one core meaning may be found, supplemented by five or six finer specifications, or maybe a set of two or more mutually irreducible meanings of Navajo conceptualizations of "nearness" can be detected. This part of the identification process thus amounts to the delineation of Navajo correlates or clusters of correlates to the UFOR entries. This procedure is undertaken and is entirely based on the material of Chapter III (eventually modified through information from the natural philosophy, chap. I). I will present an analysis of one such set of terms/expressions and their meaningful relationships with each other in detail, and then proceed to the results of all further analysis of the complete set of Navajo expressions given in Chapter III.

Step 3: Interrelationships and Semantic Constitution

In this third and last phase of semantic analysis, an attempt is made to determine the basic structure of the total Navajo spatial lexicon that was examined. At this level the notion of "constitution" becomes of central importance; it will be explained later in this chapter when the actual analysis is carried to this level. Suffice it to say that a semantic model of Navajo spatial talk will result at that stage.

Each of these steps results in a determination of meaning at each level of abstraction:

a) Local meaning: each particular Navajo term or expression has its own specific meaning, more or less elaborately presented in the material of Chapter III. For example, under the UFOR entry of near/separate/contiguous a list of terms was treated (processed as described above), and local, particular meanings for each of them were reached: binaa, whóshdę́ę́', etc.

b) Regional meaning: at a second level of analysis more general domains or regions of meaning are to be construed. They should "summarize" the meanings of all local analyses under the same UFOR entry and hence make a formulation of the Navajo correlate to each of the UFOR entries possible. Here, the Navajo notion of, for example, nearness, or that of volume, and so on, is proposed. A detailed example of this step is shown in the semantic study as presented below.

The regional meaning identifies especially the spatial components that make up the minimal and distinctive meaning of the spatial constituents in the Navajo lexicon and conceptual system. At the same time, by means of the analysis of all regional meanings listed, the list of meanings, which this particular Navajo spatial category serves as a constituent or a semantic building block, is given.

The regional meanings thus consist of two parts, distinguished as "Const. H" and "Const. I," respectively, in the following way:

a) Const. H (Has as Constituents): (follows the list of spatial differentiations that are observed to be constituent of [serve as semantic building blocks in], all terms or expressions referring to this particular Navajo region or UFOR entry).

Const. I (Is a Constituent of): (follows the list of spatial differentiations in the Navajo spatial system of which this specific category appears to be a constituent).

The specific set of Const. H's and Const. I's defines the semantic content of a given Navajo spatial category. There can sometimes be slight, or sometimes considerable differences in correlating categories in other cultural knowledge systems, for example in the Western spatial differentiation system.[2]

b) Global meaning: A third level of analysis aims at the structure of the spatial world of Navajos. The particular relationships (Const. H's and Const. I's) are summarized and represented in an englobing diagram.

c) The universe of meaning: the spatial categorization of Navajo language and thought has to be understood, evidently, in the total system of world knowledge that is theirs. This part of the more general anthropological study of Navajo culture is not undertaken here, although some indications are given through the discussion of basic characteristics of space.

Semantics: Between Scylla and Charybdis

A still more general orientation in the field of semantics is necessary in order to bring out the advantages of the present approach. It must be clear from previous sections that the classical approach to semantics, including Katz's efforts, represents a pitfall for the present investigations. At the other extreme is lexicographical semantics.

First of all, I understand semantics to be at a metalevel. My lexicographical and indeed fieldwork aimed at describing the meaning of particular terms or expressions. Each term or expression enters a "category" of Navajo spatial knowledge that corresponds to, but is still somewhat different, from the correlate notions in the Western cultural knowledge system and in the frame system (UFOR) that is used here as a universal basis of understanding and comparison. Now "Navajo" semantics proper deals with concepts, notions, and categories in this sense, and not primarily with the particular terms or expressions examined. The latter are but instances and in fact (to some extent) differentiations of the category under investigation within the Navajo language.

My criterion of relevance for selecting material for the semantic analysis proper (called "regional" and "global" analysis in following sections) is unique in the tradition of semantic analysis and deserves more explicit comment.

2. Comparison with the particulars of spatial conceptualization in Western thought is possible via Piaget's work (Piaget and Inhelder, 1947; cf. also Pinxten, 1976).

I look for components or characteristics that appear in the analysis of all terms and expressions gathered within the same "category," and select only those characteristics as relevant for semantic analysis proper that appear in the analysis of each and every individual term or expression. For example, when I found that six different expressions were acceptable to Navajo consultants to render the meaning of "nearness," and they all agreed on this set, I then checked it throughout the whole Navajo language work in different tests and cross-checkings. Only "volumeness/planeness" was recognizable as a component of each and every one of these six mutually differentiated expressions, while several other meaningful aspects were relevant for one, two, or more of these terms, but not for all of them. Consequently, I decided to delete all information, except the component status of "volumeness/planeness," as irrelevant for my semantic work proper. This procedure is followed for all UFOR entries (in the correlates determined by our Navajo consultants), leading to a series of "minimal characterizations of semantic categories" (of Navajo "nearness," of Navajo "volumeness," etc.), each time selecting the components that have relevance for the entire set of expressions and terms examined (in other words: selecting those components that are observed to function as "building blocks" in each and every term or expression examined within a given range).

The "system" of Navajo spatial semantics, then, is construed exclusively from information selected in this way.

One of the unusual aspects of this procedure (and certainly of its results) is the lack of clear "definition" or "paraphrase" of the semantic characterizations given. In other words, the semantic analysis of any notions (Navajo "nearness," Navajo "distance," etc.) does not finally produce a neat determination on the content of such Navajo concepts, or reach a clear definition of the notion under investigation. Rather, it points to "building blocks," semantic components that were found to be necessary in order to understand the Navajo notion involved. And that is all. It does not produce an exhaustive list of spatial (and maybe nonspatial) characteristics, but rather (a) some minimal spatial characteristics that typify all terms and expressions in native spatial categories (Navajo "nearness," etc.); and (b) the relationships between Navajo spatial categories as defined through the former procedures in a total system of "spatial knowledge." The latter is construed exclusively on the basis of the selected characteristics, that is, on the minimal semantic characterizations that formed each notion or concept behind a set of concrete (and often varyingly specified) terms and expressions.

The present notion of semantics (semantics proper) differs considerably from lexicography in that the latter is taken to be but the first step in the analysis. A much more abstract level of analysis is reached than is the case in lexicography to get at the structural and systemlike level of semantics proper.[3] On the other hand, the present analysis differs from Katzian seman-

---

3. It is well known that lexicography either shows immediate circularity (dictionary entries generally refer to each other within four or five steps, at the most), or probably unwarranted

tics in its denial of the importance and even the relevance of full-fledged definitions or paraphrases in semantic analysis. I claim that the system of minimal interdependencies of purely structural and formal relationships is more important than the content-centered and redundant (quasi-lexicographical) model that Katz defended (1972). In a way, this approach aims to get closer to the thesaurus idea of meaning than to the dictionary model.

Now, how can all this be defended?

The question is answered in an indirect way. I formulate two criteria of adequacy with which a good semantic model has to comply. These criteria of adequacy are

1) a semantic model must describe the structure of the (spatial) lexicon adequately and efficiently, and

2) the semantic model has to enable one to bridge the gap of "untranslatability" between different languages, or, more strictly, between the cognitive systems that are expressed in two different natural languages. The actual analysis and the construction of the model in the present study will answer the question, in showing how the present model overcomes the inadequacy of the others in complying with these criteria.

The first criterion will be dealt with in detail at the end of the present chapter, and the second will be dealt with in more detail in Chapter V. The latter is dramatically highlighted in the current inefficient and alienating communication between the two systems of cultural knowledge (the Navajo and the Western system) in the schools. The existence of this gap and the incapacity to bridge it, even in the best schools on the Navajo reservation, makes the relevance of this criterion painfully obvious.

Detailed Analysis of Regional Meaning: Near/Separate/Contiguous

The present section presents an example of semantic analysis on the regional level. All similar analyses are left out of the present report and only the results are mentioned. But, in order to enable control and insight in the actual way of performing this type of semantic study at this particular level, one example is worked out in full detail.

Near

I was told repeatedly by the Navajos that they clearly distinguish between two general categories of "being near": an absolute identification of nearness giving details on the relationship between any two items in a general

---

hierarchy (taxonomy per se) as a structure of lexicons. This may be due to specific outlooks on semantics and on semantic analysis.

sense, and a relative identification, stressing the relationship of anything in the vicinity of the speaker (ego). The distinction is represented, as such, at this level of semantic analysis.

Absolute

Two expressions are found in this group differing in meaning but having at least the absolute sense of describing the spatial relationship between any two items in the outside world.

1) áhání and its derivatives define such a relationship of closeness or nearness between any two or more items in the environment. None of the items has a privileged status to any other, and the relationship remains very ill defined. There is certainly no information precise enough to allow for any measurement to be relevantly sought for.

2) binaa rather stresses a neighborhood or nearness set: it can be applied to items in a situation of áhánígi to each other, and moreover specifies that the sum of these items forms a minimal structure that is differentiated from any other item in the environment.

Both expressions, at least, have enough in common to be said to inscribe a very unspecific relationship between items, or better still, between aspects of the world that are at least instances of volumeness. The latter expression is somewhat more specific and comprises a vague reference to a notion of center. Both expressions are absolute differentiations in space, that is, they exclusively define the relationship between any two items in space.

Relative

The expressions found in this group always refer to a privileged position in the spatial relationship network. Most of the time the reference (implicit or explicit) is to ego, the speaker, or perceiver.

ch'į', whóshdę́ę́' and t'áá'áhą́ą́digo all point to the nearness of an item to the observer/actor, specifying that the distance is shortening still. t'áá' ághídíghi is similar in meaning, but does not imply any actual movement or displacement on the part of the item. A characteristic of all these expressions is the way nearness is expressed through the capacities of the actor/perceiver to whom the item is said to be near: the consultant stressed that items are near in the sense of these expressions "provided they can be acted upon, reached, or grasped quite easily." In other words, the relative aspect is understood very clearly in terms of the possibility of actions on the part of the referent (ego) involved.

Taking into account all these expressions and examining the general meaning that pervades all of them at once, I come to a very general and rather vague Navajo "kernel" meaning of nearness: items, instances of volumeness (or planeness) are said to be near one another provided they appear to be easily reachable to each other (when one of them is an agent), or provided they appear to be clearly in relationship though at a loosely defined distance from each other.

In the framework of the constitution model of semantics that I am defending in this work, I must now look for the minimal requirements of Navajo semantic differentiation of "nearness" (as exemplified in all expressions analyzed). It appears that some notion of instances of volumeness (or planeness) is used in the semantic characterization of all expressions. That is, nearness is invariably defined in the Navajo lexicon as a relationship between items that have some (undefined) extension on two or three dimensions; in other words between unspecified volumes ("objects" or "things" we would say in our cultural knowledge system) or surfaces ("flat objects," "places," etc.). In some cases, namely in the relative expressions on nearness, one of the related items can be the perceiver, ego. The meaning of each expression is specified more or less particularly by supplementary characteristics: in several instances movement (or action) is codeterminant of the meaning of an expression, while in another instance the notion of center plays a role. No characteristic, apart from volumeness/planeness, has the status of semantic building block in all expressions examined.[4] Therefore, the distinction of "volumeness/planeness" as the only characteristic that is relevant throughout all expressions having to do with nearness in Navajo is singled out and is considered to be a necessary, though nonsufficient, semantic component in the Navajo semantics of terminology related to "nearness" notions. This conclusion is rendered as such:

"Nearness" Const. H: volumeness/planeness. That is, "nearness" (in Navajo terminology) has as constituents the notion of volumeness/planeness.

It should be borne in mind that, as mentioned in a previous section, in my approach it is not considered the task of a semanticist to come to a full definition, or even a detailed paraphrase of any specific Navajo expression in this chapter.

The information that results from such an analysis will then be used in the construction of the semantic model, that is, the structure of the Navajo spatial semantics, in a specific way. Indeed, having determined in like manner the "component set," or better still, what is called the "constituent set" of each and every spatial category, I can then proceed to reiterate the relationships between all notions in the Navajo cultural knowledge system. If, for example, nearness, dimension, center, and width all have this same notion of "volumeness/planeness" as a constituent (the example is fictitious), then their semantic similarity in this respect will appear in the model that is constructed of the total meaningful domain of Navajo space.

A second part of the semantic characterization of any notion or category (e.g., nearness) is missing, however. Each notion is not only determined by one or more other semantic actions (e.g., volumeness in this case), but codetermines the meaning of other notions as well. In other words, any notion

---

4. Only this material is taken up for the further semantic model while all other information is deleted from the final systematic picture.

can be a constituent of any of the other notions in the semantic domain of spatial terminology in Navajo. Looking through all "Const. H's" characterizations of the notions examined, one easily gathers the set of notions that "nearness" is a constituent of. This information is represented as follows:

"Nearness" Const. I (followed by the list of notions that "nearness" is a constituent of). It will be read: 'nearness' is a constituent for (list of notions).

Both sets of information, the set of Const. H's and the set of Const. I's, in fact determine the semantic relevance of the notion treated (i.e., "nearness").

The former paragraphs should suffice to make clear the procedure that is followed in order to get at the information deemed important for further semantic modeling. I now present the results of similar procedures to determine the semantic relevance of all spatial notions examined in detail in the Navajo spatial vocabulary and spatial knowledge. The procedures as such are not given in detail, since that would take a huge and rather boring volume to analyze properly. Rather, I have decided to present only the results of these investigations. The reader can always retrace at will any specific procedure through the indications given with the detailed example in this section. Again, of course, the analyses are based on the material that is given in Chapter III, which is based in turn on painstaking fieldwork on the lexicon and the nonverbal spatial differentiations.

III | Linguistic Material on Navajo Spatial Meaning

In the present chapter I compiled all linguistic material necessary for a better understanding of the way specific terminological distinctions of spatial relevance carry meaning and are used in the Navajo language. Through reference to this material, the analyses and model building in Chapter IV acquire empirical weight, and thus validity, to enable thoroughgoing discussions on relevance, adequacy, and particular benefits and fallacies of the model for semantic analysis.

A few restrictions must be stated explicitly:

1) It is doubtful as to whether there is something like *the* Navajo language (and spatial terminology) to be worked upon in a significant way, through semantic analysis. The present material focuses on the use of the terms listed by people of a relatively small part of the present Navajo reservation, mainly the more traditional part extending between Lukachukai and Rock Point, situated in the Chinle area. The consultants were native to this area.

2) The complete list of terms and expressions that is presented was worked out, in its entirety, with Frank Harvey and with TB (monolingual consultant). Apart from these older and more eloquent speakers of the language, detailed sets of expressions and terms (ordered sets or just occasional groups of words) were worked upon, discussed, analyzed, compared, illustrated with drawings, and the like by several other consultants in occasional sessions (one or two for each consultant): LB, BB, BW, KB, LT, CM, M-AL, RB. The main consultants in fact worked through the whole list of terms and expressions up to four times: once word by word, provisionally ordered according to the translations that were found, once in systematic cross-reference to other, semantically related terms (asking for mutual distinctions and similarities, for appropriate contexts of use of each of the seemingly related terms, etc.), once with the use of nonverbal aids, primarily to determine meanings and mutual distinctions (drawings, clay structures, body positions, the "Test on Topological Notions" using drawings of presumably cross-culturally valid topological relationships), and finally the first draft of the material was reviewed to correct, elaborate, and refine the first understanding. The total sequence was followed systematically with FH while it was done in a more synthetic way with TB (doing drawings and exemplifications in the same sessions). The reference to both consultants is omitted from the following text since both worked on all

the material concerned. Only supplementary consultants are mentioned in the text, with their particular input.

3) Organization of material: I started out with all entries on space to be found in the several dictionaries,[1] ordering the material according to translations, in categories that were drawn from the UFOR (Appendix B). In the process of investigation, the material was reorganized several times, ending up with the present order, again on basic distinctions and concepts in the UFOR. It goes without saying that the actual categories of Navajo terms differed during the process, while the basic UFOR characterizations remained workable and efficient throughout.

From the different consultants a wealth of information, insights, examples, and the like were gathered on each of the terms and expressions. It is impossible to present all of the material. In the first place, the number of examples given with any one term was often considerable (it ranges from 5 to up to 15 example sentences per item investigated), while the results of the "Test on Topological Notions" would require a separate monograph to explain what they are all about. Therefore, a concise presentation of the results was favored. With any term discussed three or four of the most characteristic examples were chosen and presented, and results of drawings, clay models, the topological test, and so forth are described wherever appropriate with reference to the linguistic material. This and other information is given in English most of the time (except for the relevant words or sentences).

The presentation and ordering of the material was done in the following way:

1) I followed the general headings of the UFOR, forming sections with the corresponding UFOR entries. Under it, in each section the corresponding Navajo terms are listed together with translations, examples, and supplementary information on use, connotations, nonverbal exemplifications, and the like.

2) The material on each term comprises a selection of sentences in Navajo (with translations), exemplifying the meaning and use of the term discussed. Before giving the examples, the term (stem or simple form of stem and pronoun) is introduced, together with its basic translation (offered by FH). Furthermore, a short text is printed with the translation, summarizing the researchers' understanding of the use of the term, of the examples not listed, of nonverbal instances of the same notion, of contexts (sacred or profane), and so on. Finally, at the end of the presentation of material on each individual term, an individual "constitutional" characterization is provided, listing a set of spatial (and some nonspatial) components that are held to be relevant for the particular term discussed. This "delineation" of the meaning of the particular term has definite characteristics: the components, again, are entries of the UFOR held relevant for this particular term (together with occa-

---

1. Young and Morgan (1942, 1980), Haile (1950–51), Hoijer (1974), Franciscan Fathers (1910), Wall and Morgan (1958).

sional nonspatial features) distinguishing the particular term to some extent, but defining it incompletely. That is, it is my conviction that semantic analysis cannot aim at definitions or full (necessary and sufficient) circumscriptions of the meaning of any term or sentence (cf. Pinxten, 1977, against Katzian semantics, and Appendix B), but can provide an understanding in the distinctive uses, the comparative meanings of, for example, all spatial terms in a specific language community (e.g., Navajos) vis-à-vis each other, structuring the total field of "spatial meaning" in such a way that the minimal or incomplete characterization of one term (e.g., border) is distinguished sufficiently and unambiguously within the given semantic or meaning field (space), from any other, similar, or opposite, or partly synonymous, or simply relevant term (e.g., line, center, but also limit, etc.). The distinction is not made absolute in any sense, rather, indicated through the different sets of components (UFOR distinctions) that go with each of the terms discussed (cf. more information on this aspect in Appendix B, and in chap. II).

The scheme of the material for any particular term is presented as follows:

Navajo term: "English translation." English description of meaning, use, nonverbal correlates, and the like.

Examples: Navajo sentences and English translation.

Components: list of relevant entries of the UFOR, making up a characterization of the meaning of the particular Navajo term. (N.B.: The little text following the English translation, as well as the list of components, is made up by the researchers; the rest comes integrally from Navajo consultants.)

The selection of Navajo terms listed and discussed was a delicate problem. By the use of singular or combined prefixes, postpositions, enclitics, and pronouns, a practically infinite set of spatial terms and expressions can be formed, each with a sometimes delicate or very minor differentiation from the next one. Following the good examples of Young and Morgan and Berard Haile's stem vocabulary, I decided to focus clearly on distinct stems before all else, presented most of the time with the third-person singular pronoun (bi- or yi-) and in the perfective mode. Occasionally, specific complex forms were added in the set of examples, not entered as separate items to be discussed. Some exceptions were made: when it turned out that particular composite forms had wide use or held an important and substantially different meaning (from the imbedded stem), the form was introduced individually, in a separate scheme (cf. above).

I certainly do not claim to present the ultimate set of spatially relevant terms. Without doubt, gaps of information will be likely, and I hold full responsibility for any omission or fault in the picture presented below. However, I hope to have gathered and analyzed sufficient material of the Navajo spatial terminology (both within the geographical and the theoretical limits discussed above) to be able to reach interesting and, presumably, educationally valuable insights on Navajo spatial meaning, its specific modeling and representation of universally relevant distinctions in spatial manipulation and spatial representation in thought and language (i.e., the entries of the UFOR). Particularly in this chapter, Young's suggestions and corrections have been very valuable. I followed his corrections, except in those cases where the Navajo sentences themselves would have been changed.

102. Near, Separate, Contiguous (Numbers 102, 202, and 302 of the UFOR)[2]

These distinctions are represented in a set of terms and expressions, all having a particular degree of generality, and having more or less specific non-spatial characteristics besides. In consequence, the list comprises terms and expressions that cover a range of meanings having to do with nearness, separateness, and/or contiguity in a more or less strict sense.

I propose to make one more basic distinction: the words relating to nearness, separateness, and contiguity in an absolute sense are distinguished from those having a relative meaning. Those having a relative meaning invariably have a referent expressed or implied with the use of the term or expression: something is near to me (ego as referent), or to you, and so on. In the absolute sense, things are near with no specification at all.

Absolute Nearness, Separateness, Contiguity

a) áhání, 'close by, a little way from'. A spatial relation is defined through this particle, without specification or referent. On the other hand, the object(s) is (are) characterized partially by its (their) relationship of nearness. No specification is further made to restrict the relevance of the term to one space: therefore, it is taken to be relevant in all the spaces O, S, and C. It refers to things that are so close "you can touch them or easily walk up to them."

Examples: naalyéhé bá' hooghandóó t'áá 'áhánígí Asdzą́ą́tsoh kééhat'į́, "nearby the store 'Big Woman' is living"; chidí naat'a'í t'áá'áhánígí yit'ah, "the airplane is flying just nearby (above our head)"; anít'i t'áá'áhání, "the fenceposts are standing just a little way from one another."

Components: near/separate; any direction; codefining items. Related terms are áhánígi (pointing more to distant places) and t'áá 'áhání (the nearness between two items).

b) binaa, 'near, surrounding'. This postposition relates to the relationship of several items, within a small area, in the mutual vicinity of a central item (LB). In this way neighbors can be located, but also the diurnal movement of the sun around the earth. The term is used in all three spaces. No precise distance whatever is implied.

Examples: atiin binaagóó dah hodiilnił, "you clean up everything

2. For the definition of each of these notions in the UFOR, cf. Appendix B.

alongside the road"; táchééh binaago tsé sinil, "there are rocks right next to the sweathouse"; kéyah binaa ahéé átiin, "there is a road completely surrounding (-ahéé) the farmland"; "there is a halo around the sun."

Components: near/separate, multiple items; center; any direction from center.

c) łah, 'separate, distinct' (but also connected). This particle and its derivatives seem very general in meaning and are difficult to render unambiguously in Western thought. In all three spaces the word, and its more common derivations, are used (O, S, C). In all cases the recognition of a division, a putting apart or separating of something else is understood; sometimes, however, it is understood to convey stress on the connectedness in space of the distinct entities. Only the several derivations are used: łahdi 'at another place'; łahgóó 'toward, along'; łahgo 'different, in another way' (-go corresponds broadly to the English -ing, -ly); łahjí 'on the other side' (-jí means 'opposite, other side'), and łahji 'part of, other part' (-ji means 'as far as, up to').[3]

Examples: díí t'áałah dilt' éhé', "that one lives just separate" (he is the only one left); díí łį́į́' łahgo łį́į́ 'át 'é, "this horse is different from (other) horses" (said of a zebra); łahgóó diné łahgo 'át'éégo kéédahat'į, "people of different places live differently; at this place more people are educated than at other places."

Components: separate/contiguous; relation between two or more items.

d) kóníghánigo, 'nearby here and there; items with little space (or time) in between'. Again, this particle essentially indicates a relation between plural items. The "spaces" between each of them do not have to be identical; rather the separation between all of them is stressed. The term describes relations of separateness, indicating the presence of space separating several objects of any magnitude (spaces O, S, C). The minimal structural feature that is further made explicit is that none of the items in this relationship should touch each other (noncontiguity).

Examples: díí kǫ́ǫ́ t'áá kóníghánigo dził daní'á, "there are many mountains around here, each at a small distance from the other"; díí kǫ́ǫ́ t'áá kóníghánigo dahooghan, "there are a lot of houses close to each other here (a house here, a hooghan there, etc.)"; stars are said to be apart from each other in this sense.

Components: separate; plural items; minimal structure: no contiguity.

e)'áłah, 'together, forming one formation'. This particle identifies a relationship of connectedness, linking several items in one constellation with a minimally defined global structure. The connection between components is the only structural information that is conveyed through this term. The word

---

3. Only spatial notions are considered. Apart from these łah as such and its derivations are used to speak about time.

is used to describe relationships between items in the objects and in social spaces; in an exceptional case, the particular constellations of stars (e.g., Big Dipper) can be said to be recognized through this relationship.

Examples: dííjį́ 'áłah aleeh jiní, "it is said they are going to have a meeting"; t'áá 'áłah, 'both together', as in : bik'idahasdáhí t'áá 'áłah ahił díínił, "put both chairs away (together)"; the medicine herbs gathered for a specific ceremony are in this specific relationship.

Components: contiguous; plural items; relation structures whole formed by items; volumeness/planeness.

f) -tah, 'together in a (nonordered) group, mixed set, among'. The relationship is similar to the foregoing, but the resulting whole is poorly structured, has a mixed-up character (FH) that blurs the boundaries of the individual items that make up the whole. It is said of a plurality of items (LB, BB). It has relevance in O- and S-spaces.

Examples: shiłį́į́ ni dibé bitah deeshnił, "I'll put my livestock with yours"; naa'ołí dóó naadą́ą́ t'áá 'ałtahgo 'azis bii sijaa', "the beans and the corn are mixed in one bag"; deenásts'áá' dóó dibé t'áá 'ałtahgo naníłkaad, "the ram and the sheep are mixed (mating)"; the relation between ink and a pen is 'ałtah; the different stripes of a rainbow, intermingling at several points (blurring the boundaries) are in that relationship.

Components: contiguous; the items in this relationship form a badly structured whole (for instance volumeness or planeness).

g) binahjį', '(being) against something'. In the O- and S-spaces this postposition is used to describe one item leaning, hanging, sitting, or the like against another, like a man against a rock, a stick against a wall, but also (in a metaphorical sense) like helping one another.

Examples: kin binahjį' sédá, "I am sitting against the house"; dził binahji' ha'agééd, "against the mountain (on its side) there is a mine"; shimá dóó shizhé'é shinahjį' hiniilná, "my parents helped me"; dził łizhini binahjį' shihooghan, "I live against (halfway up) Black Mountain."

Components: contiguous; volumeness/planeness.

h) ahinááadíí'á, 'they meet, are connected'. This verb refers to the coming together, the meeting of two lines in one point. The stress is on the fact that they reach, touch each other, in a clear contrast to those that do not quite reach each other and leave some space between.

Examples: díí'ídzoh ahinááadíí'á, these lines form an angle, meet each other; in a slightly different meaning, only one other derivation is used: ahíhodíít'i (meeting at the end of something).

Components: contiguous; plural; form specific surface or volume.

i) shaazh, 'knot, something that has been broken and was put back/has grown back together'. The verb (and/or noun) describes a specific form of contiguity between two parts of an object. It is used mostly to speak about the visible knob on a part of the body, as a result of the growing back together of a once-broken bone. Only in O-space.

Examples: hastiin bíchį́į́h shaazh, "the man has a knob on his nose";

tł'óół shaazh éíyá, "the rope has a lot of knots." People distinguish different knots, made with a cattle rope: yishzhazh or square knot (with two ends), and dashzhazh or lasso knot.

Relative Nearness, Separateness, Contiguity

All the following terms are relative in meaning by the specific referent that is stated or implied. Something is near to me, to you, and so forth. The personal pronoun is either made explicit in the term or expression used, or with the verb or adverbial expression that follows.

a) t'áá áyídígi, 'near (ego), closer to (ego)'. The meaning of this particle is almost the same as that of áhánígi and its derivations, except for the fact that a referent is implied. The use of the term is restricted to O- and S-spaces.

Examples: Tótsohńlį́ndóó t'áá áyídígi shighan, "I live close to the Totso wash"; shighandóó t'áá áyídígi tó hasgeed ná'á, "there is an irrigation ditch close to my homestead."

Components: near/separate; relative to ego; volumeness/planeness; plural.

b) -ch'į', 'toward (ego)'. This postposition (completed with personal pronoun) indicates a movement in the direction of the referent, closer to him or her. The referent does not have to be reached totally (touched, as it were). The term is also used in the metaphorical sense, denoting closeness of relationship or feeling (much like in the English "close"). It pertains to the O-space exclusively.

Examples: gohwééh shich'į' niní'aah, "bring the coffee closer to me";[4] shimá shich'į' niníyá, "my mother walks up to me"; shicheii shich'į' haasdzíí', "my grandfather was always more near to me (gave me a lot of good advice)"; nahasdzáán shimá nilch'i bii'gistíín shich'į' át 'é, "the heart (spirit) of Mother Earth is ever closer to me" (in a traditional religious way of speaking).

Components: near; relative to (ego); movement (narrower distance to ego).

c) wóshdę́ę́', 'come nearer to (ego), this way, this direction'. The particle is used to describe a situation where something or somebody moves from a position away from the referent straight up to, touching the referent. It primarily denotes items in the O-space, sometimes of the S-space. In a traditional way of speaking, one can ask a Holy One or a spirit to come close to one.

Examples: ńléí tsénikánídóó wóshdę́ę́' yas, "it snowed from Round Rock (mesa) all the way up to here (me)"; ńléí dá'ák'ehdóó wóshdę́ę́' atiin 'ayóígo hodiwol, "from my farm (over there) the way up to here the road is rough"; woshdę́ę́' dah sédá, "move closer to me."

---

4. It does not have to reach me, in the spatial sense. If one would say shaa ní'aah (lit., move it terminatively to me) the movement would be more final: put it into my hands, hand it over to me.

Components: near/separate relative to (ego); movement; reaching (ego): contiguous.

d) ák̯ǫ́ǫ́: 'from here to there, thither'. Particle. The referent (ego) himself or space around him/her is the point of departure and the general direction is away from him/her. The stress is on the general direction 'no matter how far'. Relevant in O-, S-, and C-spaces.

Examples: naalyéé bihoghangóó ák̯ǫ́ǫ́ déya, "I go from here to the trading post"; tséhootsooígóó ák̯ǫ́ǫ́ déya, "I am going (from here) to Fort Defiance."

Components: near/separate; relative to (ego); direction; broadening separate from (ego); volumeness/planeness (place directed to).

e) t'áá 'áh̯ádígo, 'close by to (ego), close together'. This particle is used to describe the relation of something to the referent so he/she can touch or grab it easily. It is only used with O- and S-spatial items. Its meaning is very similar to that of áhání' and its derivations. This term implies a readiness or ease in handling the item that is close.

Examples: yówehédi dah sínídá, "sit a little farther away (from me)"; díí diyogí linígíí ndaa' t'óó'tahdi t'ah yówehédi nda 'iiłnih, "the rugs, like these, are worth more just a little farther away" (i.e., explaining rugs are better paid for in Farmington, N.M., than at the local trading post).

f) yówehédi, 'a bit further away from (ego)'. The term is the exact opposite of wóshdę́ę́' and describes a situation where something or someone is asked to move or is actually moving a little away from the referent. It pertains to O-space items primarily, though sometimes also to S-space phenomena.

Examples: yówehédi dah sínídá, "sit a little farther away (from me)"; díí diyogí linígíí ndaa' t'óó'tahdi t'ah yówehédi nda 'iiłnih, "the rugs, like these, are worth more just a little farther away" (i.e., explaining rugs are better paid for in Farmington, N.M., than at the local trading post).

Components: near/separate relative to (ego); movement; noncontiguous; broadening separateness with (ego); volumeness/planeness.

g) ńléidi, 'over there, in that direction (from ego)'. This is a very widely used particle, designating an unspecified distance away from and in front of (ego). It is often accompanied by the pointing of the lips in the direction indicated. The direction can only be in front or, eventually, above the individual pointing. In a general sense the place or area or object pointed at can only be said to be away from (ego), be it a yard, a mile, several hundred miles, and so on. The general criterion appeared to be somewhat the opposite of áhání: the item referred to cannot be touched or reached easily (a praxiological criterion). The term can be used on items in all three spaces (S, O, C).

Examples: ńléidi na'niłkaad, "he is herding sheep way over there"; ńléidi tsénikání si'ą́: "Round Rock mesa is way in the distance (from us)"; yádiłhił ńléidi sikaad, "the sky is stretching a way above us"; ńléidi dah sínídá, "you go and sit over there."

Components: separate; direction; up or front; relative to (ego); volumeness/planeness.

h) bits'ą́adi; bits'ą́ąjį', 'at a place not far away', 'on the opposite side', respectively. Both postpositions are relative to (ego); no direction or specific place is implied. The mere broadening of distance is expressed. The terms can be used in all three spaces (O, S, C).

Examples: shicheii łį́į́' bits'ą́adi yóó'ííyáálá, "my grandfather's horse walked away from him"; shimá shizhé'é bits'ą́adi yóó'ííyá álá, "my mother's husband (my father) walked away from her"; diné t'óó' ahayóígo chį́į́h yee adilohii yits'ą́ąjí danlį́, "a lot of people are against the elephant (the Republicans, that is)."

A different instance of the same stem is 'ałą́ąji, 'against each other, on the opposite side of each other.'

Components: separate; relative to (ego); nonspatial: opposition, or difference; volumeness/planeness.

i) 'adaah, 'meet (alter from ego out)'. The postposition is used to describe the meeting of people, or of one person with a place, implying the covering of a certain distance to attend the meeting that is to take place. It is restricted to items in S- and eventually O-space.

Examples: nimásání bidááh nínááh, "you (go and) meet your grandmother (over there)"; dóghózhii bii' tóódóó wóshdę́ę́' shidááh díínááł, "wait for me at, meet me at this side of Greasewood"; shidádę́ę́' níyol, "the wind blows in my face."

Components: contiguous; separate; relative to (ego); direction; movement, volumeness/planeness.

103. Part/Whole Concepts (Numbers 103, 203, 303 of the UFOR)

To me, at least, the elicitation of information about part/whole distinctions seemed difficult, even cumbersome. When comparing this finding with the information on the natural philosophy of Navajos (cf. chap. I, especially "dynamic nature" and "interrelatedness") there seems to be a point: the Western, highly segmented static world induces a prominence of part/whole relationships, of partitions in every realm of reality. Indeed, even clearly dynamic or systematic units (the body of a living being, time itself) are easily divided into subunits, parts with a formally uniform character. One sometimes speaks about the spatialization of time in exactly this sense: time as constructed out of formally identical units, rods as it were.[5] All this is rather odd to Navajos, it appears, a circumstance that may explain the difficulty in deal-

---

5. The discussion on the "psychological moment" is a case in point, although more fundamental research on these topics is certain to be found in physical and philosophical literature (e.g., Smart, 1964 for an excellent overall view; Reichenbach, 1958).

ing with part/whole relations in the general and widely used sense of the Westerner.

Still, some different words having to do with part/whole were discussed with consultants, partly through question-and-answer procedures, partly through drawings and manual modelings by ethnographers and consultants alike.

a) the personal pronoun: several consultants pointed out that part, in the sense of body part, is simply expressed through the use of the personal pronoun added to the noun in question. When asked (in a question, and through drawings) "my arm is part of my body," they simply said, "shigaan" (FH, TB, KB).

On the other hand, parts of an animal were indicated in this way, or through this expression complemented with an emphatic bich'į' (cf. section on nearness). In this way, the heart of a sheep, even when taken out of the animal, is expressed through: dibé bijéí bich'į' ('the sheep, her heart, with her, towards the sheep's heart').[6]

One consultant pointed to the use of reduplication to express, in the most emphatic way, the part/whole relation. In this sense, "my own leg" should be translated as shí shijáád (TB).

b) łahjį', 'part of'. This particle (cf. section on nearness also) is sometimes used to express part/whole relations, however in a slightly different way from the Western distinction. According to FH the term is used in a specific expression, pointing mainly to a missing part. It can be used in all three spaces (O, S, C). KB agreed on this point.

Examples: łahjį' bąąh dahaz'ą, "a part is missing" (said of somebody who is ill, or of somebody who lost a limb, etc.); łahjį' chidí bąąh 'íícho', "a car part is broken."

-łahgo, 'part'. As mentioned earlier, łahgo means 'different, apart, separate in some way or other'. In a certain expression, it takes the meaning of 'part', in much the same way as the Western notion. What seems to be different in the meaning is the much reduced stress on the distinction between a part and its whole, resulting in a stress on an organic unity, rather than division or distinction in Navajo.

Examples: nahasdzáán bikáá' diné łahgo bił dahaz'ą, "Navajos are part (of things) on top of the earth"; łahgo bił haz'ą, "part of my property is for her or him" (in the case of a father, part of whose land is being used by daughter or son). It was emphasized that the whole remained unchanged, that it was still the property of the father, but that a part of this is considered of a particular character since it is given in use to a child of the owner. What comes, according to our opinion, out of this view, is a much more "graded"

---

6. Individual differences may occur here. FH, at least, made it a point of respect to consider the heart of a butchered animal as still a part of the animal, or rather still its heart, etc. Werner mentioned a consultant who clearly disagreed on this point.

notion of the part/whole distinction: the strict dichotomy in the Western notion, illustrated and emphasized in the physical connectedness and the physical boundaries between parts and the whole, is not held in the Navajo notion. Rather, there is a dynamic, somewhat organismic functional unity that pervades any so-called partition. Further examples may make this clear.

A typical instance occurred while discussing land ownership with one consultant (FH). He confided to having land on the reservation (only trust land, of course) at several places: a piece of land at Lukachukai, one on top of the mountain, one in the Many Farms area, and finally of one in Lukachukai. But this spatially fragmented whole was spoken of in a singular way: my land, as if it were a solid unit. The Westerner would be inclined to use a plural, at least, because of the divided character of the lands. The consultant insisted on the unity, linked to his own person, because of the functional or "organismic" unity: all these parcels served to insure the survival of him and his family under his sole guidance, under his sole authority.

c) other words: in the same sense, but more directly stressing what we called the "organismic" character of part/whole relations, our questions concerned two very common and well-known instances: body parts and auto parts.

The question: "How would you express that your arm, heart, intestines, head, etc. are part of your body?" yielded the immediate counterquestion: "You mean, how do all these things work together to make the human being function as a system?" The latter question probably provides an insight into the Navajo way of dealing with part/whole in the clearest way.

The answer to these questions, then, was: bee na'anishí t'áálá'í bits'íís siléi bii' (lit.: 'by means of it, it works, as one [unit], his body, they lie [like a rope, line], inside'), "all parts form one group to make the body work."

Auto parts: the question asked for a Navajo name at all the auto parts stores on the reservation. The answers pointed out a strict comparison with the human body: chidí bits 'íís siléi t'áá ałtso bee bi'oonishí (lit.: 'car, its body, they lie, all of them, with it, it works'), "all auto parts." The same notion was detected while discussing the way to deal with the whole, as contrasted to the parts. KB stressed two ways of speaking about the whole:

Examples: chidí bee hadít'éíí (lit.: 'car, by means of it, it [the car] is dressed, manufactured'); chidí bee hadilyaa (lit.: 'car, by means of it, it [the car] was created, was made into being').

Typically, both ways of referring to the whole (i.e., the car) as a system, a dynamic unity point to the interrelationships between all unspecified items (bee: 'by means of') that make the system up. The first example was given by KB as a sort of present tense (in English, of course) stressing the actual manufacturing, while the second example referred to the resulting system qua result according to KB (and thus more or less to the past tense in English: the car upon completion, having been formed).

The "organismic" sense of part/whole relations may be clear from these examples. The clearly functional meaning of wholes (and consequently parts) follows from additional information: in the human body the intestines, the heart, and so on are parts, but so are breath and blood pressure, since the body cannot exist, stops functioning without them.

Components: volumeness/planeness; part/whole; function.

d) hóló, 'to have, to be or exist for (ego)'. This verb has a meaning that is somewhat the inverse of the expressions like łahgo and łahjį', denoting that which has parts, rather than the parts themselves.[7] When consultants were asked to speak about a unit and its parts in different ways, they easily came up with an expression built up around the -łah stem, and one using hóló instead. The verb can be used in all three spaces (O, S, and C). Again, KB's suggestions have been most valuable here.

Examples: shidibé dóó shiłį́į́' dahóló, "I have livestock (sheep and horses)"; bee ńtséskees hóló, "to have a good mind"; ba'át'é'hóló, "to have his mind in the wrong way" (e.g., to be quick tempered); you can also say, łahgo bił haz'ą́ in this case ("something is missing").

Components: part/whole; volumeness/planeness; function.

104. Bordering, Bounding (Numbers 104, 204, and 304 of the UFOR)

In terms of action (the praxiological approach), two different types of border can be distinguished: an obstructionlike border, dividing two parts of the same unit and requiring a modification of the action to overcome it (go around it, climb over it, etc.) and continue action on the unit, and, on the other hand, an ultimate border marking the end of a unit, and requiring a change of action, a reorientation to cope with the new unit, the new territory on the other side of the border. The distinction may appear pretty abstract. Examples will make it stand out more clearly, and will illustrate its actuality in Navajo.

In general the center of the hooghan can be considered as an in-between or obstructive border: you are never supposed to cross the center; rather you go around it. The figures in the east on a Sandpainting have a similar meaning: they keep bad spirits out, and form an entrance for certain spirits only. The (most often circular) boundary of the Sandpainting on all other directions clearly marks the ultimate limit of the "world" that is depicted inside it. In a similar way, Lukachukai Mountain and Black Mountain are considered in between borders limiting a central part of the Navajo world (FH, BW, TB), but do not enter an entirely different territory. On the other hand, while passing the "border" constituted by the four Sacred Mountains, you enter enemy land, ana'i bikéyah; you have to behave quite differently (FH, BW, CM). The beliefs and practices to deal with this "other world" exclusively, illustrate the meaning of "ultimate border" dramatically (Enemyway).

---

7. I am indebted to Professor Oswald Werner, who pointed out this peculiarity.

Obstruction Border

a) -ch'ą́ą́h: 'in the way, barring the way'. This postposition, with a personal pronoun added, expresses the fact that someone, something comes in the way of me, you, and so on, thus obstructing the normal path that was followed, causing the agent to go around, get rid of the item barring his way or any similar action. Its use is restricted to O- and S-space.

Examples: t'áadoo shich ą́ą́h sínízíní, "quit standing in my way! (barring my view)"; łį́į́' bich'ą́ą́h sézį́, "I am standing to bar the way to the horse (so it will not come out of the corral)"; 'áłchíní bich'ą́ą́h dádi' níłkaał, "close the door on the children (so they will not come through here)"; also, in a metaphorical sense: shiłį́į́' shich'ą́ą́h 'ííyá, "the horse came in my way (died instead of me)." [8]

Components: obstruction border; relative to (ego); front/back; movement or not, volumeness/planeness.

b) -k'ą́: 'to set on a small ridge, border space between two items'. This verb is generally used to specify a characteristic of a rock or other social spatial item, but sometimes applies to small things, like a knife or other object. It has a connotation of scariness: a small ridge on the edge of a canyon (you might fall into), or a very sharp knife, and similar instances. This may explain the aspect of "turning over, uncertain balance" that is apparent in the meaning of the word, be it used in a literal or in a metaphorical sense.

Examples: dah hodik'ą́ 'ííyá, "he walked on the narrow ridge" (during the Spanish occupation around Canyon de Chelly, people are said to have slept on small ridges in the canyonwalls to escape from the Mexicans); béésh bee nahagizhígíí bikáá'góó t'óó báhádzidgo dah hodik'ą́, "the knife you cut with, when you sharpen it, you just cannot run it across your hand"; TB (monolingual) referred to the four lines on a piece of paper in this way: dį́į́'k'ą́ ('four; ridge').

Components: obstruction border; volumeness/planeness; horizontal; pluridimensional extension (narrow); connotation of scariness.

c) biníká, 'through'. Postposition. Terms with this and similar meanings also have to do with a relationship of in and out. Still, it seems reasonable to handle them under the present heading, since a certain notion of border is apparent as well. This particular term is used to describe things you can see through, thus restricting its use to O- and S-spaces.

Examples: shiwoo' biníká i'íínil, "he drilled (a hole) through my tooth"; tsah shá biníká níłt'ééh, "put the thread through the needle for me"; hoghan biníká hoodzą́, "there is a hole passing through the hooghan (a man-made hole)."

Components: obstruction border; planeness/volumeness (a hole in something); in/out; motion.

d) bighá, 'through, forming a hole through', cf. section on open/closed.

---

8. I was assured that this is a usual thing to say among older people: when somebody dies, he is said to die in your place (cf. chap. I: the life-taking role of the sun).

Ultimate Borders

a) -dzoh: this general verb stem is used in a lot of complex terms. We will consider some of them, disregarding however the particular forms in the circumscription. Words based on this stem have a very broad use, ranging over phenomena in all three spaces (O, S, C). They describe any type of border, from the simple mark to indicate a boundary, to statelines or heavy walls.

Examples: t'áádoo shihoodzoh bii'na'nı́łkaadí, "don't trespass (herd) on the inside of my border line (don't step on my land, or cross my border line)"; Mexico border hoolyééji' 'éí Naakaii bił hahoodzoh, "people on the other side of the Mexican border are called Mexicans"; tsásk'ehdę́ę́' dahonít'ídóó 'asdzoh díí nihonít'í'jj', "from this end of the bed a border (edge) goes down all the way to that end."

Components: ultimate border; volumeness/planeness; motion or not; lengthwise; plural items.

b) 'aneel'á, 'at the end of a formation, at the most remote part'. The verb is used in all three spaces (O, S, C) and points to the limiting part, the end of a formation, whether flat or voluminous. As such it is a surface or volume itself, rather than a mark or line.

Examples: ńléí kin nineel'ą́ądi shighan, "I live at the very limit of the village"; naabeehó bikéyah kojj'nineel'á, "this is the remotest part, the limit of Navajoland"; a special form is, for example, ahíhoneel'ą́ąjj' ('to the end of a leveled place'): ńléí 'ahíhoneel'ą́ąjj' shá nihodiyííłdlał, "you will plow my field up to the limit of this leveled surface."

Components: ultimate border; volumeness/planeness; part/whole; direction/motion; succession (order).

c) 'adáád, 'at the edge'. This noun is used to describe the edge, the absolute limit point or line of something, "the end of the line," marking a discontinuity in space. Beyond this point is a wall straight up or a deep cliff, or any other insurmountable change. It is relevant in O- and S-space.

Examples: 'adádí, "the edge," is the name of a place over Lukachukai Mountain, all surrounded by a volcanic wall (game was trapped there and then caught); díí'shidáłł'óół, "my doorguard or gate" (when completely closed off); shizis 'adáátł'óół, "the piece of rope on top of my bag (to close it tightly)."

Components: ultimate border; volumeness/planeness; succession; part/whole; discontinuity; horizontal; up/down.

d) 'anít'i', 'something extends in a thin line, fence'. Verb. The second translation is broadly used, although a more general meaning of anything that bars your way, in front of you, is more appropriate in the case of this verb. The fact that it can be used in all three spaces (O, S, C) may make this point clear.

Examples: shimásání, 'ákǫ́ǫ́ 'anít'i', "grandma, there is a fence crossing right here"; 'ákǫ́ǫ́ tł'óół nít'i', "the rope is lying right here (before you)"; ńléí e'e'aahjí k'os 'ałts'óózí nít'i', "in the West a narrow string of clouds extends"; yikáísdáhí nít'i', "the Milky Way is going across (before your eyes)"; tsinanít'i', "wood wall."

Components: ultimate border; volumeness/planeness; front/back (facing, or up/down); movement; line (extension along a line, path).

e) biná 'ázt'i, 'a border, fence around it'. The verb is a composite form of the former stem, having to do with fencing, bordering. The main difference is the stress on a specific type of bordering, encircling some place rather than cutting or barring it. It is relevant in O- and S-spaces only.

Examples: shikéyah biná'ázt'i', "I have a fence all around my farm"; béégashii' biná'ázt'i', "I have a fence all around the cattle"; dził biná'ázt'i', "there is a fence, border all around the mountains."

Components: ultimate border; volumeness/planeness; movement; line; open/closed; part/whole.

f) tábąąh, 'water's edge, shore'. This particle is specific, pointing to something like a shore, a beach, the space of dry land alongside any water. Thus, it is more a surface than a line. It is restricted to S-space.

Examples: tábąąhgi tábąąstíínléi' sitį́, "right on the edge of the water sits an otter"; tábąąh góde 'atiin, "there is a road up the shore"; ńléí tábąąhgi tééhooltsódii leí' sizį́, "way down on the shore a big monster is standing."

Components: ultimate border; volumeness/planeness; laterality; horizontality; water; plural (i.e., water and land).

g) ní'á, 'it extends in a line (as a mountain range)'. The verb is used to express the extreme, descending edge of something solid, like a mountain or any kind of voluminous structure. Anything linelike, a road or a path, is not appropriate. The verb is used for items of O- and S-spaces.

Examples: díí dził yaa ní'áadi béésh łigaii haagééd, "there is a silver mine down at the end of this mountain"; shíchį́į́h yaa ná'á, "at the bottom end of my nose"; dził bikáádi yas ayóíáníłtsogo ná'á, "on top of the mountain the snow is very deep"; 'atiin gónaa 'áhí ná'á, "there is fog bank lying across the road."

Components: ultimate border; volumeness/planeness; part/whole (the extreme part); up/down.

h) bílátah, 'its end, butt, tip'. This particle describes the uppermost tip (eventually volume) of an item. Again the bordering "top" is considered as part of the item of which it is the top. The term can be used in O- and S-space.

Examples: sitsii' bílátah, "the end (the tip) of my hair"; dził bílátahdę́ę́' háá'át'ááh, "the sun rises from the highest point of the mountain"; tsah bílátah hááhaashchii', "a needle has a sharp point (top)"; shikélátah gónaa nidininiih, "I have a little pain in the tip of my toe"; naaniigo bílátah, "at the end of a horizontal formation"; deigo dóó yaago bílátah: "at the upper and lower end of something."

Components: ultimate border; volumeness/planeness; part/whole overlapping; any direction.

i) 'éé'ńléít'į́į́', 'horizon'. In a discussion on distance (with words like nízaad and dooshónízaad da), I asked these words to be applied to the ultimate distance, the horizon. It was agreed that similar words could be used as specifiers of the qualities of the horizon, though not for the translation of "horizon" itself. (Indeed, where the former word [nízaad] points to places in a certain direction, this cannot be said of the horizon: it moves back farther still if you try to approach it.) The more general, functional description, then, is expressed in the word 'éé'ńléít'íí', pointing at the limits of visibility, no matter what direction and no matter how far. All depends "on your eyesight, on your position, and similar conditions." Evidently, the term is only used with relevance to S- and C-space.

Components: ultimate border; horizontal path; visibility, volumeness/ planeness; part/whole.

105. Overlapping (Numbers 105, 205, and 305 of the UFOR)

Overlapping is the general term used to speak of every possible instance of one object, figure, or space covering or stretching out over or sitting upon or in some way screening a second one. There need not be any further implication of contiguity, complete or partial covering and the like. The relation (or the operation) is considered to be an independent, presumably rather basic spatial relationship, to be understood generally like the relation of overlapping in Western logic (e.g., the notion of ⊃ in Venn notation). In this sense, shadows could be understood to overlap part of the ground,[9] but also stones overlap the piece of ground they lie upon, or professional domains could even overlap, all depending on the way similar situations are rendered in a particular language or culture (cf. Pinxten, 1975).

In Navajo it seems reasonable to distinguish two, slightly different, types of "overlapping": (1) exclusively active and (2) active and/or passive "overlapping." The former consists of the kind of overlappings that define or at the least necessarily imply an action or a process of covering, of crossing, and the like. The latter may or may not imply an action or a process. That is, a situation where one rock is clearly extending over and thus in a sense "overlapping" another one (passive) is described with other words than the action of placing a rock on top of another one. The difference is not essential, but still real enough to be taken into account.

Active Overlapping

a) báátis, 'up/over it, crossing it'. This postposition expresses the crossing of something solid or big in extension. It follows the term of whatever is crossed, overlapped. The movement, expressed through the verbs that go with it, is generally slow or at least takes a certain amount of time, a certain stretch (excluding a jump, a quick and sudden move, and the like). This

---

9. This is so in the Dogen description of shadow, where they use a term that means "hiding," in fact (cf. Pinxten, 1975).

would constitute the main difference between this and the following term, bitis. The postposition can be used for displacements in all three spaces (O, S, C). It can only describe the crossing of the outside of something (LB).

Examples: k'os dził báátis ahííkaad, "the cloud is stretching out over the mountain"; tó na'nízhoozh báátis ahííkaad, "the water is spreading, running over the bridge"; díí dził báátis chidí bee doo ngigháah da, "you cannot cross this mountain by car"; díí tł'iish doo báátis ngigháah da, "you cannot step over this snake"; [10] díí awéé sháátis ee'na, "this baby crawled over me (over my body)."

Components: overlapping (active); motion (slow); volumeness/planeness; horizontal; nearness/contiguity.

b) bitis, 'over it, to the other side, crossing it, stepping over it'. This postposition expresses the same relation (as báátis), only modifying the way of going over something (BB). The actor jumps over the obstacle, crosses it quickly, can go over it with one step, and the like. It is relevant in all three spaces (O, S, C).

Examples: anít'i' bitis dah' diishwod, "I jumped over the fence"; tó t'óó ahayói ńłį́į́ léi' hajoobá' ígo bitis ííyá, "you cross the wash that flows very deep by going on the rock in it"; adínídíín bitis dah diishwod, "I jumped over the sunbeam (on the ground)"; tsásk'eh bitis yishná', "I crawl over the bed" (small, relative to me).

Components: overlapping (active); motion (quick, short distance); volumeness/planeness; nearness/contiguity; horizontal dominantly.

c) ná'á: 'lying down, extending out over'. This verb expresses the position, movement, expansion of something solid over something else. It is used most commonly with solid bodies like rocks, rock formations, even mountains. Several verbal prefixes can be added, specifying the meaning, or stressing the basic idea of a solid body that is stretching out. It has relevance in O- and S-space.

A second, often encountered aspect of meaning has to do with the ultimate parts, the end of a solid body lying over something: When speaking about a mountain using this verb one often implies, if not always, that it is visualized as a formation with ends coming down, or a hilllike formation, leveling out near the end of its length. The discussion of what is solid, and thus, what can be described through this verb, is rather intuitively loaded: pebbles are too small to be called solid, while a table is big enough. The general form of a human nose again is liable to be called solid, basically, it appears, because of the "coming down at ends of a one-piece form" (i.e., the head).

Examples: ńléí nízaad dził łizhin ná'á, "way over there lies Black Mountain"; siníkéé sinilí bita' naná'á, "the bridge of my glasses (piece lying between, extending over)"; héél ba' naná'á, "the bundle lies over across (the

---

10. This rule applies in general for snakes, snake trails, bear trails, dead bodies. The sanction on the breaking of these rules is severe and brings about serious diseases that can be cured only through costly ceremonies (Mountain Chants, Shooting Ways).

pole, your shoulder . . .)"; tsé'naa na'nízhoozh naná'á, "the bridge goes straight across" ('across, bridge, goes down over').

Components: overlapping (active); border; volumeness/planeness; horizontal; down; motion (or not).

d) aháą́h niilá, 'I folded it (something flexible)'. This verb denotes the actual event of folding something over or, with the same verb, of something folding over itself. As such, the meaning is rather specific, but still illustrates a clear form of overlapping. The verb has relevance for O-space, eventually for S-space.

Examples: beeldléí aháą́h niilá, "I fold up the blanket"; łį́į́' aháą́h shiniilá, "the horse threw me over"; aháą́h shiniilá, "he folded me up (in a fight)"; k'os aháą́h siniilá, "the cloud folds over (itself)."

Components: overlapping (active); motion; volumeness/planeness; contiguity; flexible.

Active and/or Passive Overlapping

a) tsé 'naa, 'over, across'. This particle expresses over or across implying that the overlapping has taken place already, or is permanent. As such it serves to make composite words (bridge: tsé'naa na'nízhoozh) or codefines verbs that express a situation of overlapping extending horizontally and always in front of the referent. It is relevant in all three spaces (O, S, C).

The general meaning can be rendered through a composite translation: something is tsé'naa to you if it goes across (barring your road in front, as it were), ahead of, or before you, and goes in a straight or direct stretch across.

Examples: yikáísdáhí tsé'naa nanít'i'yá ałníí gónaa, "the Milky Way crosses right through the middle of heaven like a (cross) line"; akónaa' tsé'naa nanílį́, "right there a stream runs across (the plain)"; áhí tsé'naa atiin niní'á na'nízhoozh nahalingo, "there is fog going straight across like a bridge"; dził tsé'naa ní'á, "the mountain lies right across (as between Lukachukai and Shiprock, barring the road between both)." A special form is 'aná tsé'naa as in: nááts'íílid 'aná tsé'naa íít'i', "you go over the rainbow" (the means of transportation of the Holy People).[11]

Components: overlapping (passive); border; volumeness/planeness; separate (from ego); front of (ego); horizontal.

b) ha'naa, 'over, across an area or space'. This particle expresses about the same situations that can be grasped with tsé'naa. One possible explanation for the difference between both terms is that ha'naa stresses something/someone, while another explanation, consistent with, though differing from, the former one, stresses the fact that ha'naa would point to the bridging of the gap, of an open space between things (BB). It will become clear that both aspects are present and combined in some of the examples (a flagstone covering a gap, for example), since both are very similar. A good

---

11. The expression aná tsé'naa is only used for special cases, e.g., transportation in the Holy Way.

example illustrating this idea was given by TB: speaking about the position of himself on the opposite side, across (the table). The meaning of ha'naa here implies a space between persons dividing their spaces of contact (open space?), and the table filling this break space, constituting a means of communication or contact for crossing the gap. The particle can be used for relations in all three spaces (O, S, C).

Examples: tsé ha'naa sikaad, "the flagstone covers the place, is lying across"; ha'naa nininá, "he moved over across (he used to live here, but moved to the other side)"; chidí ha'naa niilwod, "the car has passed the wash"; áhí ha'naa na ná'á, "the fog lies across like a rock"; nááts'íílid ha'naa na nít'i', "the rainbow stands like a sun halo."

Components: overlapping; volumeness/planeness; border; horizontal; front.

c) ni'góó, 'along the ground, on the earth'. This adverbial expression derives from ni', 'ground, surface of the earth'. The expression describes anything covering, extending over the mud or earth. Only phenomena that are in some way or other spread out, covering some surface can be described thus. The direction is always horizontal, and, from the point of view of the referent (ego), downward (as is implied with the translation 'along the ground' as well). The expression has relevance in O- and S-spaces.

Examples: ni'góó tó nílį, "the water is running along the ground";[12] ni'góó ch'il hólǫ́, "plants are spread over the ground"; níyol ni'góó, "the wind blows over the surface of the earth"; beeldléí ni'góó sikaad, "the blanket spreads over the ground or floor."

Components: overlapping; volumeness/planeness; border; extension; horizontal.

d) ałná, 'crossing, crisscross, exchange'. This prefix has a lot of meanings, some of them implying an overlapping. In these cases, two or more units are covering one another partly, making up a cross or any similar figure. In a metaphorical sense, the same notion of crossing, going over to the other side, and the like, has very definite relevance, most of all with respect to death. The prefix is used in expressions having relevance in all three spaces (O, S, C).

Examples: ałná'asdzoh, "a crossmark, a cross, an x-mark"; ałnáda'oostiin, "the intersection of roads"; jóhonaa'éí yá ałníí' gónaa ałnánádááh, "the sun usually crosses (its own path) in the middle of the heaven"; ałnáá baa', "the woman who goes crossing her own path"; tsin ałnáago dah sinil, "the sticks are crosswise on top of one another" (the sticks form a cross); shash ałnádabikéé'go eekai lá, "the bears walked away with their feet lopsided" (this corresponds to the way the shoes of dead people are put on, initiating them into another world); tsin ałnádabikéé'go haal'á, "the trees (uprooted) are lying one toppled over the other, scattered all over the place."

12. ní- with high tone as a prefix to the verb denotes a downward movement, directed to the earth. In the sentence, then, the leveling out (ni'góó) and the downward movement are combined.

Components: overlapping; contiguity; direction (and inverse); volumeness/planeness.

e) the forms bikáá' and bi'ąą (on top, going over, and over it, stretching out) and bik'i (on top) are treated under a separate heading (cf. section on up/down), since their meaning has to do primarily with this distinction, though implying a certain kind of overlapping as well.

106. Internal/External; Central/Peripheral (Numbers 106, 206, and 306 of the UFOR)

The general qualitative notions of in and out, internal and external, inward and outward, and the like, can again be grasped most readily in the Navajo vocabulary through the actions expressed with them. The several differentiations in meaning, varying slightly from one to the other, that are rendered primarily through the use of specific terms, express differences in the actions, or modifications in a phase of actions that are described. In this way the "in" of going into some place or some building is expressed by means of an adverb or prefix other than the "in" of extending into something. For several phenomena the characteristics can be specified (as in any culture) by restricting the use of a particular term to inside/outside peculiarities (e.g., there is a term denoting the inside corner of a room or house in Navajo, tł'ah, and several to denote the outside corner; naanáz'á: outside corner of a street; naaná'ázt'i': outside corner of a fence). In a similar way the span of an angle is most often identified with the smallest span of an angle (on the inside, so to speak), leaving out any description of the outside aspect). These terminological fine points will not be dealt with in this section. Part of it will be found under proper, dominantly presented headings (e.g., the section on corner, angle); others will be omitted. Still, their existence points to the relevance of the notions of inside and outside in Navajo and reminds us that the already abundant material in this section is subject to expansion. Only the more general and exclusive notions are withheld here. A few old rules of social behavior illustrate the prominence of the in/out distinction in keeping peace and order. All of them focus on the hooghan as the definite unit of social (and other) organization: the shift of behavioral rules in trespassing the threshold (or rather the cloth covering the entrance hole in the traditional way) points to the importance of the in/out distinction. In this way, it is forbidden to look from the outside in (and the other way around), over the cloth, while any person who is admitted inside is said to have the right to look around and inspect the inhabitant's affairs at will.[13] People inside the hooghan should learn to live on their own, without the assistance of Holy People in everyday life, but the lat-

---

13. Not only was this the opinion of consultants, but I often experienced its veracity personally, whenever my landlady came into the room, first knocking at the open entrance while hidden on the side of the entrance and then, invariably, looking around and inspecting very openly and thoroughly once she was invited inside. The same was done by other people, even children, differing only in zeal, but not in basic attitude.

ter do come around and are said to "check on the people inside the hooghan" early in the morning, just before waking up (BW). Similarly, when a healing ceremony is performed inside a hooghan, Holy People are invited. They are expected inside the building where they join in the doings, while invariably, specific figures on the Sandpaintings that are used to guard the entrance of the place of healing (and in some way of the hooghan) permit the entrance of some spirits, while preventing others from coming in.[14]

The concept of "center" is considered a specification of the in/out Navajo distinction, in that anything that is said or held to be central will consequently be treated as inside or away from the outside of something. Again, beliefs and rules concerning the hooghan give a major meaning to the center, the place where the fire is kept, as well as the place where the patient is to sit during a healing ceremony. Similarly, in traditional belief the center of Heaven and Earth have a very sacred status, due to the fact that main events in the mythic history of the Navajos are said to have taken place there (place of emergence from the former worlds, place of creation of deities; cf. the section on Boundedness; Center in Chap. I).

Internal/External

a) bighi', 'inside (a container)'. Postposition. It specifies an object or phenomenon in relation to a container, that is, the object is inside the container. As such only characteristics of the container, or the position of an object relative to a container, or an action bound to take place on the inside of a container can be meant when this postposition is used. There is no movement implied, no transition between in and out. Phenomena of any magnitude can be dealt with (in O, S, and C spaces), since the turquoise set in a ring, but also oil inside the earth or thunder in the sky are expressed with the same word.

Examples: díí'azis nimásii bighi', "inside this sack are potatoes" ('this sack, potatoes, inside'); tónteel bighi' łóó 'tsoh hólǫ́', "the ocean, inside of it are sharks (or whales)"; k'os bighi' déę́' nahałtin, "rain comes from the clouds (from inside the cloud it rains)."

Components: in/out; volumeness (inside of which is dealt with); border (container notion); defines spatial unit (i.e., the inside of something).

b) bii', 'in it, inside (a relatively closed container)'. Prefix, with a meaning that is synonymous with that of bighi'. When asked for the difference between both terms, one is told that bii' is used for something in a container, or something that is inside a container for a long time, a nearly permanent characteristic of the container. It is used for phenomena in all three spaces (O, S, C).

Examples: aghaa díí azis bii', "there is wool in the sack" (consultants pointed out that, were the sack open, one would have to use bighi' instead; FH, TB); díí'jish tádídíín bii' siłtsooz, "inside this medicine pouch is some

---

14. These figures are, for example, the Bat, the Horned Toad: cf. in Reichard and Newcomb (1975), and Newcomb et al. (1956) for excellent descriptions.

corn pollen"; hooghan bii' shighan, "I live in a hooghan"; dił yá'át'ééhgo 'ii' hólǫ́ǫgo yá'áhoot'ééh, "if good blood is inside somebody, he is healthy" (a person with good blood is healthy); bii'gistiin dóó bii'sizííni át'é, "spirits (inside forms) and souls (inside standing ones) do exist" (the permanence implied in the use of bii' is emphasized through its use with these particular aspects of Navajo reality: see chap. I, section 4, which points out that these spiritual aspects are the "backbone" of anything existing and living in Navajo metaphysics, and are considered to be prerequisites for its subsistence).

Components: in/out; volumeness/planeness; defines spatial relationship to volumeness/planeness; relative permanence (time presupposed); border (container itself).

c) biih, 'in, into something (a container)'. Postposition, indicating a movement from outside something to within it, a transition from out to in. The difference between this expression and the two former terms lies in the active aspect that is implied in the use of biih.[15] It clearly specifies an action (linguistically, a verb) rather than an object or static phenomenon. No further restrictions on the direction of the action or movement should be mentioned, stressing exclusively the transition from outside something to its interior. It can be used for transitions of this type in all three spaces (O, S, C).

Examples: gohwééh biih níjááh, "put coffee into it (container)"; ne'éé' biih nínááh, "put on your coat" ('your coat, into it, you go'); chidí bitoo' biih dííkááł, "you must put gas into your car"; hooghan biih nínááh, "go into the hooghan"; shiih yilwod, "it (illness . . .) goes into me, into my body."

Components: in/out; volumeness; border; motion.

d) biih yí' áago, 'extending into, sticking into'. The word is complex, comprising biih (into) and áá (slender rigid object is), together with the personal pronoun (bi-, 'his, its') and the enclitic -go; the total meaning then denotes some relationship between an object and a container. The object itself exemplifies the transition between in and out: it is half in and half out of a container; the stress is on the part that is in, rather than the part sticking out (still). Examples would include a pole sticking out of the water (but only partly so) or a thorn sticking into your finger. It can be used with respect to all three spaces (O, S, C).

Examples: béésh tó biihí'áago sitą́, "the gun (or knife) is sticking into the water container"; tsin hooghan biihí'áago sitą́, "the pole is sticking into the hooghan"; béésh łeezh biih yít'i', "the wire (flexible) is sticking into the mud."

---

15. Hoijer (1974) distinguishes between several aspects in verbs, specifying in this way the particular connotations of action, permanence, repetition, and the like that modify any general meaning of a term or a stem. For example, if some movement through space is implied with the use of a term it is characterized as "active" or as "agentive" (if the movement is induced or brought about by an agent), "passive or neuter" (no movement implied), etc. The idea is correct, but further specification should be found, as is attempted here for each term (cf. also chap. I, section on the dynamic nature of the world).

Components: in/out; volumeness/planeness; border; defines transitional phenomenon (part is in, part not); direction inward dominant; part/whole.

e) bináká, 'through (an opening in it)'. A postposition, defining a transition from outward inward, or the other way around, through an already existing opening or penetration through. (See section on Border; Obstruction Border, C, this chapter).

f) bighá: 'through something, completely through it'. The meaning of this postposition is very close to that of bináká, with minor specifications. While the latter may be used to describe the looking through a window or hearing through a wall (TB), the former tends to be used to describe a hole that goes completely through. Consequently, it cannot be used in a cosmological space, since no such holes exist in the universe (at least in the traditional beliefs).

Examples: tségháhoodzání, Window Rock (a rock south of the reservation with a hole going completely through it); tsin bigháhoodzá, "a hole all the way through a log"; biih hoodzá, "it has a cavity" (i.e., a tooth). The term thus seems more specific than bináká, since it is restricted in use to holes, tunnels, and the like that have two open ends, or that go completely through.

Components: obstructed border; in/out; volumeness/planeness; motion; two outer borders.

g) kóne' or akóne', 'in here' or 'in there'. These verbal prefixes already have a more specific meaning than any of the foregoing. The main distinction of inside and outside remains, but is modified: kóne' is only used for a direction that goes in and downward, in a literal or a metaphorical sense. In this way, its meaning should be rendered 'down and in', implying a movement to make the transition (from out to in) or not. The downward direction is always seen from the point of view of the referent (ego). It can be used in expressions dealing with all three spaces (O, S, C).

Examples: gahásh kóne' yah eelwod? "did the rabbit go (down and) in there?"; wóláchíí' kóne' bighan, "the red ant lives in here"; pointing to a trail in a forest, you can say, kóne' éí'etiin, "there is a trail going in here"; nííltsá k'os bighi' kóne' silá, "inside the cloud the rain is lying" (bighi' specifies the inside of the cloud, while kóne' tells us the thunder is lying 'in that [interior] part of the cloud').

Components: in/out; volumeness/planeness; border; motion or not; downward (from the referent's point of view).

h) wóne', wóne'é, 'inside something, completely inside it' (also góne'). This particle expresses another modification of the general notion of inside, stressing the absoluteness of a state of being inside (or going inside). Like akóne' it seems to point to closedness, invisibility from the outside, covering up, and the like. Again, it can apply to phenomena in all three spaces (O, S, C).

Examples: shimá dóó shizhé'é wóne'é siké, "both my mother and father are sitting inside (completely)"; gah a' ááwóne yah eelwod, "the rabbit ran completely inside of its hole"; chidí bighi' wóne'é deesdoi, "in the car, in its interior, it is hot."

Components: in/out; volumeness/planeness; border; open/closed (invisible, totally inside, etc.); defines spatial unit (volume).

i) tł'óo'di: 'outside, out.' This term is the opposite of wóne'é, and serves to describe the place, the spatial disposition of anything that is not inside, in whatever sense or degree. It denotes a very unspecific place, in reference to an inside place (house, corral). In other grammatical forms a direction outward, toward the open or outside can be expressed (with enclitic -jį'). The term can be used with phenomena in all three spaces (O, S, C). Typically, in the cosmological order it could be applied to anything on the outer surface of earth or heaven, that is, anything "above the earth's surface or beneath the sky."

Examples: naalyéhébáhoghan tł'óó'di, "outside of the trading post"; tł'óó'di níchííl, "it is snowing outside, in the open"; dibé t'áá tł'óó'di naakai, "the sheep are on the outside." Another way of speaking about your own position is through the use of another expression: ch'íníshaah, "I am in the act of going out" (TB).

Components: in/out; volumeness/planeness; border; open/closed; motion or not (opposite of ghóne'é); defines spatial unit (volume).

j) ha-, 'up, up and out'. Verbal prefix that is used in several expressions, all pointing to the movement of rising, popping out, and the like, with a direction from downward to upward, from a rather closed space into the open. Only the complete verbal expressions will be mentioned in the examples. The basic meaning of the prefix will stand out clearly through each of them. It can be used for moving bodies in all three spaces (O, S, C). In this way, the sun rises every morning out of the horizon, from below the earth, in the traditional belief. With the same prefix an ant's coming out of the anthill is described, and so on.

Examples: hajíínáídę́ę́' tązhii akéédę́ę́' haayá, "with the emergence the turkey was the last to come up" (hajíínáí is a term used to refer to the mythical "coming on top of the present world," emerging from former worlds in the Navajo cosmogonical myth); jóhonaa'éí ha'ii'ą, "the sun rises (comes up and out)";[16] wóláchíí' haayá; "the ants pop out, come up out of the anthill; something is sticking up out of the ground"; see also the section on Up/Down.

Components: in/out; volumeness/planeness; up/down; motion; direction (out and up); border or relatively closed space as referent.

k) ch'é'étiin, 'the way in or out, doorway'. This noun, derived from the general stem -tiin (path, road), specifies the path of the transition between the inside and outside of something. In this sense, it can be used to speak about the doorway or entrance of a house or hooghan exclusively (TB), or

16. This description is said to be accurate up till about noon, when the sun does not rise anymore, as it is near the zenith.

about any way or path that connects inside and outside (FH). It can be used to describe similar places in all three spaces (O, S, C).

Examples: kojígo ch'é'étiin nish'náájígo ła éí níłts'ą́ą́jígo ch'é'étiin, "here is a doorway on the right side and another one on the other side"; tsékooh góyaa ch'é'étiin, "there is an exit road passing down in this canyon"; ni'ałníí ch'é'étiin át'é, "the center of the world is a passthrough" (like a doorway, i.e., to the other world).

Components: in/out; path; motion; connection between in and out (contiguity); volumeness/planeness.

l) yah aninááh, 'come inside'. This verb, used with humans and animals only, expresses an invitation to come inside, to make the transition from the outside. In the descriptive aspect yah'ííyá ('I, he/she come in'), somebody's entrance is described.

Components: in/out; motion of transition; direction is inward; volumeness/planeness; (what is entered); border (as space of transition).

Center/Periphery

We only came across words pointing to center position; no word or expression typically expresses the notion of "periphery" or "out of center," unless the more general term binaa (around, in the surrounding; cf. section on nearness/separateness) is considered like that.

a) atníí', 'center, middle, half'. This verb (to become the middle on both sides) defines a particular spatial unit, a very general order, or a division of some bigger unit in two, or all of these in one. Whatever the dominant meaning, no strict metric distinctions are implied. Any body, volume, or surface can be structured by ascribing to it a center, even without further mention of the character of this center (point, hole, or surface). Centers can be discerned in phenomena of all three spaces (O, S, C).

Examples: ni'ałníí'dóó yá'ałníí'shich'į'hózhǫ́ǫ́ doo, "from the center of the earth and from the center of the sky, may I be blessed"; tónteel ałníí'di da 'ahijikááh, "in the center of the ocean they deliver a (final) battle"; ńléí tó ałníí'góó adííłkǫ́ǫ́, "swim to the center of the water (surface)"; kin ałníí' gónaa na'íítł'in, "there is a partition in the middle of the house (up or across or . . .)"; shiníí, "the middle of my body"; shíchį́įhałníí'gi neezgai, "I have a pain in the middle of my nose"; shiníí gónaa sis, "a belt around my waist (middle)."

Components: center; volumeness/planeness; defines space, order or units; part/whole.

b) biníí', 'in or around the center, its/his/her middle or waist'. The verb/noun has a broad meaning, having to do with center and/or surrounding of a poorly defined center. In this way, it can be used to express one's position in a crowd, as well as the middle of a wall (in horizontal direction). It is only used in O- and S-spaces, while its reference to cosmological matters always seems to imply a metaphorical meaning of both the phenomena and their center (e.g., referring to the middle of the world with this word, one speaks in a metaphorical, symbolic sense, not of the physical center).

Examples: hooghan biníí' gónaa' njígai, "there is a white stripe across (gónaa) in the middle of the hooghan (that is, on the wall, all around)"; hooghan biníí'góne' ahoodzą́', "inside the hooghan there is a hole in the middle (not the floor or the roof, but in the middle of the wall)"; diné biníí' hastiinaléi' sidá, "a stranger is sitting amidst a group of people (a crowd)."

Components: center, in/out; volumeness/planeness; horizontal; near/separate; border (across); defines space; part/whole.

c) wóniidi, 'way back in the center of the hooghan'. The term is highly specific and refers to the place in the back of the hooghan, facing the entrance, where medicine man and patient are supposed to sit at the beginning of any ceremony.

In a similar, ceremonial way it can refer to the corresponding position on earth in the West.

107. Open/Closed (Overt/Covert; to Open/to Close) (Numbers 107, 207, and 307 of the UFOR)

Generally I tend to conclude that only actions and direct correlates of actions having to do with openness and closedness are the domains of meaning of corresponding terms in Navajo, excluding virtually all purely perceptual instances that would certainly strike Westerners as examples of openness or closedness. Put another way, only that kind of opening/closing that you can walk through, pass through, or where water or any other substance can pass through, or is blocked off in its way, would be likely to have terms corresponding to open and closed in Navajo.

All of these have to do with a particular kind of action or movement implying a passing through, the crossing of some type of threshold, and the like. The more strictly perceptual instances of openness and closedness that cannot directly induce actions will have less relevance here in Navajo. This conclusion was reached through the analysis of the linguistic material I list below, supplemented with two additional and independently presented tests, stressing this particular point. In the topological test a list of drawings were presented, two at a time, all displaying the crucial distinction of open versus closed, in pairs of drawings like a C and an O, a Ω and a Ω , and the like. The monolingual and the bilingual consultant invariably pointed to the similarity of both members of the pair. After pressing for more information, they would both try to determine minor deformations in one or both members of each pair, however, systematically neglecting the open/closed distinction. The reaction as well as its unanimity was so striking[17] that I went on to present

---

17. Both consultants live in Apache County, though thirty miles apart, with no observable kin relationship and no means of transportation of their own.

an explicit question on openness and closedness on a similar case. For this second analysis I used some of the drawings in the Segall, Campbell and Herskovits (1966) volume to investigate perceptual illusions (especially the figures on pp. 13, 17, and 59), showing geometric figures where some of the lines do not touch or cross and leave a small open space. Asking the consultants about the name of these openings directly, I always got answers with verbs like honít'i' and dahazt'íí (cf. below).

As pointed out in Chapter I, the world as such is considered to be complete and closed: nothing can really be added, nor can anything escape, except through contact with neighboring tribes (including the whites, of course) which invariably amounts to bad consequences (and requires healings through specific ceremonies). Even if this belief is not firmly held any more, the fear of misuse of these specific "doorways" between the Navajo world and outer worlds clearly exists in present-day Navajo society.[18]

a) dá kał, 'to close (with force)'. This verb describes the closing of a stiff or solid unit like a door, a tumblerock (a flat rock that closes off a cave), and the like by an agent. The closing of a curtain or cloth will never be rendered with this word, but rather with the one just below. Some people prefer to give other verbs instead (as e.g., TB), like da'anít'i (one recognizes anít'i, the fence, the long, linelike phenomenon that bars the road) to describe the closing of a door. The verb has relevance only in O- and S-spaces.

Examples: dádi'nítkaał, "close the door tight" (or with a key).

Components: closed; volumeness/planeness; completely (tight, with key); solid item; motion.

dádiníłtsooz, 'I closed smoothly, (flexible material)'. The expression dates from the time the hooghan was closed off by a curtain or cloth, instead of a wooden door. It is not commonly used now (according to TB), although some people would use it now to denote the closing of the door as well. Again, it has relevance only in O- and S-spaces.

Example: naak'a'at'áhí dádiníłtsooz, "I closed the curtain, the cloth."

Components: closed; volumeness/planeness; flexible object, motion.

b) ąą, 'open (particle) or to open (verb)'. This verb is used both as a verb and as an adjectival form to describe the opening or the being open of something. As far as we could investigate, it is a very general way of speaking about the action or the corresponding state, confined to O- and S-spaces.

Examples: shá ąą ályaa, "opened up for me"; tséso' ąą át'é, "the window is wide open"; díí atiin ąą át'é, "the road is wide open"; ąą'ííshłaa, "I opened it"; ąąnoot'íít, "they are increasing."

Components: open; volumeness/planeness; motion or not.

---

18. The author was frequently asked what he would do with the knowledge gathered, once "outside" (of the reservation), and whether he was planning to take along some of the more sacred products (drum, basket, cradle) to the world of the white people. In a similar way, a complex process to retrieve several of the major medicine pouches of Navajo medicine men (deposited in the Santa Fe Museum, i.e., outside of the reservation) was thoroughly and repeatedly discussed during this period.

c) another, completely different way or referring to open/closed involves the description of the fact that specific spatial configurations allow
room for the passage of something, or that such configurations come into existence. Derivations of two different stems make up such verbs.

haz'á as in dahaz'á, 'there is room, or room opened up'. In contrast to
the verbs above, there is no agent necessarily involved: a natural setting can
be like that, or a wash can produce such a situation, and so on. The verbs,
again, have relevance in O- and S-spaces.

Examples: ałts'ą́ąhjí ałts'íísígo eh'idahaazt'i', "there are small openings on both sides" (like an old wooden log in the ceiling); łahgo bił haz'á, "a
part of it is for him/her" (there is room for her); łahji' bąąh dahaz'á, "part is
missing" ('on opposite side, border, there is room').

Components: open; volumeness/planeness; part (constitutes open
form); defines volumeness/planeness.

d) ahoodzá, 'hole, cavity'. a'áán, 'hole (in ground), burrow'.

These words constitute instances of openings in a certain sense. However, since I feel they are more accurately represented as in terms of space or
volume in Navajo, I treat them in that place (cf. no. 109).

108. Converging/Diverging (Numbers 108, 208, and 308 of the UFOR)

These notions were formerly held to be specifications of other entries
in the UFOR (cf. Pinxten, 1975). Their abundance and importance in Navajo
language and thought led me to reconsider this status and to introduce them as
genuine and separate entries. The change is not only due to their appearance
in great number in the Navajo world view, however. Rather, the Navajo experience led us to reconsider the basic meanings that could possibly be bestowed
on these notions and terms. I came to the conclusion that those spatial distinctions cannot be reduced to other entries of the UFOR without severe loss of
meaning, and this led to their constituting a separate entry on their own. The
enlightenment I gained from the discussions with Navajos on these points cannot be rendered in full.

This aspect of Navajo space is found with different living things in the
Navajo world, and has relevance for human beings as well. A basic process of
expansion out of one center and final return to that same center was discussed
earlier (cf. chap. I, section "The Dynamic Nature of the World, Time,
Being"): creation out of the center of the world and ultimate return to this
center is an instance (CM).

a) da' nííts'ą́ą́', 'in all directions, spreading out'. This expression can
describe a movement (going in all directions), as well as the position of various places or groups, as visualized by the center referent. In some cases it can
be used to speak about the mind or thought of human beings (mental probing
in many directions is a proper way of living for a Navajo) or of songs. The
expression can only be used in O- and S-spaces.

Examples: béégashii dah nííts'ą́ą́jigo deikał, "the cattle are spreading out in all directions"; da'nı́łts'ą́ą́jigo adahayóı́go nı́łtsą́, "it rained all over the place, in all directions"; dah nı́łts'ą́ą́jigo adáhagééd Peabody Coal Minedóó: "people are hauling out coal in every direction from Peabody Coal Mine."

Components: divergence; center; horizontal; motion or not; separate; plural things.

b) ałchishdę́ę́', 'from both sides; from different directions to one place, coming together'. The opposite of dah nı́łts'ą́ą́ji is expressed: there is direction, movement from an ill-defined and poorly structured periphery toward one center. The words are relevant in S- and O-spaces.

Examples: Lukachukai hoolyéegi da' nihiłchishdę́ę́' diné'áłah ałchishdę́ę́' dahazlı́ı́'go Késhmish dahasłı́ı́', "at the place called Lukachukai people from everywhere came together for the Christmas reunions"; ałchíní da' nı́łch'ishı́dę́ę́' jı́'ólta'ági da'ólta', "children from all different places are students at the day school"; bééso ałch'ishdę́ę́' adayiiznil, "money was brought together by people from everywhere" (for donation); also: łı́ı́'da'nı́łch'ishı́dę́ę́' deíkááh, "horses are coming in slowly from every direction"; wóláchíı' ałchishdę́ę́' yisnil, "the ants come together (in anthill) from all directions."

Components: convergence; center; horizontal; motion or not; near; plural things.

c) ahibidiikéé', 'tracks come together'. This verb expresses the joining of tracks, footprints, and the like, of one and the same or of different animals or people. The expression is rather specific, restricted to these phenomena. Still, the general notion of convergence is illustrated by it. The verb has relevance for S-space only, since it implies the relationship between agents of some sort.

Examples: ahinihidiikéé', "we come together (our tracks come together)"; łééchąą'í dóó dibé ahibidiikéé', "there are dog and sheep tracks coming together"; diné dóó asdzáni ahibidikéé', "a man's and a woman's tracks come together."

Components: convergence; path, track; center; horizontal; motion; two or more items; near.

d) ałts'ábíkéé, 'tracks separate, diverge'. This verb is the exact opposite of the foregoing one. Again all characteristics apply.

Examples: łı́ı́' ałts'ábíkéé', "the horses separated (the tracks separated)"; mą'ii dóó dibé ałts'ábíkéé', "the tracks of the coyote and the sheep separate."

Components: divergence; tracks; path; center; horizontal; motion; two actors; separate.

e) ałtso'íít'i, '(parties) coming together in a line for one person'. This verb is a complex form of íít'i (in a row, in formation). Again, it is only used to speak about the gathering of people, and even then restricted to a specific purpose (S-space).

Examples: ałch'ishdę́ę́' ałtso' íít'i, "from both sides they come together in a line" (for politicians of different opinions, on their own responsibility).

Components: convergence; near; motion; center; horizontal.

f) ałta'neets'ee'ii, 'crisscross, mixed together, interlocked, knotted'. This noun expresses a strong kind of convergence, realizing an intertwining or mixing together of the phenomena involved. The prefix ałtah- ('mixed up') may be the main component here. Still, the noun is taken up under the present heading (convergence), because a movement from separate positions toward a center and a complete mix in the center is expressed. It is relevant in O- and S-spaces only.

Examples: saad ałta'neets'ee'ii doo nisinda, "I do not like any mixed-up talk, any propaganda"; tł'iish t'óó'ayóígo ałta'neets'ee'ii, "there are a lot of snakes crawling up, intertwined"; ni'dah da'atiin to'óó'ayóígo ałta' neets'ee'ii, "on earth you have a nexus of roads (some highways, some dirt roads, some paved roads . . .)."

Components: convergence; contiguity; volumeness/planeness; line-like items; plural items; overlapping, center.

g) shaazh, 'knot, broken thing put back together'. This noun refers to any knot, or any joint, or even any little hump on the body resulting from the growing together of a once broken element. It has relevance in O- and S-space only.[19]

Examples: shigaan shaazh, "the knot on my (once broken) arm"; tł'óół shaazh éíya, "the rope has one knot after the other"; dashzazh, "a lasso knot".

Components: convergence; overlapping; part/whole; contiguity (cf. also the section on nearness/separateness/contiguity).

109. Volumeness/Planeness (Numbers 109, 209, and 309 of the UFOR)

These characteristics turn out to be of major importance in Navajo spatial structuring. They represent the most qualitative or experientially basic differentiations in the person's coping with his body and the outside world through action and perception, structuring the world in different sets of spatially determinable forms: forms that prove to have three-dimensionality or rather that extend in all possible directions in which one can handle or perceive them, versus forms that extend in only two orthogonal directions and thus are plane or flat forms (cf. Rucker's excellent elaboration on the classical Flatland tales, 1977).

Not only is the fact of "having extension, being extended" along two or three orthogonal directions recognized, but vague, fuzzily bordered categories of volumeness and planeness are represented in the lexicon of any culture, including that of the Navajos. Their specific characteristics differentiate them mutually and from any other spatial notion represented in the lexicon: you can have cuplike forms, solid or compact forms, and so on as instances of volumeness, or planeness. Many of the other spatial notions were found to

19. TB stated firmly that he would use the word exclusively for knots.

imply the existence and recognition of any general or more specific instance of volumeness or planeness in their specific use and circumscription: bikáá' is preferably used on top of something "solid, compact," while deení applies to the top of a pointed volume, and so forth. Consequently, the identification and differentiation of different, common instances of volumeness and planeness in the lexicon could prove of considerable value for the better understanding of Navajo space in the same way that (or more so than) the identification of different meanings of "border," proved interesting to that goal.[20]

The Navajo lexicon contains a set of verbs that were claimed to be of utmost importance in understanding the Navajo way of dealing with the outside world. These classificatory verbs specify different aspects of substances and different ways of handling, moving, or seeing substances (cf. Hoijer 1945–49; Garrison, 1974). They are included in the present section, because, in our perspective, they deal with the delineation of spatial forms (volumeness and planeness), apart from other functions.

In the present section, then, three subdivisions were introduced: (1) specific units of physical, sociogeographic, and cosmological space, (2) the classificatory verbs, and (3) some modificational processes with respect to space.

Specific Units of Physical, Sociogeographic, and Cosmological Space

Without any doubt a lot of common spatial units in the Western (say the English or American) culture are not named: the delicate geographical work of Gould and White (1974), searching for the mental counterpart of people's behavior in geographic representation and decision making, at least urges us to keep in mind that a lot of processes seem to escape any conscious level. Consequently, naming of the resulting units and relations is not always to be expected. We conjecture that a similar situation may be expected, mutatis mutandis, with other cultures, notably with the Navajos. Somewhat more explicit and accurate naming and description could be encountered, in view of the Navajo stress on thorough perception. Still, it would be foolish to expect full and accurate differentiation and identification of all possible perceptual and praxiological distinctive units of space. In consequence, only those units that are named in Navajo can be taken into account here.

Since this set is very extensive still, we decided to withhold those distinctions that prove substantial, that define a clearly different spatial unit. The latter criterion has resulted in the elimination from the list of a considerable

---

20. Whenever a clear notion of order is introduced in similar differentiations, a metric notion is reached. I will then speak about "volumes" and "surfaces" (cf. sections 124 and 128). Terms that clearly imply such metric aspects are not included in the present section.

number of derivations of complex forms, though the simpler forms themselves are introduced.[21]

a) ahoodzá, 'hole through something, there is a cavity'. This verb (verb stem -dzá, 'there is a tunnel, hole') indicates the piercing through a rock, or a pipe, anything rather solid with a hole going right through it. Most tunnellike holes are termed this way, no matter how solid or big, the substance is. The hole/tunnel can lie in any possible direction. Specifications are, of course, possible: to speak of nahadzá' specifies the hole more as a tunnel than merely hoodzá (BB). Rather than the direction or movement, however (as in bighá), the spatial form defined in the substance is referred to: therefore, the substance, object, or whatever serves as phenomenon with a hole is always mentioned (rock, pipe . . .). The verb is used in all three spaces (O, S, C).

Examples: ni'bighi' hoodzá, "there is a tunnel or hole through the ground" (within the ground); tsé bighá hoodzá, "there is a hole in/through the rock"; Tségháhoodzání, Window Rock (cf. previous example); yá bigháhoodzá, "there is a hole through the sky"; shíchį́į́h bii' ahoodzá, "there is a hole in my nose"; kin łánídi ayóí áníłtso ahoodzá, "at Flagstaff, there is a huge crater hole."

Components: volumeness; defined on volumeness/planeness; in/out; border; dominance of longitudinal dimension; no specific direction; open.

b) a'áán, 'hole in the ground, pit, burrow'. This noun, in this and similar constructions, refers to a cavelike, holelike space against a background of homogeneous material: in the above word the background is earth. It could be mud (łeezh'áán), rock (tsé'áán). In contrast with the -dzá forms, the 'áán forms are said to be animal holes, mostly moving downward. Moreover, the latter have only one open end and cannot be tunnels. The noun(s) can be used in all three spaces (O, S, C).

Examples: łees'áán ííshłaa, "I made bread (on a dirt oven)"; atsá tsé'áán góne' bighan, "the eagle has his home in a hole in the rocks"; gah ba'áán, "the rabbit's hole, mound."

Components: volumeness; defined on volumeness/planeness; in/out border; down; open/closed.

c) yíldiz, 'ditch in the earth'. This noun is specifically limited in use to natural or manmade ditches, small horizontal and lengthy furrows in the land. Evidently, its use is limited to O- and S-spaces.

Examples: yíldzis góyaa íítłizh, "I fell into the ditch"; yíldzis góyaa tó ńlį́, "the water flows down the ditch"; yíldzisgo łeezh hayiską́ągo yíldzis ayíí'ą́, "you remove (turn over) the earth to make a ditch."

Components: planeness/volumeness; defined on volume (soil); horizontal; dominance of one dimension; depth (not dominant).

---

21. Indeed, the set of derivations, combinations, modifications through the use of prefixes, postpositions, and enclitics is virtually infinite. Most of the time, however, the meanings of any specific complex form can be derived from the stem and the meanings of each of the encountered modifiers. We especially thank Professor Oswald Werner and Mr. Allen Manning for information on these points.

d) dził, 'mountain, mountain range'. This noun denotes some very solid formation, having a considerable height. The main distinction between hills (k'id) and mountains seems to reside in the height: whenever a formation is taller than "any imaginable house or tower," or when you have to characterize it through its solid extension upward and horizontally (ná'á is appropriate), the formation is considered a mountain. A hill is an object that one can see over, with a definite form in all directions.

Examples: Lukachukaigi aláádhi dził ná'á, "the mountain lies all the way down on the side of Lukachukai"; dził bąąh áhí, "there is fog on the mountain"; díí kǫ́ǫ́ t'áá kónighánigo dził diná'á, "there are several mountains close to each other right here" (Black Mountain, Lukachukai Mountain, Navajo Mountain).

Components: volumeness; extension in all directions; high; order; solid.

e) yílk'id, 'hump, hill'. The verb stem refers to any hump, hill, bump, and the like, from a very small to a large and relatively high formation. It is also said of speed bumps, anthills, but genuine hills are also called k'id. The upper limits of height (cf. the section on dził) are fuzzy, but can be vaguely defined "as high as a house or tower," giving any hill some connotation of man being able to see over it, or to work it.

Examples: tójí k'id át'é, "on the other side of the wash is a hill" (the wash here points to the scale of the hill in a way); díí k'id dah ats'os bikáági shighan, "I live on that coneshaped hill"; Dziłízhiin bikáá'di k'id dah ats'os dah si'ą, "on top of Black Mountain is sitting a coneshaped peak/hump."

Components: volume; upward; extension in all directions; order; small.

f) ni', kéyah, nahasdzáán, these three terms all have to do with a distinctive extension on the surface of the earth, ranging from object, to social and cosmological space.

ni' is used to refer to the ground, or earth in your immediate vicinity, the ground you stand on, live on, and the like. Sometimes however, it is used as a generic term to deal with the earth's surface. This use is apparent in most specifications of the surface formation as well as in specific names for specific or peculiar places.

Examples: ni'ałníí' shich'į' hózhǫ́ǫdoo, "from the center of the earth's surface, may I be blessed" (mythological use); ni'hadohołt'éégi shigan, "I live on a good, smooth land";[22] beeldléí ni'góó sikaad, "the blanket is spread out on the ground"; t'óó'ahayói tónteel nihookáá' bikáá' sinil, "there are different (several) oceans on the surface of the earth."

Components: planeness; horizontal; no or fuzzy border; part/whole.

---

22. This word, like nihookáá, can be used in a common context, but is most of all used in ceremonial matters: ni'hadohołt'é is a smooth, spotless place selected for the offering of jewels by a medicine man or his patient. Nihookáá refers to the surface of the earth, again most of all in religious or mythological contexts.

kéyah refers to a unit of the earth's surface, as defined through a boundary. It can be the boundary of a private domain, a family resort, a nation, as long as it does not cover the whole world.

Examples: diné bikéyah dóó Washindoon bikéyah sinil, "Navajoland (the reservation) and the United States of America (the land of Washington) both exist"; nabeehó bikéyah kojí nineel'á, "the land of the Navajos ends right here"; B.B. bikéyah ayóigo niteel, "B.B.'s land is very wide."

Components: planeness; horizontal; part/whole; ultimate and strict border; overlapping (by family, group, population . . .).

nahasdzáán, 'earth, earth's surface'. This noun refers always to the totality of the earth (either, traditionally, the Navajo earth between the four Sacred Mountains, or recently, the total earth of the Westerners). It can be used in a holy or traditional sense (Mother Earth, cf. chap. I) or in a common sense.

Examples: nahasdzáán bikáá't'áá ałtso hóló', "a lot of things are growing on the earth"; nahasdzáán náánihidlaa łeeghi' adeit nííłgo, "when we die we go back into the earth (into the dirt of the earth)"; nahasdzáán ał'ąą aná 'niił, "the world/earth changes again and again" ('earth, different kinds, again, change').

Components: volumeness/planeness; horizontal; whole; order (biggest extension).

g) bii hahookaad or bii habii kaad: 'shallow surface without a rim'. This verb (in both forms of the same stem) is composed of the following parts: bii ('in, inside, on the inside'), ha or hahoo ('upward or outward/there is room'), and -kaad ('stretching out in a flat surface'). The idea that is rendered is the form of a rather shallow plate, tray, and the like, the shallow inclination of the slopes of the bottom of a lake, of a valley, and so on, or the form of a rimless dish. The form has important mythological connotations since, in the traditional belief, the earth and the sky both have this particular outlook (CM, BW, TB, though not anymore with Western-oriented people like HT, the earth has a dishlike form and the sky tops it in an upside-down dishlike form). The surface covered is considerable, with respect to the lack of depth of the form, so that a horizontal expansion seems dominant. The verb is relevant in all three spaces (O, S, C). Bii hahookaad is considered somewhat deeper than bii habiikaad (respectively, like a dish and a saucer).

Examples: nahasdzáán bii hahookaad, "the earth is concave, stretches out in a smooth dishlike form"; be'ek'id bii hahookaad, "the mountain lake has a dishlike form"; shits'aa'habii kaad, "my wedding basket has a dishlike form."

Components: volumeness/planeness; extension; border; horizontal; depth; curvedness.

h) háádahazts'aa', 'any kind of shallow place, valley'. This verb (stem -ts'aa', 'be bowlshaped') expresses a range of bowlshaped, dishlike, hollow formations, irrespective of the depth or relative flatness of the structure. The general outlook of a surface, rather than the volume, remains: the structure is nowhere covered by a ceiling or anything similar, unlike, for example, a cave or hole. The verb can be used in O- and S-spaces, but seems mostly restricted to parts of landscapes.

Examples: háádahazts'aa'gi tó háálį́, "there is a spring in that valley" (hollow place); dził bitahdi shikéyah háádahazts'aa, "my land extends in a bowl shape between the mountains."

Components: planeness; horizontal; depth; border; open; curved; order (i.e., as deep as the bii hahookaad example).

i) bii'halts'aa, 'cuplike, roundish hole'. Again, the meaning of this verb is very close to that of the former one (having the same stem), but here a hole, a cavelike structure is clearly distinguishable inside and under a surface. The hole should not be covered, but is sufficiently different from the rest of the surrounding surface that it is selected as a hole. Its relevance is primarily in S-space, and to some extent in O-space.

Examples: bitsii'bii'halts'aa', "there is a little hollow place inside the skull of his head" (this refers to the fontanels); Tsénikáni bikáá'bii'halts'aa', "on top of Round Rock mesa there is a depression (with water in it)."

Components: volume; volumeness/planeness (background); part/ whole; roundish; deep; open; border.

The Classificatory Verb Stems

As was explained earlier, the classificatory verb stems cannot be considered as spatial terms in themselves. Still, their role in detailing spatial constraints and sorting out mutually differentiated types of objects is so important that their treatment in an analysis of Navajo space terminology is required. The use of a specific classificatory verb stem delimits a range of objects also in their spatial characteristics. Therefore, rather than present a list of components for each of the stems themselves, I restrict the list to a statement of what spatial characteristics can be ascribed to the set of objects implicitly delineated in the use of a specific grammatical form: third person singular, perfective mode.[23]

a) sitą́, 'a stiff, slender flat object is in place'. The verb specifies the group of objects it can be used with: anything rather stiff, rigid, generally elongated, standing up or lying down in any direction. One object at a time is referred to, always primarily characterized through its length, or, what amounts to the same, by dominance through its extension along one of three dimensions. Furthermore, I found the verb is only used in the object space (not in S- and C-spaces).

---

23. The very thorough work by Ed Garrison (1974) helped a lot to come to grips with the problem of the classificatory verb stems. His analysis served as a basis for the semantic analysis of the specifically spatial aspects involved in these: I hope to be complementary in offering the spatial study rather than to focus on the verb stems' global meaning.

Examples: bee 'ak'e elchíhí sitą́, "the pencil is lying down"; łeezh bee hahalkaadí sitą́, "the shovel is in place"; tsin sitą́: "a stick is in place (milepost)"; kodóó naalyéhé bahoghanjį' t'áálá'í tsin sitą́, "from here to the store is one mile away" (the milepost is referred to and used metaphorically to denote the distance of one mile).

Spatial type: one object with dominance of one of three dimensions, stiff. This characterization of "spatial type" differs somewhat from the interpretation of other authors dealing with the classificatory verb stems (Hoijer, 1945–49; Garrison, 1974). This may be because of the restriction of scope in the present analysis, exclusively to spatial aspects. An important difference, however, is precisely in the way the spatial features are dealt with. Whereas in dictionaries up to now, and also in Garrison's profound analysis, space is taken for granted as built up necessarily and represented most naturally as a coordinate system of Cartesian nature (i.e., with three sophisticated, metrically defined dimensions, each orthogonally defined with respect to the others). I do not adhere to such assumptions and instead present more qualitative, more directly praxiologically based dimensional notions: The characteristics of an object are defined through the ways in which it can be manipulated (as expressed in the classificatory verb stems), where dominance on one dimension rather than equal extension on all three (volume, compact form) or dominance on two (flat thing) induces another way of attaining an understanding of it. Nowhere, until then, are metric specifications implied. They can be, of course, if necessary.

b) siką́, 'a mass or a set of things is in place in an open container'. The crucial distinction between this and a form like sighį́ is that the container is clearly distinct from its contents, whatever its nature may be apart from that. A further distinction with, for example, siłtsooz is the relative rigidity of the container: when siką́ is used the container tends to be rigid, like a wooden barrel or a steel container. However, no decisive evidence could be found on the latter and consultants would sometimes use this verb to describe the matter inside a sack or bag as well. Relevance in O- and S-spaces.

Examples: tó siką́, "the water is in the container"; tł'iish łeeyi' siką́, "the snake is rolled up in the mud" (as if lying in a container); hashtł'ish siką́, "the mortar is in the container"; bilasáani siką́, "an apple sits in an open container."

Spatial type: a plurality of objects or a mass inside a clearly bounded space, with closure of the only opening. No dominance of any one dimensional extension. The contents as well as the container are characterized primarily as instances of volumeness.

c) siyį́, 'something massive lies, is in place'. This verb is used to describe big amounts, great volumes of things being present. As such it is often used for fluid or not very solid matter. It can be used in all three spaces.

Examples: tó ahííghį́, "the water is extended out without end"; Tó dzís'á siyį́, Wheatfield Lake, Arizona; bik'i dah siyį́, "a big belly bulging out (a beer belly)"; dah sighį́, "something sits still in a whole amount" (on a table, for example).

Spatial type: the being in position of a mass, without specification of the actual form, or the dominance of extension on one or more dimensions. A notion of order is implied since it is stated that the amount must be big, considerable.

d) si'ą, 'a solid, bulky, or roundish object is in place'. This verb has a very general meaning, dealing with phenomena of any extension, in all three spaces. On modeling different forms in clay and asking whether si'ą or any other verb would apply, we gained answers like: it could be si'ą because "it [the form] is solid" and "it can sit flatly without moving," but also "the form is lying solidly," without the dominance of any dimension or combination of dimensions over the other(s). It is relevant in all three spaces (O, S, C).

Examples: Tsénikáni dah si'ą, "Round Rock mesa is lying solidly, in one piece"; bikáá'adání si'ą, "the table is sitting"; sǫ' si'ą dóósǫ' silá, "a meteor is lying [near Flagstaff] and a pair of stars [meteors] lies [near Crystal]"; tsé názbąs nahalingo si'ą, "the round looking rock is in place" (si'ą is more general than any rather geometric form like round, názbąs).

Spatial type: si'ą refers to a very general, topological form of volumeness, but then is used generally to deal with any specific volumes as well (ball, box, cube . . .). It refers to the handling of one individual solid or compact entity (without specification of the values on any particular dimension), or the being in place or sitting up of the entity.

e) sinil, 'they (two or more) are in place'. The meaning is similar to that of si'ą, but pertains to plural objects. A minimal order is required, since otherwise haal'á (scattered) would be used (TB, BB). Typically, the same connotation of solidity is required: For example, coins can be said to be sinil whereas paper money cannot, because of the criterion of solidity.

Examples: tsé sinil, "rocks are lying side by side, or piled up"; dził sinil, "the mountains are lying in a formation"; bééso báhoghan bééso sinil, "money is deposited in the bank."

Spatial types: cf. under si'ą, but for plural objects.

f) sikaad: Garrison (1974) correctly distinguishes between two homophonic words here, with clearly different semantic features. We can only confirm his findings on this distinction, and will speak accordingly of sikaad A and sikaad B.

sikaad A, 'something extending out flat, like a rug, along a surface'. This form stresses the surface or horizontal extension, the covering of a certain surface. It is this form that was encountered previously when discussing the dishlike form that was to represent the traditional conception of the earth: bii hahookaad, habii kaad, haskaad.

Examples: tó sikaad, "a thin layer of water is spread out, standing still"; diih dikǫn tsin sikaad, "a wooden floor is spread out, in place"; one cannot say kéyah sikaad (rather than kéyah si'ą) because land has a certain thickness; linoleum sikaad, "the linoleum is spread out"; Lukachukaidóó Tsénikáni góyaa náhoodeeskaad, "from Lukachukai down towards Round Rock mesa there is a wide space stretching out" (only the surface is dealt with, and its flatness is described).

Spatial type: the very notion of "planeness" seems to be expressed here, giving minimal information on the characteristics of the flat space described, and certainly refraining from implying any specific, metric, or sophisticated surface notion (as was clear in the valley examples: humps, irregularities, and the like are neglected in favor of the general appearance of a flat space). The third dimension (verticality) is completely deleted from the picture.

sikaad B, 'it grows like a bushy or leafy tree'. One individual living thing is erected in position and extends upward through time. Typically, the verb applies to growing things, and, at the same time, to things that stand still, are in position.

Examples: ch'il sikaad, "one plant is standing/grows up"; gad sikaad, "a cedar tree is standing"; nahasdzáán bikáá'góó t'iis dah sikaad, "the cottonwood is standing on the earth (with roots in it, growing upward)"; ch'il naazkaad, "plants are standing all around" (all individually).

Spatial type: the vertical dimension is emphasized exclusively, deleting any reference to other dimensions. The range of applications of this stem is restricted to living things, with fixed location, that grow upward.

g) silá: Garrison (1974) distinguishes between three different uses or forms of the verb, each having a slightly different meaning. For the purpose of this investigation this distinction is unnecessary, since all three presumably separate forms have the same spatial typology that goes with them. Therefore, I handle silá as if it had but one uniform meaning.

This verb indicates something in a formation like a string, a rope, a stream, or something extending lengthwise without interruption or discontinuity. A main connotation distinguishing this spatial type from the one indicated through the verb stem nít'i (extending lengthwise, as a fence) is that the object or phenomenon that is said to be silá is touching upon or well imbedded into the background, the substance it is articulated upon. In this sense, a rope on the ground and the like are silá, whereas a wire extending above the ground and other, noncontiguous lengthwise extensions are described more properly through the verb nít'i.

Examples: tooh silá, "a river is extending far out" (like the San Juan and the Rio Grande); ałts'oostsoh silá, "an artery is lying (all through the body)"; hoodzoh silá, "the border line stretches out"; béésh silá, "the iron pipes lie on the ground"; even metaphorically, one could say: dził silá, "the mountain stretches out like a string."

Spatial type: the verb indicates the handling of something in a horizontal position, touching the background it is lying upon and with absolute dominance on the lateral or the depth dimension.

h) shijool, "noncompact matter, not too solid, is in place." The verb deals with substances like wool, cotton, loose grass or hay, and the like, provided they are folded up, packed together. The spatial characterization is restricted to their being in a volume, though without any container (i.e., without outside borders). Its use is restricted to O- and S-spaces.

Examples: beeldléí shijool, "a blanket is lying there, all folded up"; béésh ałts'ózí shijool, "the loose bundle of wire, folded up in a bunch, is lying"; akájí shijool, "the [tanned] hide is folded up"; metaphorically it can be said of old people: hastiin sání yishjool, "the old man is lying in a pile, a heap, hunched."

Spatial type: much like si'á, the verb sijool stresses an extension on all three dimensions. The main difference seems to reside in the nonspatial characteristics of the objects it speaks about. They are flexible, not solid. The main difference with the verb siká can be sought in the lack of the container.

i) siłtsooz: Here, again, we follow Garrison's distinction between two forms having distinct semantic meanings.

siłtsooz A: 'a plurality of things in a small bag, together constituting a new unit'. The emphasis is on an instance of volumeness, formed by the putting together of a plurality of items in the container (like groceries in a bag). The form is used in O- and S-spaces.

Examples: łeezh siłtsooz, "the mud is in a bag"; aghaa' siłtsooz, "the wool is contained in the bag"; tádídíín siłtsooz, "the corn pollen is held in a sack."

Spatial type: a plurality of things forms one volume unspecified for the different dimensions. The container codefines the form of the volume.

siłtsooz B, 'a flexible, soft material is in place'. Anything flexible, smooth, woollike, paperlike, and so forth. The main difference between this term and sijool lies in the latter's stress on a volume, a three-dimensional formation being the result (cf. also Garrison, 1974), whereas the objects wtih siłtsooz can be extended flat, horizontally, or in some sense folded or piled.

Examples: she'éé' siłtsooz, "my shirt is lying" (but, yistłé háadi silá, "where are my socks?" (silá, since they are a pair); bich'ah háádi siłtsooz, "where is his scarf hat [of the medicine man]?" (whereas for a common, stiff hat: shich'ah si'á, "my hat is in place, like a solid thing"); naaltsoos siłtsooz, "the sheet of paper is in place."

Spatial type: one or more items, flexible, horizontally extending.

j) Other words, specifying further peculiarities, have little relevance for spatial knowledge: shijaa' (plural objects, like seeds, lie), sitłéé' (mushy matter lies), sitį́ (animate subject lies), shitéézh (two animate objects lie). Robert Young (personal communication) pointed these out for the sake of completeness.

Spatial Modifiers

This heading does not refer to a grammatical category, but rather stresses a semantic group. Some Navajo terms, discussed here, express an action or an event of creation of space, modification of spatial units, redefinition of spaces at the physical, sociogeographical, or cosmological level.

a) haz'ą́, 'there is space (for); it is lacking'.[24] This verb, composed out of ha(z), ('there is room/space'), and the stem -ą́ ('be in a position') has a variable meaning, depending on the linguistic context it is used in. As mentioned in the section on part/whole (section 103), it can be used to denote an empty space, that is, a space from which the object or occupying item is said to be missing (łagho bił haz'ą́). On the other hand, meanings more neutral, or less implicit, can be mentioned merely by describing a certain space (minimally). It can be used in all three spaces (O, S, C).

Examples: shimá bikéyah łahji' bił haz'ą́, "my mother has her own farmland" ('my mother, her farmland, separate, for her, there is room'); ánih-wii'áhi łahgo bił haz'ą́, "the judge has a place of his own" ('judge, part, for him, there is space'); díí hastiin bąąh dahaz'ą́, "that man is always sick" ('that, man, alongside him, there is room' [repetitive]); shichidí bąąh dahaz'ą́, "my car is broken" ('my car, alongside it, there is room'); náhásdzo haz'ą́, "the acre is empty, the empty acre" (nothing grows or is planted there).

Components: volumeness/planeness, part/whole; border (cf. also section 103, part/whole).

b) ná hooł'aah, 'make (a) room for someone/something'. This composite verb can be used to refer to the act of making room (literal or metaphorical), allowing time for something, and the like. It differs from haz'ą́ in that this verb expresses a decision or action from a human being (while the former is transitional to an event, a natural process or situation). We found it used only in O- and S-spaces.

Examples: áájí náhoo'aah, "they make room [for you] up to that point"; five o'clock góóbąąh dahooł'aah, "we start our work from five o'clock on"; nihá náhooł'aah, "you make room for us repeatedly."

Components: volumeness/planeness; part/whole; border; motion.

c) ákohgo, 'that amount of space (or time)'. This particle might be used primarily for time (as stated by TB), but was encountered in spatial reference as well. It refers to the precise date or time set to do a certain task, and to the amount of space accorded or covered. In this sense, it is used as a rather vague measure of distance, most of all expressed in time (x days walking, and the like). It is primarily used in O- and S-spaces.

Examples: New Yorkgóó ákohgo déya, "in the direction of New York I go that far [only]"; shikéyah ákohgo sikaad, "my land stretches out that far"; shikéyah ákóniteelgo sikaad, "my land stretches out that far in any direction [in width]."

Components: volumeness/planeness; pluridimensional extension; unit of measure is temporal (day, sun, etc.).

---

24. Young and Morgan (1942, p. 96) only mention a nonspatial meaning ('can, is possible'). The spatial meaning which holds my attention here is not mentioned; however, it seems related to the more strictly spatial meaning I found.

110. Succeeding, Ordering (Number 110 of the UFOR)

The relation of succession, as defined in the UFOR, is a very general notion. It is considered to be the most general way to visualize, think, or speak about order, in the spatial context. When one makes a row, putting one item next to, on the side of, above, under, in front or behind, to the right or left of another item, an ordering relationship is introduced. While most or all of the above ones would be conceived of as rather specific in our culture and thought (having to do with horizontality or verticality), the general pattern, the formal relation that is present and identical in all of them is called "succession" or "order" in the UFOR. This relationship can exist between two or more items, and can be more or less absolute (logicians speak about a complete versus a semiorder that depends on whether each item can be placed in a unique relation of preceding one and succeeding another; some items have to "share" a place with each other, respectively).

In the Navajo language and culture, order is as important as (if not more important than) in Western culture (cf. chap. I, section on closedness of the world, order). Therefore, a considerable number of terms and notions to be found in the Navajo vocabulary, specify a more-or-less general type of order. Some distinctions are thus required in order to assure a readable account.

I would like to introduce the simple (possibly oversimplified) distinction between order and semiorder: Items are said to be in an orderly relation to each other if each item is unambiguously placed with regard to every other according to, or through this relation. There can be no vagueness as to which one is bigger, longer, and so on, and no two items are to be irrelevant to each other. Things are said to be in a relation of semiorder to one another if not all of them can be placed as distinct from each of the others.

Furthermore, within each of these types distinctions can be made as to the number of dimensions that are considered relevant. Some items are ordered in a row, as if in a line, implying the dominance of one spatial dimension. Others are ordered in a plane or in a volume (two- and three-dimensional ordering, respectively). These distinctions are clear more often than not; they will be introduced in the text.

Finally, a difference between strictly spatial and not strictly spatial notions can be pointed out. The former ones imply notions that are used practically exclusively to order a set spatially; the latter are broader notions, pointing to order that may be spatial, but is sometimes also (for example) temporal.

Order
a) shizhoozh, 'one next to the other (slender rigid objects)'. This verbal form expresses the movement or position (being, extending in place) of items parallel to each other. No specific direction is implied, as long as the items or individuals involved have a certain length, and extend next to one another lengthwise. The verb has the connotation of bridging, making some-

thing one can walk over. This is true for human beings and animals (even ants, bees . . .). The verb or a derivative form should never be used to describe the rainbow, though. It has relevance in O- and S-spaces.

Examples: tsin t'óó 'ahayóí naaniigo shizhoozh, "there are a lot of poles lying one next to the other horizontally"; tsin t'óó 'ayóí t'ayíí bihízhoozh, "there are a lot of poles piled up, one on top of the other"; tsin tsé'naa na nízhoozh, "the wood is making a bridge across [the water]"; diné shizhoozh, "people are lying one next to each other on a slant."

Components: succession (order); volumeness/planeness; contiguity; overlapping; any direction; extension on one dimension.

b) dinééskááł versus ndánééskááł, 'in a straight, orderly fashion', versus 'in a disorderly or zigzag formation here and there'. These verbs express a strong sense of order (versus a specific disorder), in that a linelike succession of items is expressed (versus the absence of a clear linelike succession), even stressing the straightness of the line formation. The fact that, when talking about the straight fence around, for example, a square, the verb dinééskááł should be repeated four times (for each side separately) adds to the specificity of the notion expressed. The verbs are used for O- and S-space phenomena. The individual items making up the formation should have some length and be erect, standing up, not lying flat.

Examples: tsin tsé'naa dinééskááł, "they put a row of poles across"; tsétahgóó tsinoolkááł, "they put a row of posts through a rocky passage"; tsin ahéé'dinééskááł, "all around there are posts in line formations" (e.g., illustrated by a row of poles along each side of a square field); dziłbigháádi tsin t'óó 'ayóí ndánééskááł, "on top of the mountain, there are many [fallen] trees lying here and there"; atsee'ch'ah baah atsee' t'óó' ndánééskááł, "on the [chief] headdresses are feathers here and there" (not in a uniform formation though).

Components: order/minimal order; volumeness/planeness; plural items; up (sticking up); linelike (respectively, not) with dominance of one dimension (respectively, loss of this criterion).

c) íít'i', 'it extends way out of sight in a slender line'. The verb describes a spatial order, or a motion realizing that order, with all items put in a row, at regular intervals, without any disruption or discontinuity. In this way, it is still somewhat more specific, stricter in meaning than any of the former ones. Again, however, the dominance of one dimension is apparent. The formation that is described with this verb covers a considerable length, so that "the line is continuously ahead of you, so you will never catch the end." The verb has relevance in all three spaces (O, S, C).

Examples: nááts'íílid íít'i, "the rainbow extends away continuously ahead of you"; díí kǫ́ǫ́ atiin baahgóó íít'i díí bééshígíí, "this wire goes continuously on along the side of this road"; ákǫ́ǫ́ 'atiin baahgóó siláałtooí íít'i', "a whole battalion is lining up along the side of this road"; sizéé' góne'i' íít'i', "down into my mouth it goes" (a thread you cannot see the end of, like a probe during hospital treatment).

Components: order; extending out, away from (ego); motion or not; one dimension, volumeness/planeness; linelike; plural items; continuous (cf. also section on continuity).

d) ałkéé'aníí'á, 'they follow one another; they extend away in a row one behind the other; going in each other's tracks'. This verb expresses a very basic metaphysical relationship in the Navajo world view:[25] the legendary twins (children of the Sun and the Earth in the Creation Myth) as well as sun and moon are said to be in this mutual relationship. So also are the younger and the older generation of Navajo people, the moments that make up a day as well as the seasons in the course of a year, and so on. It is also used in a common, less sacred sense.

Examples: ńléí góyaa dibé ałkéé'aníí'á, "the sheep run down here one after the other"; ńléí gódei anít'i'bijaad ałkéé'aníí'á, "up there are fenceposts following one another"; jóhonaa'éí dóó tł'éhonaa'éí ałkéé'aníí'á, "the sun and the moon go in each other's track."

The Holy Ones who go in a pair like that (the Twins, the Dawn People, the Twilight People, etc.) are called ałkéé'naa'aashii ('the two who follow each other', BW).

Components: succession; path; volumeness/planeness (items); plural items; one dimension; discontinuous (space between items).

e) nizhóní, 'in an orderly way, good, ·the right way'. This verb (also used in nominal form) has been translated in diverse ways (from 'pretty' to 'in balance' and 'in good order'). I only want to consider it in the more directly spatial meaning, thus restricting myself to its relevance in understanding the notion of order. Even then, there is no spatial meaning strictly speaking, but at least some uses will not be considered. In view of the criterion in Navajo tradition that anything good or desirable tends to be in accordance with a certain (ill-defined?) order, the latter has a broad range of meaningful applications, difficult to grasp (cf. Wyman, 1975).

In contrast to the foregoing expressions, this verb is not used to detail a particular characteristic or relationship between individual items, leaving out any further aspects of the items for the time being. Rather, any item or group of items that is subject to this characterization is treated as a whole, as if no dimension and no detail of it could be abstracted when it comes to referring to something using this verb. Phenomena of all three spaces are liable to be categorized in this way.

Examples: When the landlady comes into the house I rent from her she looks around and comes to the conclusion, made explicit: nizhónígo ('everything is in good order, as it is supposed to be'); a table on which things are lying about is cleared: afterwards the state of the table is nizhóní ('orderly'); a person who leads his people in a good way is termed nizhónígo diné ałáaji'

---

25. John Farella has worked thoroughly on the meaning of these terms in Navajo beliefs; we owe him a lot for clarifying the exact meaning, as well as the importance of the notion expressed.

yá'sizį́ ('in a good way, the people, foremost, he stands'), "he is a good leader for the people."

Components: order; volumeness/planeness; part/whole; all dimensions; one item (or group considered as unit).

f) ałníí': See section on in/out, center.

Semiorder

a) aláąh, 'foremost, first in line'. This particle, and several derivatives (aláahdi, aláąjį') define a partial order or semiorder in that only one specific position of a row or set of items is characterized, leaving all others unrelated to each other. The one position defined is the first or farthest, or extreme vis-à-vis all others. It can be used in all three spaces (O, S, C).

Examples: díí ashkii aláąjį' eelwod, "this boy won the race" (came in first); díí hastiin aláąjį' dah sidá, "this man is the chairman" (sits in the head position); díí ashkii ałchíláąjį'go yiláąjį' naaghá, "this boy is the first born (born first of all children)"; aláahdi dah íní, "go and sit down at the end [of the row]"; díí sǫ aláahdi si'á, "this star is placed the farthest away, at the farther end."

Components: semiorder; border; plural items; part/whole; all directions; one or more dimensions; volumeness/planeness (= item).

b) sitł'in, yistł'in, "stack, pile anything." The verb expresses a very incomplete way of ordering: several different or similar things are put on top of each other in a heap or pile. The items are solid things. They are piled up in a lengthwise order, that is, the end result could be a wall or just a heap. The verb is relevant for O- and S-spaces only.

Examples: ak'áán azis bee sitł'in, "stacking up the flour" ('flour, bags, by means of it, stack up'); chizh sitł'in, "the firewood is piled up"; tsé yitł'in, "a stone wall was made" ('rocks stacked up').

Components: semiorder; volumeness/planeness; plural items; horizontal/vertical; part/whole.

c) binaa, 'surrounding'. See section on near/separate (two- or three-dimensional order).

d) bílátah, 'top one, uppermost, end, tip'. See section on border (one-dimensional order).

e) ałch'ishjí, 'on both sides, on each side'. This particle, in this and another form (ałch'ishdę́ę́'), defines a minimal order through the separateness of two items: They are located each on one side of a border or a space, or an object. This particularity gives them a vague opposition in space toward each other. The expressions can be used in all three spaces (O, S, C).

Examples: díí kǫ́ǫ́'shighanígíí ałch'ishjí tó nílį́, "here in this house I am living in, there is water on both sides"; chidí bikee' t'áá ałch'ishjí niiłtsǫǫz, "the tires on both sides are flat"; łį́į' ałch'ishdę́ę́' toohjį' deíkááh, "horses are coming from both sides to the water"; atsį' yá'át'ééhgo naalyéhé báhoghandi ałch'ishjį, "there is fresh meat in the stores on both sides [of the village]."

Components: semiorder; separate; volumeness/planeness; center; border.

Other words denoting a specific order among things are not taken up in this section. They have a more clearly specific emphasis of height, distance, or even volume and the like, and are thus dealt with under those headings.

111. Preceding/Following (in Front of, in Back of) (Numbers 111, 211, and 311 of the UFOR)

Both directions or spatial positions are most naturally embedded in the body structure of human beings; the possible experiences a person can have in his frontal fields are clearly distinct from his back through the specific way each of these fields is liable to be seen, heard, felt, smelled, and otherwise sensed by the human being. Therefore, it is to be expected that this distinction will be voiced in every language, including Navajo. In the course of the preceding sections several connotations of "in front of (ego)" or "beyond, behind x" were encountered with terms or expressions that had primarily to do with other spatial characteristics (near, border, etc.). These will not be taken up again, limiting the present section to terms that have dominant relevance for front and back distinctions.

a) bine', 'back of, behind'. This postposition, and its various derivatives, denotes the rear of anything. The direction is unimportant: the back of the earth is under the earth (in traditional belief) while the back (or far side) of Shiprock is further to the east than Shiprock (from the point of view of Arizona citizens). For all these the same postposition is used. It has relevance in all three spaces.

Examples: Tsé bit'a'í bine'di shighan, "I live beyond, behind Shiprock"; nííłch'i nahasdzáán bine'jí ádin, "there is no air on the backside, behind/under the earth"; hooghan bine'déé' ha 'íí'á', "the sun came up from just behind the hooghan"; díí' hooghan bine'déé' tsin haayá, "a pole sticks up from behind that hooghan."

Components: back; volumeness/planeness; any direction.

b) biláaji', 'first, foremost' (see section on semiorder). The expression has a strong connotation of 'in front, ahead of him'. It can thus be used to express the "farthest away in front of you, in the direction you are facing."

c) bidááh, 'meet it, face it'. This postposition, and its derivatives, relate to a movement or situation confronting (ego) and liable to come to touch with (ego). It has relevance for O- and S-spaces.

Examples: shidááhdi níyol yigááł, "the wind comes [walking] towards me"; nimásání bidááh nínááh, "you go to meet [come in front of] your grandmother"; díwózhii bii'tóódóó wóshdéé' shidááh díínááł, "you will come and meet me this side of Greasewood"; ma'iitsoh shidááh níyá, "the wolf came up to me."

Components: front; volumeness/planeness; nearness/contiguity; motion. (Cf. also section on near/separate.)

d) bikéé', 'behind it and following it'. This verb is used to denote a trail, a track of human beings and any beings that can move around. In a specific use, intended to be highlighted here, it refers to the following of someone, the "going in the tracks of someone." Evidently, it is restricted to O- and S-spaces.

Examples: shiljį́' bikéé' yishááł, "I am following my horse" (I am walking along behind it); shimá bikéé' dah sídá, "I am sitting behind my mother"; níyol bidááhdę́ę́' dóó níyol bikéé'dę́ę́', "the wind has a front and a back" ('wind, from its front, and wind, from its trail'; against the wind and with the wind).

The form bik'eh has a similar metaphorical meaning, though it tends also to be used in (if not preserved for) sacred speech.

Examples: hooghan bik'eh da'nítiingóó yishááł, "I am going from hooghan to hooghan down in the line"; diné yá'át' ééhgo na 'niłtiní bik'eh yishááł, "I follow the person with good advice"; są'ah naagháí bik'eh hózhóón, "a long and strong life along the path of beauty and happiness" (a blessing, the translation of which is abundantly discussed: for example, Haile, 1947, interprets the second part as 'along, beauty', or 'guided by beauty and happiness').

e) bikáá', 'on top, the surface of it, above it'. This postposition has, together with a second one forming a pair, a very deep and at the same time pervasive meaning in Navajo mythology and world view: biką́'ii dóó bi'áádii is always rendered as "the male and the female one" (the one on top and the one somewhat remote).[26] The couple are found with the stars (see below), but also in several instances on earth, always referring to this basic relationship between above and beneath or, amounting to the same notion in directly dynamic terms, male and female. The postposition can be used in all three spaces. We gathered that while bikáá' is similar in meaning to bik'i, the former overlaps more solidly and covers more surface than the latter.

Examples: náhookǫs biką́'ii dóó náhookǫs bi'áadii, "the male and the female North Stars" (cf. also Haile, 1947, p. 4: "Big Dipper and Cassiopeia"); shibid bikáági dah'alshin, "I have a speck [birthmark] on my belly"; toohjí tooh bikáágo yaa haskaad, "all along the river [e.g., the San Juan], a flat water surface stretches out"; nahasdzáán bikáá'diné łahgo bił dahaz'ą́, "the people are part of the world" ('the earth, upon surface, people, part, with her, there is room'); tsénikáni bikáá'góó łeezh sikaad, "mud stretches out all over the surface of Round Rock mesa" (there is a layer of soil on Round Rock).

Components: up; volumeness/planeness; overlapping; horizontal; contiguity; two dimensional extension.

f) bą́ą́h, 'passing it by' and bąąh, 'alongside it'. These postpositions express a kind of contiguity, however, most often with a meaningful aspect of verticality.

26. Again, I am indebted to John Farella who did major work on this conceptual couple. A basic principle valid in every major process of Navajo reality is the process of persistence and expansion of things in the world through this relationship.

One consultant (TB) claimed that this postposition should only be used for the relationship between a solid or a stiff main object and a plurality of smaller items upon it (e.g., pinions on a pine tree). The minor attributes should be attached only to and near the top end of the main body. It is used in O- and S-spaces.

Examples: shich'ah ńléí tsinbąąh dah si'ą, "my hat is hanging on that tree"; shé'éé dáádílkał bąąh dah siłtsooz, "my coat is hanging on the door [maybe on the doorknob]"; díí awéé' bąąh dahaz'ą, "the baby is sick all the time" ('that baby passing him/her, there is room'); béésh bąąh dah naaz'ání, "the councilmen" (the ones who always had badges on them); yéigo tł'óół bąąh dah síníłį, "you pull hard on the rope" ('lie, strongly, on the rope').

Components: back; path, trail; motion; two items or more; order (one leading the other); horizontal; volumeness/planeness (= items).

g) shich'ą́ą́h, 'in my way, barring my way' (cf. section on border). There is a strong connotation of "in front of (ego)" that goes with this term, implying that one could either interpret the expression as a specific peculiarity of "what is in front of (ego)" or as a specific form of border (notably, one in front of [ego]).

112. In Perspective (Number 112 of the UFOR)

No specific term or expression could be found or elicited covering this highly sophisticated notion. It should be borne in mind that the distinction is not a necessary requisite in order to build a model of space, or even a geometry (like Euclid's). Its development in an explicit and controllable way in Western tradition dates merely from the sixteenth century (cf. Dürer in Newman, 1960).

113. Deep, Far (Dimension of Depth) (Numbers 113, 213, and 313 of the UFOR)

In this section the focus is on the dimension itself, as it is constituted by a (presumably infinite) sequence of front/back relations in a stretch. It is most clearly illustrated by human vision: the field of objects in the distance slants slightly to form a linelike constellation at the horizon. The space or plane extending in front and in the back of (ego) is abstractly grasped through the depth dimension explicit in language or actions, perhaps most of all because of its evidence in everyday experience. Probably, the horizontal plane (constituted by the depth dimension and the lateral dimension) is a more significant structure in consciousness and language (cf. also in Hopi; Whorf, 1950).

In Navajo no direct and englobing form or expression seems to exist. Instead, a very general word referring to anything in the position of the horizontal plane, and a term describing the frontal direction (from [ego] out forward) were found.

a) naaniigo, 'crossways, sideways'. The term seems to describe a two-dimensional characteristic, however, with stress on the horizontal, in the sense of lateral extension. In view of the experience of horizon in every direction around a perceiver, eventually to be viewed as a wide circle around the perceiver, the notion of "horizontal plane" acquires significance, while the notion of "depth" or "front/back dimension" becomes secondary. Therefore we will deal with naaniigo in the section on "horizontal."

b) ákónaa, 'across there'; kónaa, 'across here'. This particle expresses a position, extension, or motion from (ego) out, in front of one and stretching out into the direction one is facing, coming up to one from that direction. Obviously, only the frontal part of the so-called depth dimension is made explicit. However, the abstractness of the meaning of this term does make it stand out as a dimensionlike notion. The term can be used in all three spaces (O, S, C).

Examples: ákónaa tó tsé'naa nanínaa, "you walk across the water there"; ákónaa tsé'naa na honít'i', "there is a good crossing right through here forward"; ákónaa na'nízhoozh tsé'naa anínááh, "you walk across (to the opposite side)"; ákónaa shé'étiin, "right through here in front of me is my road."

However, in some cases the postposition is used in slightly different, less unambiguous ways: kónaa adíízoh, "you make a straight line across here" (pointing to all four edges of the square table, one at a time), and díí atsi' ákónaa aháních'iish, "saw the meat right through here" (in the direction of the visual field facing the agent).

Components: depth dimension; front; path; motion or not. See also section on "horizontal."

114. Distant (Numbers 114, 214, and 314 of the UFOR)

This section focuses on more or less metric notions of distance: any number of steps, hours of walking, and so forth along the depth dimension. Several measures can be found, some more conventional than others, some more precise than others. A few of the present expressions in Navajo are, without doubt, of recent date, as is shown, for instance, by their exclusive application to Western distinctive phenomena (mile, yard).

The way distance is conceived of and actually measured is basically the same as the Western pattern: a stick is used several times in a row to measure off a piece of cloth, a man walks a certain number of steps to mark off his land, and so on.

a) nízaad, 'it is far away, at a great distance'. The distance expressed through this verb could be relatively far (a few miles), to extremely far (from coast to coast). Normally, the verb is used to express a distance along the front/back direction; sometimes, however, it can also be used to speak about the considerable depth of something (a canyon, for instance), or its height. However, the ultimately distant points along any dimension cannot be expressed through it (see below). Therefore, the verb is relevant only with respect to O- and S-space, and in fact marks a distinction between these and the C-space.

Examples: tsénikáni Lukachukaidóó doo nízaad da, "Lukachukai and Round Rock are not far apart" (in fact, only fifteen miles); bee'aldíildah sinil hoolyéégóó nízaad, "from here to Albuquerque is far [along the road]"; deigo nízaad, "it is a long way up [I cannot reach the ceiling]"; tséyi' góyaa nízaad, "the canyon is deep down."

Components: distance; path; horizontal or vertical.

b) dooshónízááda, 'very far, farther than you can see'. The imaginary "rod" of this distance is the extension of the visual field: there is said to be an absolute limit to it, and dooshónízááda is a place or extension beyond that limit. The places indicated through the use of this expression are clearly farther away from the referent than those that are simply nízaad. It is used in S- and C-spaces.

Examples: Salt Lake City dooshónízááda, "Salt Lake City is very far away") (from Arizona out); Grand Canyon góyaa dooshónízááda, "the bottom of the Grand Canyon is awfully deep"; jóhonaa'éí dooshónízááda bich'į', "the sun is very far away"; ha'a'aahjigo dooshónízááda, "from here to the East, the place of sunrise is further than you can see."

Components: distant; unit is "range of vision"; path; volumeness/planeness; depth; horizontality/verticality; border (i.e., beyond range of vision).

c) doo deighánída, '(very) far in a straight path from (ego) out'. This expression implies, contrary to any of the former ones, a straight path. It is impossible to decide on any measuring unit that would be understood with reference to it. The expression is used in S- and C-spaces.

Examples: Belgium hoolyéégóó doo deighánída, "it is very far (straight out) toward the place called Belgium"; jóhonaa'éí ha'a'aah doo deighánída, "straight toward the place where the sun sets is far away"; sǫ'tsoh doo deighánída, "straight up toward the Big Star is very far."

Components: distant; path; straight line; volumeness/planeness; any dimension.

d) tsin sitą́, 'one mile, one yard'. Literally, the expression means "the stick is in place," referring to either the measuring stick or the milepost (that designates each mile covered). The expression is, evidently, of recent date, since before these Western conventional measures only arm's width, step, and the span between thumb and middle finger (called after wóóshigíshí, the measuring worm or caterpillar) were used. Since the measuring is not originally Navajo, we shall refrain from any further comments on it.

115. Up/Under; Above/Below (Numbers 115, 215, and 315 of the UFOR)

These distinctive aspects of the vertical dimension are considered to be more directly distinguished, at least in the Western culture, than, for example, the aspect of verticality, of height, and so on. They stand for any distinction of relationship where one object is upon another, above another, sitting on top of it, under another, or having the other object upon itself respectively. We agree that there is a difference between the relations of up, upon, and under on the one hand and those of above and beneath on the other. Still, the same basic directions are apparent (probably best illustrated again with positions vis-à-vis the human body), a situation that strengthens the above presentation.

In order to render the Navajo distinctions in an understandable way, I will subdivide our material according to the differentiations referred to: particular terms have to do with the distinction of above or upward and beneath or downward, while others center on the more properly contiguous relations of upon and under.

The relevance of the distinction between the upward and downward directions, and their distinctive identification, in Navajo thought and culture has already been illustrated: While most events and objects in the Navajo world can be oriented to the system of the four cardinal directions, their location with the phenomena of the lower versus the upper part of the universe (earth versus heaven) is certainly just as significant (cf. chap. I). For several natural phenomena a heavenly and an earthly instance can be pointed out (e.g., są'ah naagháí bik'eh hózhóón as the name of two stars/heavenly principles and as the principles underneath and on top of the surface of the earth, may be very profound examples in the Navajo world view).

Upward and Above Versus Downward and Beneath

a) deigo dóó yaago, 'upward and downward'. Both particles (deigo and yaago) have a general meaning, referring to the respective directions, the mutually opposite positions, and, in combinations like those in the sentence presented above, to the alternating movement between upward and downward directions. In all three spaces, events and phenomena can be characterized through these particles.

Examples: ni'dóó deigo ahool'á, "it extends endlessly from the ground upward"; gah yaago ellwod, "a cottontail ran straight down [into its hole]"; tó yaago nínílį́, "underneath, the water is running"; chidínaat'a'í deigo yit'a', "the airplane flies up in the air"; kóyaa nínína, "you walk downward this way [to ego]".

Components: up/down; movement; volumeness/planeness; direction.

Derivations have similar, though somewhat particular meanings: gódei ('way up there, into the heaven, high upward'), góyaa ('way down, deep down'), biyaa ('underneath it, downward from it'), and so on. Dei and yaa can be used as verbal prefixes as well.

b) ha- 'up and out'. This prefix expresses a direction, an extension from the ground or referent (ego) upward. In contrast to dei, there is a connotation of "out of something (else)" and upward, pointing to a ground or background, from where the direction is visualized. The prefix occurs in several complex verbs, being used in the description of phenomena and events of all three spaces (O, S, C).

Examples: ha'íí'ą́, "the sun [roundish object] comes up" (in the traditional view the sun comes up and out of the space under the earth, cf. chap. I); hooghan bąąh tsin ha'íí'ą́, "alongside the hooghan a pole is sticking up and out"; when presented with a triangular figure, this was described as bílátahjį' háá'á, "sticking out along the points [extremities]"; tó háálį́, "the water is flowing out [up and out], overflowing"; tsé nooltł'iizhgo bąąh ha'íít'ą́, "there is something sticking out from the rock in zigzag form"; nahasdzáán tsin bąąh, "sticks, plants, etc. are sticking up and out of the earth"; dził ha'áz'á, "the mountain is sticking up above" (a second one).

Components: (cf. also section on in/out, number 106) up; in/out; movement; direction; volumeness/planeness (background).

c) náá'á, 'from above going straight down'.[27] This verb is introduced as the opposite of háá'á (going straight up). The prefix means downward in a somewhat different way from yaa: whereas yaa can be used for a downward movement in any degree (from slightly slanting to a straight down direction), náá refers to a movement that goes down, ultimately reaching the ground (at the lowest end). It can be used in all three spaces (O, S, C).

Examples: dził yaa náá'áádi nidáá', "there is a squawdance at the very downward end of the mountain"; níchį́į́h náá'á, "your nose comes down at the end"; hoghandóó haaz'éí náá'á, "a stepladder down from the hooghan."

Components: down; contiguity; volumeness/planeness; movement; direction.

d) hók'ą́ą́', 'up on top (as on a summit of a hill)'. This expression bridges both directions, describing the direction from down or level with (ego) to above (ego). It refers primarily to phenomena of S-space (in myths).

Examples: ńléí hók'ą́ą́ jį hasínááh, "you climb up to the top of it over there [above me]"; ńléí hók'ą́ą́'di hooghanléi' yaa'á, "I see a hooghan sticking up on top of that formation over there"; hastiinléi' ńléí hók'ą́ą́ dóó dah sidá ninitéé, "a stranger is sitting away on top of that formation, above me."

Components: up (relative to [ego]); direction; volumeness/planeness; contiguity; separate from (ego).

e) kóshdę́ę́', 'from down there up toward here'. This particle expresses a somewhat similar situation or direction, except that the place finally pointed to or the destination of the movement is the referent (ego). This aspect of the meaning, then, is the opposite of the former one: Now (ego) is standing above the place of origin of the movement. It has relevance for all three spaces (O, S, C).

Examples: kóshdę́ę́' tsé'naa naníná, "cross this way [through the water] up to me"; kóshdę́ę́' dibé aníłkaad, "herd the sheep over here"; kóshdę́ę́' beeldléí'ánílééh, "move the blanket over this way."

Components: upward; direction; movement; volumeness/planeness; near (ego); contiguity or center (is ego).

See also section on near/separate/contiguity (number 102): whóshdę́ę́'.

---

27. The near-homophonic prefix naa (instead of náá' in náá'á) means across, as in tsé'naa. It is not discussed here.

Upon Versus Under

a) yá and ni', 'heaven, earth's surface respectively'. These nouns denote the slightly bent domed shape spreading out above us, and the surface of the earth beneath the human beings (cf. chap. I, although Western-oriented Navajos refuse to acknowledge this traditional view, and speak of heaven and earth as nímasi, round, sphere-shaped structures: HT). Stars are said to be hanging under and from the shell of the heavens, while plants, animals, human beings, and anything valuable to humans are on or just below the surface of the earth. Ni' is also used in expressions to describe the position or movement of phenomena on or under, but mostly attached to the earth's surface. While both nouns refer to C-space, the derivations can be used in C-, S-, and O-spaces.

Examples: nááts'íílid nihidíít'ih, "the rainbow comes down in a streak upon the ground"; ni'góó dah sedá, "I sit on the ground"; tsé ni'góó haal'á, "all kinds of plants are scattered over the earth's surface."

Components (of ya and ni'); up, under respectively; volumeness/planeness; contiguity; surface.

b) álátah, 'top, tip (or on top)'. See section on border (number 104).

c) aghá, 'above others, the uppermost or farthest'. This particle is used in both a literal and a metaphorical sense to point to the top position, the one object on top of or crowning all others. As such, it is used to speak of the top job, the uppermost power, and the like, as well. It is used in O- and S-spaces. We did not come across its use in C-spaces.

Examples: aghá ndláadi, "I sit upstairs"; diyin 'ay'á' át'eii aghá hoo'áadi dah sidá, "God all alone stands above/on top of everything else"; President Carter t'óó hodíina'go aghá hoo'áadi dah sidá, "President Carter will hold the highest position"; díí tł'óół akǫǫ sinilígíí, háidííyísh aghá ánítneez? "of these ropes lying here, which one is the longest [the top one in length]?"

Components: up; volumeness/planeness; order; contiguity; defines spatial unit (top one).

d) dah, 'up'. This particle and its numerous derivations all have to do with a general way of being "upon something":[28] the direction with reference to (ego) does not matter primarily, that is, sitting on top of, or leaning against, or sitting on a slope of something, all illustrate the same "on top of, upon" notion, although the reference directions may vary from horizontal to oblique to vertical. It is in this general sense of "upon" that dah is used.

The particle and its derivations apply in all three spaces (O, S, C).

Examples: dah alzhin, "a black speck, a dot" ('on top, black'); da' nítts'ą́ąyi t'óó'adahyói níttsą́, "it rained a lot all over the place" (on different places); sitsék'eegi dah ńdaah, "you sit on my lap"; tsé bik'idah si'á, "the rock is lying on top of the other one"; díí ashkii'adah tó yiih yiyí, "this boy fell from above down into the water" ('adah, 'from on top of something downward');

---

28. It should be mentioned that dah is sometimes used as "away from upon" or "upward": for examples tsásk'eh dah diil'ááł, "lift the bed up(ward)"; diné dah sitį, "the man is on the run."

tsídii hódah sidá, "the bird sits up there" (on a tree; hódah, 'up in the air, high up'); díí kin dah 'azká nahalin, "that house looks like a mesa" (dah'azká, 'flat on top, mesa').

Components: up; volumeness/planeness; overlapping; contiguity; direction; motion or not.

e) k'i', 'up on top of something'. The meaning of this postposition varies from spatially "on top of something" to "away from, off." Metaphorically, the form can be used to express someone's accusation (on top of X). Its meaning is similar to that of dah with the restriction that k'i' always stresses the overlapping of something else, and seems to be used primarily in instances where movement is not implied. Sometimes, the combination of both, for example, bik'idah, is used (see above). It can be used in all three spaces (O, S, C).

Examples: shich'ah shik'i dah si'á, "my hat is sitting on top of me" (I have my hat on); beeldléí shik'i sikaad, "the comforter is spread out over me"; béésh bik'i sitá: "a pipe lies on top of it"; tsák'eh bik'idah sidá, "he sits on top of the bed"; hastiin léi' bik'i dah sézí, "I am standing on top of a stranger" (to reach for something).

Components: up; volumeness/planeness; overlapping; contiguity; border.

f) biyaa and bitl'ááh: Together, these terms could stand as the combined opposite meaning of 'bikáá'. The postposition biyaa means 'under it, below it', implying that it is not necessarily touching the referent object under which it is (cf. above deigo dóó yaago), while the postposition bitl'ááh refers exclusively, as far as we could elicit, to the situation of something under and stuck halfway into or hidden by something else.[29] The connotation that was stressed in the use of the latter term was that of "it is under something of considerable weight, so you cannot see it, it is completely covered by the heavy thing on top." Eventually both terms can be used in all three spaces, although use in O- and S-spaces is by far the most relevant.

Examples: nahasdzáán shimá biyaago yádilhil shitaa', "Mother Earth lies beneath/under Father Sky"; chidí bitl'áahdi sinil, "the tires are under the car, on its bottom"; k'os biyaadéé' nikihoníltá, "it rains from under the cloud"; tsásk'eh bitl'áahdi béésh sitá, "there is a rifle attached to the underside of the bed."

Components biyaa: under; separate; volumeness/planeness; overlapping (partial or total overlapping by object on top); two- or three-dimensional extension.

Components bitl'ááh: under; contiguous; volume/planeness; overlapping; order of two- or three-dimensional extension (big, voluminous reference object and small object being covered).

---

29. This finding is at variance with Minnick (1975, p. 60 and ff.), who doubts whether there is an implication of hiddenness, or coveredness. A difference in use with reference to distant locations might be a possible explanation here.

116. Vertical, Upright (Dimension) (Numbers 116, 216, and 316 of the UFOR)

The problem discussed under "depth dimension" arises: it is very difficult to point to any specific term or notion that would grasp the synthetic concept of "verticality."

117. High/Deep (Metric) (Numbers 117, 217, and 317 of the UFOR)

Some of the metric concepts in Navajo have specific reference to height
or depth, while most of them describe two and three dimensional extensions. In
the latter group, however, some do show a dominance of the vertical aspect
(e.g., big in volume, mostly in height; small, mostly short). All these cases will
be treated here.

a) neez, 'tall, long, high'. This verb stresses considerable extension in
height. It is used most of all with persons, or with sticklike objects.

Examples: hastiin nineez, "he is a tall man"; tł'óół nineez, "a long
rope"; asdzáán nineez, "the woman is tall."

Components: height; volumeness/planeness; dominance of vertical dimension; order; upward extension.

b) yázhí and ashéíí, 'small, short'. Both verbs are not primarily concerned with height, but have a dominant meaning of short, not tall. The first one
is used most of all with children or small people, expressing their being rather
short, not full grown. The second one is used exclusively and describes an
abnormally short person, a midget, somebody who grew less than average.

Examples: shiłį́į́' yázhí, "my little pony"; ashkii yázhí: "a small, young
boy"; ayáázh ayóíłikan, "young/small people are very sweet"; Ashéíí, Shorty
(name of a local woman); kónéshéíí át'é, "a short piece is left."

Components: opposite of neez: neez > yázhí +shéíí.

c) ditą́, 'deep, thick'. This verb expresses a measure vertically, from
the ground downward into the earth, or from a level surface downward. The
general direction of measurement is from a surface on which the referent is
positioned downward.

Examples: shé'éé' ditą́, "I have a heavy, thick coat"; éí tooh t'óó ayói
ditą́, "that water [lake] is very deep"; hashtł'ish t'óó ayói ditą́, "the mud is
pretty thick"; another form is íídéetą́ą́', 'thick, deep', as in k'os íídéetą́ą́', "the
clouds are very thick"; sitsį' ayói íídéetą́ą́', "my flesh is very thick."

Components: depth; volumeness/planeness; dominance of vertical dimension; order; extension, along the horizontal plane.

d) ałt'ą́'í, 'thin'. This expression is used for any meaning covered by
thin (thin man, thin layer), thus applying along any dimension. It can be used as
much to denote thinness on the vertical dimension, as to express the thinness/
thickness of paper lying flat, of water in a lake, and the like. It then tends to
be the opposite in measure of ditą́: one consultant, stated ałt'ą́'í could be used to

speak of the thickness or depth of anything up to about an inch; more than that ditą́ should be used.

Examples: díí naaltsoos ałt'ą́'í, "this book is thin"; díí tooh ałt'ą́'í, "this lake is shallow"; beeldléí t'óó ayói ałt'ą́'í, "the cloth is very thin." Components: see ditą́, but thinner than ditą́ > ałt'ą́'í.

118. Lateral, Next to (Numbers 118, 218, and 318 of the UFOR)

a) bąąh, 'beside it, alongside it'. This postposition has a rather specific spatial meaning, combining nearness with being next. It seems to be used primarily to describe the position or movement of something along the horizontal extension of something else: along the side of a river, next to a tree, and so on. It can be used in all three spaces (O, S, C).

Examples: tónteel nahasdzáán bąąh siyį́, "the ocean stretches out alongside the earth" (in traditional belief); dziłbąąh lók'aach'égai sikaad, "the big reed spreads out alongside the mountain"; tabąąhgi tabąąhstíín léi' sitį́, "right at the edge of the water some sea lion is lying"; hooghan bąąh gódi atiin, "there is a road passing next to the hooghan."

Components: next to; volumeness/planeness; near; horizontal, eventually deep or vertical; motion or not.

b) bitah/bita', 'between'. The prefix was already introduced in the section on Near/Separate/Contiguous (number 102). It has relevance here, insofar as it is used with exclusive spatial meaning. Some examples may suffice.

Examples: chézhin dah yisk'id bita' deez'á, "the volcanic rock points forward between two hills"; bits'áál bita' deez'á, "something is pointing outward between the boards [two] of the cradleboard"; ashkíí tsé bitahgi sidá, "the boy is sitting between the rocks"; diné t'óó ayói ahííkaadgo bitah naashá, "I walk among a mass of people on an overpass."

Components: See section on Near, number 102. Also: next to, contiguity; volumeness/planeness.

c) ooshk'iizh, 'on the side, along the side, side by side with'. This postposition is used to describe the position of an item along the side and covering the side of a person, animal, and so forth. It is used primarily to point to the position of bridles, belts on one side of the person, and similar objects, describing the situation on one side only, or the side of a body itself. Its use is restricted to O- and S-spaces.

Examples: łį́į' booshk'iizh sínítíígo nilį́į'doolyeed, "lift yourself over on the side of a horse and have a good ride"; díí ashkii yázhí ákǫ́ǫ́ oozhk'iish yibał, "this young boy always grabs [his mother] on the side when swinging"; ooshk'iizh nít'i' ígíłła' sits'ą́ą' k'inídláád, "one of the sidestrips broke away." Components: lateral; horizontal; contiguous; overlapping; motion or not; volumeness/planeness.

d) báałk'iisjí, 'beside it, close to it'. See section on Nearness/Separateness/Contiguity, number 102.

e) ałts'ą́ą́hjí and ałch'ishjí, 'on both sides, on each side'. These postpositions express a mutual relation: The first one is a special form of the stem encountered with bą́ąh ('passing by': see section on Up/Under, number 115); the second one is related to several forms encountered with Convergence/Divergence (section 108).

Both have the same meaning, we conjecture, though the former is used rather in a sense of parallelism, that is with items stretching out over a certain length, while the latter merely points to positions on both sides of an object or a place.

Examples: of two rails of a railway it is said that they are ałts'ą́ą́hjí doo ninít'i'í íít'í, "they stretch out endlessly on both sides"; shighandóó atiin ałch'ishjí, "where I live a road passes on both sides"; atsį' yá'át'ééhgii naalyéhé bhaooghandi ałch'ishjí, "they have good meat in both stores, on both sides of the village."

Components: lateral; separate; opposition; volumeness/planeness; eventually divergence (Cf. also near/separate, section 102, and the section on convergence/divergence, number 108).

f) ałnaashii, 'alternate, side by side, opposite each other'. This particular form of ałnaa ('cross'; cf. section on overlapping, number 105) is sometimes used to describe the spatial relationship of being side by side, with some space between each item. It is used in all three spaces (O, S, C).

Examples: ałnaashii naalyéhé bádahooghan, "[in town] there are stores on both sides of the street"; ałk'idą́ą́' ałnaashii jideezhdéél jiní, "years ago, they say, they were laid side by side [i.e. the sexes separated]"; tó ałnaashii ninílį́, "the rivers end side by side" (like the San Juan and Rio Grande at some point); sǫ ałnaashii, "stars are side by side, opposite each other."

Components: lateral; volumeness/planeness; two (or more) items; separateness.

119. Left/Right (Numbers 119, 219, and 319 of the UFOR)

These spatial characteristics are, of course, much the same as the former ones, only somewhat more defined. The determination of left and right seems to be most of the time, if not always, by means of reference to the human body (cf. Needham, 1974). In Navajo, at least in the terminology used here, there is no way of confirming this observation.

a) nish'náájí, 'on the right side'. This expression points out the right side of the body. A direction is specified rather than a definite place, which again confirms the basic dynamic interpretation of the word as expressed in Navajo language (jí: enclitic stressing a direction).

Examples: shighosh nish'náájí honeezgai, "my right shoulder hurts"; łį́į́' nish'náájígo ooshk'iizh dah sidá, "I sit on the right side of the horse"; díí ashkii nish'náájí sizį́, "this boy stands on the right side."

Components: right; lateral; volumeness/planeness; direction; motion or not.

b) nishtł'ají, 'on the left side'. nishtł'a, 'being left, lefthanded'.

The above expressions are, of course, the counterpart of nish'náájí. The verb, to be lefthanded, expresses of course the exception among Navajos, as elsewhere. I did not find any specific connotations with this peculiarity, except that the shaking of hands is carried out somewhat differently: while shaking hands with your left hand is considered a sign of inimical feelings in normal conduct, the lefthanded person can do it in the proper way while extending his left hand to a person and turning it over 180 degrees. I never witnessed this kind of event.

120. Horizontal (Dimension) (Numbers 120, 220, and 320 of the UFOR)

Again, it can be questioned if a proper term for "horizontal dimension" or 'horizontality' can be found in Navajo. I did not find a specific term, but was able to investigate two terms that seem to deal with horizontality in a somewhat exclusive way.

a) naaniigo, 'crossways, flat, (horizontal)'. This particle is, as stated above (cf. section on depth dimension, number 113), rather unspecific. That is, it cannot be said to be restricted to the horizontal dimension as understood here (laterality), but deals with any angle of direction, any plane or linear (and probably even voluminous) extension within a horizontal field, or a slice that extends dominantly along the ground, along a broad, flat surface. The particle can be used in all three spaces (O, S, C).

Examples: tsin t'óó ahayói naaniigo shizhoozh, "there are many logs lying sideways/flat one next to the other"; tsin naaniigo sitą́, "the pole lies flat, straight across."

Components: horizontal; volumeness/planeness; straight (linelike); extension.

b) dení'á, 'lying flat in line, extending flat, sleeping'. This verb, composed out of the prefix dei- ('upward') and the verb ní'á ('extend horizontally'), can only be understood by transcending both components' meanings, I conjecture. It is an expression used typically to speak about the sleeping position of a person, but it could also be used to refer to the completely flat stretching out of, for example, the earth. The use of dei in the latter case is consistent with similar information on the "way of lying" of the earth: It is said that deigo, 'upward', can be used to speak about the East, while yaago, 'downward', can be used to refer to the West on earth. Similarly, dení'á is 'lying to the East', while yaaní'á means 'lying, extending down to the West'. Apart from this meaning, the verb can be used in several cases to denote something that lies flat, completely stretched out: łį́į' t'áá dení'á, "the horse is lying dead" (just lying); chidítsoh dení'á, "the truck [fell over and] lies there."

Components: horizontal; extension; planeness; no verticality.

121. Wide; Broad (Metric) (Numbers 121, 221, and 321 of the UFOR)

A few terms and expressions describe primarily metric extension along the horizontal dimension. They are the counterparts of Western broad, narrow, wide, and the like.

a) hóteel, 'wide'.[30] This verb ('there is a wide, flat, broad extension') gives a rather imprecise characterization of measure: It can be used to describe wide open spaces, valleys, and the like. In nominal forms (e.g., tónteel, 'the ocean') the same meaning of horizontal extension, as a flat surface rather than a line (laterality) is apparent.

Examples: díí hastiin bikéyah hóteel, "this man has a wide ranch, farm"; díí hastiin t'óó niteel, "this man is wide, broad" (has broad shoulders); tónteel e'e'aahjí, "there is an ocean toward the West"; tsé nteel dah sikaad, "the flagstone is lying flat."

Components: wide; horizontal; planeness; measure without unit.

b) ts'óózí (or ts'ósí), 'long and slender, slim'. This verb stresses measures on two dimensions (vertical and horizontal), or rather the disproportion or striking difference between values on two dimensions; it is said of people and objects that display considerable length and at the same time a lack of thickness or broadness. It is relevant to O- and S-spaces.

Examples: Hashk'ąą Ts'óózí, Skinny Yucca Fruit (the name of a man near Rock Point; in view of the late introduction of bananas on the reservation, the same word is used for banana, entailing the translation "Skinny Banana" as equivalent); béésh ts'óózí, "the thin wire, the wire is thin"; tó ts'óózí, "the small water" (seepage).

Components: slender; horizontal and vertical; order; major vertical and minor horizontal extension; volumeness/planeness; measure unit; difference between vertical and horizontal extension.

c) tsaa, tsááz, and tsoh: All three have to do with broadness, thickness, horizontal extension. However, they are all applicable only to volumes, bodies, and the like, and cannot be understood without this three dimensional context. Therefore they will be dealt with in a subsequent section (pluridimensional extension: number 124).

122. Cardinal Points, Cardinal Directions (Numbers 122, 222, 322 of the UFOR)

Consistent with the explanation on the horizontal field, it must be stated that the main cardinal directions in the Navajo world are oriented inside the horizontal field constituted by the relatively flat surface of the earth. The basic significance for the orientation, the existential, and the social reference

---

30. Hoijer (1974) lists two forms, one with high and the other with low tone in the second part. I systematically came across the low-toned form, and decided to leave the other one out.

of these directions cannot be underestimated, as is illustrated through the systematic and abundant use in Navajo daily life and ceremonial practices alike: the hooghan's only doorway is oriented towards the East. All water is said to flow to the West (at least in the Arizona part of the reservation), all prayers are directed to all four directions (starting with the East and going around clockwise), the Sandpaintings are invariably directed toward the East (that is, have their single opening toward the directions the Holy Ones will come from, the East), in each direction a Sacred Mountain is situated within which a specific couple of Holy People are housed, and so on.

The four main directions illuminate the course of natural phenomena: the diurnal course of the sun is found explicitly in the names of East, South, West, while the North points to the movement of a mythologically important pair of constellations of stars. Finally, the vertical directions are clearly defined upon the horizontal constellation. Two centers are pointed out (like the nadir and the zenith in our knowledge system) as the two farthest places, up and down, in the universe, both visualized as holes in the sky- and earthshells: their character of "center" begs the question "center of what?" The answer is that the centers of the two shells align themselves in the horizontal world, oriented along the four cardinal directions. This can also be explained the other way around.

a) Examples and explanations: ha'a'aahdéé' háá'at ááh dóó ha'a' aahdéé' hanéílkááh, "from the East the sun rises and from the East the daylight [dawn] comes up." Clearly, the very name of "East" (ha'a'aah) signifies the 'coming up and out of the sun'.

b) shádi'ááhjí ayóígo deesdoi, "in the South it is very hot"; haigo shádi'ááhjí ní' dít'ááh, "during the winter time the sun goes on the South side [of the earth]." Again, the very name of "South" (shádi'ááh) means 'the place where the sun starts', referring explicitly to the course of the sun at its zenith.

c) e'e'aahjígo jóhonaa'éí aná'át'ááh, "the sun sets westward"; e'e'aahjí nihimá asdzáán ná'ádléhé sidá, "our mother, Changing Woman, lives in the West." Again, the very name of "West" (e'e'aah) means 'it [the sun] is going down'.

d) náhookǫsjí' ayóígo deesk'aaz, "it is very cold on the North side"; náhookǫsdéé' nihaa'nát'nih, "the sickness always come from the North side"; chíshch'íjdi náhookǫsdi kéédahat'í t'áá'éí' hak'az diné'é, "the people who live on the North (pole) are the Shortnosed and the People that Never Freeze (cold people)."

Náhookǫs, constructed with the verb stem -kǫs ('to turn over, turn around in a horizontal plane') and the prefix náhí- ('over, around'), expresses the rotation or revolution of a stiff, slender object. The object in question can only be the constellation of the Big Dipper (náhookǫs biká'í, 'the above/upper rotating one'; cf. also Young and Morgan, 1942, p. 122; Haile, 1947, p. 2). As such the expression 'náhookǫs' refers to the physical process of the physical object that characterizes the ultimate Northern part of the Navajo world.

e) It is clear from the literal and etymological meaning of the four terms, as well as from their use in the orientation of all things and forces in the present world of the Navajos (cf. again chap. I), that all four directions constitute one cycle, one structural and functional unit. However, other combinations of members of this set of four directions are presented as well: 1) All four can be considered separately (cf. examples above). 2) Two pairs are selected out, each pair constituting an ordered set: ha'a' aahdóó e'e' aahjígo can be considered as one basic direction to be translated as 'from East to West'. The East should be mentioned initially (order). Sometimes, the expression deigo dóó yaago ('upward and downward') is used synonymously, since East has a connotation of "deigo," while West has the connotation of "yaago." Shádi'ááhdóó náhookǫsjígo constitute the second basic direction (from South to North, in that specific order). 3) Recently, other combinations, refinements in orientation were introduced, following the Western specifications: for example, the direction "southwest" can be rendered in Navajo as shádi'ááh dóó e'a'aah bita' hóló ('[it] exists between South and West'), and so on.

f) Complementary to these directions and orthogonal to them are the zenith and nadir:[31] yá'ałníídę́ę́' nááts'íílid, "the rainbow stands from the center of heaven"; yá'ałníídę́ę́' adínídíín, "a light comes down from the center of heaven"; dinétahdi ni'ałníí át'é, "the center of the earth is Dinétah [region near Gobernador Knob]"; ni'ałníídę́ę́ hajíínáí, "from the center of the earth [everything] emerged, came into existence."

Both terms are derived as centers of sky and earth respectively. The two are never combined to form one direction, as far as I could discover. This fact is consistent with the lack of, or the refusal to consider an englobing notion for earth and heaven/sky, corresponding to the Western notions of universe or world. The combination cannot be made validly, according to several informants (FH, BW, TB), because it would imply the contact between, more particularly the mating, of Mother Earth and Father Sky, an event which would necessitate the elimination of the distance (the separating space between both) and entail the end of the present world (cf. chap. I).

Each of the directions has, according to my data, similar components. Therefore, a general characterization of components is presented, applying to all six distinct directions. The combinations will be dealt with in the following section (coordinate systems).

Components: cardinal directions; directions; center; path; motion.

123. Coordinate Systems (Numbers 123, 223, and 323 of the UFOR)

The only explicit coordinate system we could detect in the Navajo language is the one formed by the combinations of cardinal directions. No other words for abstractions such as dimension or set of dimensions (like the Carte-

---

31. Both terms are used primarily, if not exclusively, in a mythological context. All consultants except one (HT), however, were found to point to precise physical referents for both

sian system) were found, although the concepts and the awareness of the experiential usefulness of similar abstractions were clearly there (in body language, body positions, etc., cf. section 111 above).

The combinations of cardinal directions were already dealt with and exemplified in a previous section (number 109). I will restrict myself to drawing the following conclusions:

a) Pairs of directions are distinguished: East–West (ha'a'aah dóó e'e'aah) and South–North (shádi'ááh dóó náhookǫs), each combining two extremes of directions evolving away from each other (with a prayer, the person saying the prayer is the center).

b) The set of all four forms is a revolving disc, a horizontal plane with a clockwise rotational movement (BW).

c) The orthogonal introduction of zenith and center on this horizontal structure introduces the third dimension, however, again built out of two opposite directions rather than one dimension (e.g., illustrated by the fact that there is no word, and no theoretical notion to consider the whole universe, but that the upper sphere of heaven and the lower sphere of earth remain substantively separated).

Components: coordinate system; volumeness/planeness; two units; cardinal directions; up/down; horizontal/vertical; part/whole.

124. Multidimensionally Extended (Metric) (Numbers 124, 224, and 324 of the UFOR)

Only a few standardized measures of surface or volume are used in Navajo. The most traditional ones were imprecise: a hooghan should be built with six, eight, or twelve sides, and not more than twelve logs high (one on top of the other); a rug is measured by the span of a woman's hand (the distance between thumb and middle finger) put in a row eight times, and the like. These are seldom used now, and are thus deleted.

a) ná hásdzo hayázhí, 'an acre (of land)'. The expression deals with a bounded space (náhásdzoh, 'surrounded by a line'), that is small (ha, 'there is space', yázhí, 'small, little'). It is the Navajo name for the American acre of land. The metric aspect is clear: the unit is defined pragmatically (fenced land), while the elementary measure (yázhí versus niteel, for example) is specified as an element of order.

Components: multidimensional extension; planeness; measure through order.

b) tsoh, 'big, fat, large'. The adjectival enclitic is a measure for volumes, objects with a certain extension in all three dimensions or rather in every possible direction. It can be used for all objects with a certain solidity,

---

terms. Ni'ałníí is recognized to be Dinétah in New Mexico (FH, TB) or a place in San Juan Mountains in southern Colorado (others), while yá'ałníí was identified by all (including HT) as being behind the constellation of dilyéhé (Pleiades).

like rocks, bags (a pack full of something), persons, and the like with a slight dominance in width.

Examples: tótsoh, Big Water (wash in Lukachukai that has a big volume of water; deep, big amounts); hastiintsoh, "big man," or "big belly"; bee'eldǫǫhtsoh, "cannon, big gun."

Components: multidimensional extension; order (big); volumeness; slight dominance.

c) hótsaa, nitsaaz, 'anything round, ball-like, or big and choppy'. This particle expresses an equal extension in all dimensions and in all directions. Moreover, the extension is considerable (big, not small). Humans and animals would be wide (nitsaaz).

Examples: asdáán nitsaaz, "big, choppy woman"; łį́į́' nitsaaz silį́į́, "the horse grew big"; tsé nitsaa deez'áhí, Rock Point, Arizona (the big round rock pointing out).

d) ts'óózi, ałts'óózi, 'narrow'. Cf. section on width (number 121).

e) áníłdííl, 'high and broad' (corpulent in a comparative sense). The term denotes squarish forms, both extended in height and width. It differs from tsoh in that the latter is extended in all directions.

Examples: łį́į́' ayói áníłdííl, "a big, broad horse" (Belgian horse); hastiin ayói áníłdííl, "a big, round man."

Components: multidimensional extension; planeness; vertical/horizontal; measure.

125. Geometric Point (Numbers 125, 225, and 325 of the UFOR)

a) dah alzhin, 'dot, speck, point'. The expression ('upon, black') has only recently come into use for the Western notion of dot or point. Originally it was used to denote a relatively small, dark spot in the distance (BB); e.g., a dark spot on a mountain or on a wall. The meaning was then, of course, imprecise, approximating a strictly geometric notion of point (space without extension).

Examples: a'áán góne' dah alzhin, "a tiny black hole in the ground"; kin bii' dah alzhin, "inside the house there is a black spot"; nizéé'dah alzhin, "shut up/your mouth is open like a black spot."

Components: point; multidimensional extension; order (smallest).

126. Geometrically Linear, Straight (Numbers 126, 226, and 325 of the UFOR)

a) t'áá ní'áagi, 'continuously in a line formation'. See section on continuity (number 144).

b) ídzo, 'line, straight line'. The verb denotes any line; if made by man, it is any 'straight line drawn without a ruler, no matter how crooked it looks'. It is relevant in O- and S-spaces.

Examples: bik'ehgo ídzo, "to draw a line with a ruler" (along with it);

atiin ídzo, "the marking of the road" (roadlines); in the topological test, any lines presented separately are called ídzo.

Components: line; extension along one dimension; approximately metric.

c) k'ézdon, k'éhézdon, 'straight, straight line'. Both terms express the straightness, the condition of being a straight formation or line. There is a slight line in front of (ego), while the latter is unimportant with respect to direction. Used in O- and S-spaces.

Examples: in the topological test the words were used to denote straight lines at the bottom of figures most of the time; tsin k'éhézdon dóó názhah, "a tree is straight and then somewhat curved"; tsé k'éhézdon haa'á, "the rock is standing erect"; k'ézdongo anít'i', "the fence extends straight out in front of (ego)."

Components: straight; planeness; direction; front/back or all directions; approximately metric.

d) názha, 'bent, curved (line)'. This verb proved to have a very general meaning, that is accounting for any type of curvedness of lines from nearly flat or straight lines to nearly closed curves (three-quarter circle or more). Through the topological test a systematic variation of curvedness in a set of lines (without sharp angles) all yielded the same answer: názha. The word is used most of all in O- and S-spaces.

Examples: názhago dah sínída: "go and sit in a curved form (with knees up)"; dii béésh názbạsgo názha, "this wire is bent like a circle" (almost a circle, but only three-quarters); tł'iish nahalin názhago sikạ́, "lying like a snake curled up"; názhahí, "squashblossom"; ałch'i' názhahí, "bent toward each other" (cf. Lukachukai Mountain and Black Mountain).

Components: line; curved; open; any direction; approximately metric.

127. Geometrically Pointing, Parallel, Being an Angle (Number 127, 227, and 325 of the UFOR)

Angles, corners, and the like are predominantly volumes and surfaces in Navajo (rather than lines as in the Western system).

Parallel
a) báálk'iisjí, 'on the side, parallel'. This particle was dealt with under "lateral" (section 118). It can be used to denote parallelism as well.

b) ahạạh, 'together, in parallel'. This postposition is used, first, to describe a situation of two objects next to each other, an object facing a person, two things sitting together, and so forth. It is also used to denote parallelism. Both meanings were elicited in the topological test, as well as in sentences. It is primarily used in O- and S-spaces.

Examples: ahạạh ídzo, "two lines running parallel to one another"; dził t'óó ahạạh sinil, "the mountains are lying parallel to each other"; ahạạh atiin, "two parallel roads"; ahạạh shitééžh, "two human beings lying parallel to each other."

Components: parallel; plural objects; dominance in one dimension; planeness/volumeness.

Points; Pointedness

a) deez'á, '(a volume) lying flat and pointing, peninsula'. The verb is used to denote rock formations, big volumes lying on the surface of bigger ones (or the earth), and pointing in a specific direction. It is used in O- and S-spaces.

Examples: tsé deez'áhí, Rock Point (a rock formation with longitudinal extension pointing to the East); t'áá díí'góó adeez'á, Four Corners ('just, from four ways, pointing out', so that the points meet each other, not the other way around); tsah deez'á, "a needle pointing out"; kéyah tsé bita' deez'á, "the farmland points out between two rock formations"; ałch'į 'deez'á góne, "the [outer] corner [of a house]."

Components: pointing; volumeness; border; out; direction.

b) deení: 'sharp; edge or point of something'. This verb denotes the sharpness of the point or line, where two or more surfaces come together to form a sharp, piercing structure (like the blade of an ax, the point of a needle, etc.). It can be used in S-space, but most often in O-space.

Examples: tsah deení, "the point of a needle"; shichíįh deení, "the tip of my nose is sharp"; k'aabéésh ayóígo deení, "the arrowhead is very sharp, piercingly sharp."

Components: pointing; volumeness; border; up/down (tip of something). N.B.: háhaashchii' refers to sharpness in a very similar sense. Here, the sharpness of a linelike form is described, rather than that of a point. The form is attributed to long blades like razor blades, the blade of a spade, a knife, and the like.

c) dah ats'os, 'in conical shape'. This expression[32] describes an upward-pointing conical shape, a volume with this form sitting on top of a solid surface or other volume. The direction of the point should be upward; if it points downward, as in some ceremonial designs (forming a V-shape), the verb deez'á is used, while any sideways extension will be rendered through heets'óóz. In the topological test the triangle sitting up on one side was characterized by this expression.

The top part should not be sharply pointed; it can be smoothly rounded (like a hill) or even flat (like a butte). The expression is relevant in O- and S-spaces.

Examples: tepee wolyéego níbaal dah ats'os, "what is called a 'tepee' is a conically shaped tent"; díí k'id dah ats'os, "that hill is tapered, like a cone"; dah ats'osgo dah azká, "the mesa (butte) is in a conical shape"; dah ats'os nineezí, 'the big coneshape' (place name near Wheatfield, Arizona).

Components: point; volumeness; border; up/down; curved surface; vertically dominant.

---

32. The verb stem ts'os ('taper, be conical, come to a point') is the basic element here.

d) heets'óóz, 'long and tapered form'. This verb was most often used to describe a form like an anthill, with a rather broad base and pointing up in a relatively small and sharp tip. However, conical shapes in other directions (pointing horizontally) can be rendered through this verb as well. Used in O- and S-spaces.

Examples: wóláchíí' baghan heets'óóz, "the anthill has a tapered form"; díí táchééh heets'óóz, "this sweathouse has a tapered form"; the triangles with broad bases in the topological test were mentioned in this respect.

Components: point; volumeness; border; up/down; curved or sharp; horizontality dominant.

Angles, Corners

With the topological test it became clear that very broad angles, when presented in any form of straight or crooked line formation (more than 120 degrees), were not considered angles any more, but were referred to either as lines or as curves (that is, názha). When a geometric figure or any closed design was presented, the corner notion was expanded to include any inner angle.

Systematically, inside corners (in figures and in line formations) are rendered with the stem tł'ah, while outside corners were described through deez'á, stressing the fact that a volume was considered to be lying horizontally in a specific direction (cf. section on deez'á). When presenting lines constituting an angle, the acute "inner" angle was named (through tł'ah), while the outer angle (considering a total rotation of 360 degrees) was inconceivable, even in terms of deez'á.

-tł'ah: 'forming an angle, an inner corner'. This verb and its many derivations are used practically exclusively with reference to corners inside a house, as well as angles when confronted with geometric figures. Corners are volumes rather than lines.

Examples: hooghan bii' báhástł'ahdi dah sídá, "inside the hooghan you sit in the [round] corner"; náhookǫsji' bee nástł'ah, "to the North there is a rounded corner [inside the house]"; k'aabéésh táá'go yistł'ah, "the arrowhead has three [inner] corners"; díí'go yistł'ah, "the four-cornered, four angles, zigzag formation" (lightning, ceremonial design); naanáz'á, "outside corner"; naaná'ázt'i', "outside corner of a fence."

Components: angle/corner; volumeness; in; any direction; border.

128. Geometrically Being a Volume, a Surface (Numbers 128 and 228 of the UFOR)[33]

This section deals with any metric notions of surface or volume, as distinct from the general, topological notions of "volumeness" and "plane-

---

33. The cosmological surfaces and volumes are left out; they comprise all celestial bodies, a study of which is beyond the present scope.

ness" considered previously (see section 109). The metric element is sometimes hard to find, but should still be clearly discernible.

a) -bąs, 'ringlike, round, circular'. The verb stem points to a formation of things or a line forming a complete ring or circle in a plane (horizontal or vertical). When it is said of objects that are in this position (forming a circle), the extension on the third dimension seems irrelevant. The verb is used in all three spaces (O, S, C).

Examples: t'iis názbąs, "the cottonwood is standing around [a hilltop] in a ring" (Teecnospos, Arizona); when presented with an almost closed circular figure in the topological test, the description was názbąsgo názha, "a figure curved like a ring/circle"; jóhonaa'éí' názbąs dóó tł'éhonaa'éí názbąs, "the sun is circular and the moon is circular"; tónteel názbąsgo sinil, "the oceans stretch out in a big circle (around Mother Earth)."

Components: surface; round; horizontal.

b) -mąz, 'round volume, ball-like'. This verb expresses a similar form, but clearly three-dimensional.

Examples: when presented with several drawings in the topological test, most were immediately understood as three-dimensional forms, volumes of some kind; bilagáanaa binahasdzáán nímąz, "the earth of the white people is like a ball"; nímasi nímąz: a potato is round.

Components: volume; round.

c) yilk'ooł, 'wave'. The progression in a regular, wavy motion is expressed through yilk'ooł. Its use is restricted to water, land, not hair or other rather metaphorically "wavy" phenomena. The form of the volume is indicated.

d) náhineests'ee, 'it (goes) winding around, it is coiled'. This verb expresses the formation of a cylinder or barrellike form. It can be used to describe the specific act of a snake, of a certain handling of the rope, sometimes of rain, and so on.

129. Geometric Figures (Number 129 of the UFOR)

No overall uniformity was found between bilingual and monolingual consultants on this topic. The bilingual tends to take into account all or some genuine Western geometric characteristics in his Navajo "translations" of regular geometric figures, while the monolingual expresses the features of the figure in much more general (presumably topological) terms; sharp edge pointing out (angle), two straight lines lengthwise and two others (four sides of a square), and the like.

Examples (without elaboration): dik'ą́ díí'go aheelt'éego ahída'ídzo, "it is square" ('square, four similar lines, drawn'); beesh'est'ógi nahalingo táá'go ahídah'ídzo, "triangle" ('like an arrowhead, three, lines/marks' [monolingual]); tsi ts'aa' nahalingo si'ą́, "cube, cylinder" ('like a box, it is in place' [both mono- and bilingual]).

No conclusions were drawn, since this topic might require considerable comparative work in different speaker groups (mono- and bilingual) and age groups.

229. Map, Scale

The description of what amounts to a map, in Navajo, again bears resemblance to the part/whole logic, as explained in a previous section (number 103). Instead of offering one word, or pointing to a fixed piece of paper or other substance, a clear guide for practical use is given or indicated: Things that have relevance or importance in transporting a moving object from one place to another. To indicate scale, the same reference to actions is used, typically stressing not the "picturelike" character of the model and the original, but rather the way the model is made after the original.

Map

Examples: bik'ehgo oodáłigíí, "a roadmap" ('that in accordance with which going takes place'); na'asdzohgo bik'ehgo na 'adáhígíí, "a roadmap" or "all the different markings of the places you can go to" ('marks, according to them, you go, in direction of'); sǫ bik 'ehgo na 'adáhígíí, "a star map" ('that with which going takes place according to the stars').

Components: map; movement, volumeness/planeness; near/separate; path.

Scale

Examples: hooghan be'elyaa, "a scale model [or picture] of a hooghan"; eventually you could use hooghan nahalin (similar to a hooghan); nahasdzáán be'elyaa, "a scale model of the earth" (we made one in clay to trigger reactions from consultants).

The verb be'eshłééh means to make a copy, so that the derivations described above to express scale model should clearly have a connotation of action, manufacturing, making something like the original.

Components: scale; movement/action; volumeness/planeness.

130–133. Resting, Moving, Direction of Movement

These entries of the UFOR are not dealt with in this study. They were covered in the fieldwork, but the material we elicited did not prove sufficiently elaborate to allow a meaningful report.

In Navajo "movement" is all pervasive, as was explained in Chapter I. In this sense, most of the knowledge to be had on movement, action, or any kind of dynamic processes of growth, change, expansion, shrinkage, and so on, is amply presented in the foregoing pages. In a sense it can be stated that most of the information presented thus far has to do with these dynamic aspects of space, since the Navajo world (and thus its space) has this essentially dynamic character. Those verbs, however, that have to do exclusively and strictly with "movement through space," covering distances, or (inversely) not moving or resting, as well as the different types of movement and rest had to be handled in the present sections. Their specific semantic characters seemed pretty similar to the information disclosed in previous sections, in fact making use of the same contextual and strictly semantic aspects that are precisely explained in those sections. Therefore, the deletion of the sections on movement proper may not produce as grave a gap as was to be expected: The same topological and other spatial characteristics may be considered to be relevant in Navajo "static" space (location, description of spatial characteristics of objects, etc.) as in Navajo "dynamic space" [34] (movement, types of movement such as spiral, zigzag, etc.). Indeed, it is only the information on types of movement and rest, on specific distinctions between different velocities and motion patterns (go, run, dash, walk, gallop, jump . . .) that will be missing here.

134. Being Spatially Random/Spatially Determinable (Number 134 of the UFOR)

This characteristic is an analog of the strict notions "open and closed set" in topology. As such the elements of this pair point to the possibility or impossibility of specifying a spatial order or relation, however general, qualitative, or even minimal they may be. In previous works the necessity of this criterion stood out, because of the apparent discrimination of so general a criterion in cosmogonies and systems of knowledge all over the world (cf. especially Long, 1969, on the role of the notions of chaos [indeterminability] versus [determinability] in cosmological myths).

It proved impossible to make similar concepts explicit in Navajo, and except for one notion, there is an absence of varying "degrees" of chaos.

a) -haal'á, 'scattered, in an unspecified and unspecifiable formation'. Verb. It can be said of plural items of any sort, of which the order is not perceivable. Consultants even claimed that, when such a set was to be cut in two halves, both subsets would have the characteristic of haal'á still ("then it's haal'á on both sides"). It pertains to items in all three spaces, typically also to the stars (which were not placed in a proper way, according to traditional belief).

Examples: ólta'di 'áłchíní t'óó' ahayóí haal'á, "at school the children are spread all over the world."

Components: spatially random; plural items; volumeness/planeness.

Apart from this verb, others can be mentioned that seem to imply this criterion. However, all of them tend to be rather more specific, pointing to degrees of order and/or disorder (cf. section on succession): nizhónígo ('beau-

---

34. The distinction between "static" and "dynamic" space, for all its relevance in Western objectifying spatial segmentation, seems very odd when dealing with Navajo space. The expressions are given in the Western context, indicated through the use of quotation marks.

tiful, orderly') and doo yá'át'ééhgo or doo baa hózhǫ́ǫ́ da ('ugly, bad, disorderly'). They will be treated in a later section.

231. Being on a Path, Orienting

These notions are considered to be entries of the S-space of the UFOR.

a) atiin, 'road, path, trail'. This verb (or noun), is the most general form expressing a kind of path you can walk, drive, or travel along from one place to another. Any kind of road can be expressed by it, provided different types of prefixes are added to specify form, condition, and so on.

Examples: łį́į́' be'atiin, "a horse trail"; ááni bee'atiin, a footpath; díí'atiin dził báátis, "a pass over the mountain"; díí'kóne'atiin ch'íníłíígóó atiin, "this trail here goes directly to Chinle."

Components: path; planeness; contiguity/separateness; extension on one dimension dominant; movement.

b) k'ézdon, 'straight path from you forward'. See section on line, straight (number 126).

c) Orientation. When asked how people would go about locating and orienting themselves, when there were no road signs or other artificial indicators, most consultants referred to natural and celestial phenomena:

At night the location of some major constellations can help: the two constellations of Náhookǫs in the North (Náhookǫs bika'í and náhookǫs bi'áadii, the male and the female turning figures), the Milky Way (Yikáísdáhí) somewhat East–West, and the constellations in the center of the sky (dilyéhé or Pleiades) most of all (AD, TB, HT).

During the day, one goes from place to place, asking instructions from people one encounters. Major landmarks in giving directions would be the sun, mesas, specific rocks (with particular structure), and hooghans. A major device to determine the cardinal directions (even when foggy or when visibility is very low) is the hooghan: the entrance is, evidently, always to the East (AD, TB, FH, HT, BW). A particularly striking experience was related to us by AD, when explaining the primary importance of the structure of the hooghan in this context. She related that once, in her youth, she climbed a mountain in order to attend a Yei'bicheii dance. On her way she got lost, but finally reached the hooghan where the ceremonial activities took place. By then she was convinced that the Yei'bicheii (dancer) had entered the hooghan from the West, although she knew this was impossible (the East being the only doorway). She told her experience to her companion. She was considered dangerously out of her mind for a short time until she could word her conviction differently that the Yei'bicheii must have entered from the East and that "the hooghan had turned around again." This illustrates the importance of good order, and of orientation in the structure of the hooghan, as well as the social and existential impact of the information imbedded in the hooghan.

Sometimes rivers, mountains, washes, and the like are considered basic prerequisite information in order to locate oneself on the reservation. This was evident from the way several consultants dealt with the major mountains in the Apache County area: Lukachukai Mountain and Black Mountain are considered the center of the reservation, with some places in between these mountains and all others relative to that huge centerpiece: Shiprock to the East, Tuba City and Navajo Mountain to the West, and so on (HT, M-AL, FH, AD).

232. Navigating (Number 232 of the UFOR)

Here, I conjecture, a similar situation occurs as with part/whole: the terminology used to indicate the navigator or navigation as a process, in fact, points to a system of interdependent events and relations.

Examples: tsinaa'eeł ndeił'eełígíí, "the navigators of the boats" ('the boats, who sail them'); yideeyáago hołííshją́ ályaa ('when one is going, to him, make understand, the way one should be taught to go').

Components: navigating; motion; direction; system.

140. Global Spatial Characteristics (Numbers 140, 240, and 340 of the UFOR)

The characteristics under this heading pertain to basic theoretical aspects of space.

The characteristics deemed important in the UFOR are five: continuity/discontinuity, absoluteness/relativity, finiteness/infiniteness, boundedness/unboundedness, homogeneity/heterogeneity. Navajo consultants presented information on the first pair only. All other aspects will be derived from the material analyzed and are discussed in Chapters II and IV.

144. Continuous/Discontinuous (Numbers 144, 244, and 344 of the UFOR)

Several Navajo expressions have relevance in this section. Different words are used for different manifestations of continuity, since a line is continuous in a way different from a plane or a massive substance.

The distinctions between all three spaces become blurred here since, evidently, the very notion of continuity implies the transgression of these distinctions.

a) doo ninít'i'í, 'the endless one, without (visible) end'. The expression is formed with the verb stem -t'i' ('fence, something extending linelike'). It is generally used to speak of a linelike extension that seems to have no beginning or end, that is, you cannot see any beginning or end to it. The line can be straight or bent, horizontal or vertical. Essentially, the distance that may exist between a subject and the beginning or end of the formation cannot be really covered or modified through motion (walking, etc.).

Examples: díí tooh doo ninít'í da, "this river is so long as to be endless, going on continuously"; shi'iiná doo ninít'i'í íít'i, "may I live on to the very point I can go" ('my life, continuously, it goes in a row'); béésh doo ninít'i'dago íít'i, "the wire extends out farther than you can see"; Yikáísdáhí doo ninít'i'da, "the Milky Way goes on continuously."

Components: continuous; line/path; horizontal/vertical; border lacking, extension.

b) t'ááni'áago, 'continuously on, extending in one section'. This expression stresses the holistic character, the "being of one piece" rather than the endless spreading out. Moreover, it is used primarily to indicate a characteristic of an instance of voluminousness, although it can be used to speak of linelike formations as well.

Examples: díí chézhin t'áání áagi íí'ą, "this volcanic rock formation stretches out continuously"; Santa Fe Express t'áá ná' áago íí'a, "the Santa Fe Railroad goes on without interruption"; Lukachukai dził t'áá ní' áago naaná'ą, "Lukachukai Mountain extends out in one continuous volume"; díí'kǫ́ǫ́ dził ní'ahígíí t'áá ní'áago íí'ą, "the mountain that goes through here extends out in one continuous chunk"; díí'áhí t'áá ní'áago íí'ą, "this fog goes on continuously without interruption" (exhaust trail of a plane).

Components: continuous; volumeness; part/whole; horizontal; extension (pluridimensional).

c) aghá deeyá, 'he is going to go ahead (of others)'. This expression emphasizes continuity in a movement, a passing from place to place. It was not used as often as the others.

Examples: díí'hastiin aghá deeyá, "this man is going ahead [of the others]."

Components: continuous; movement; extension.

d) t'áá ałtsogo: 'everywhere, all over'. This expression is clearly different from all previous ones in that a characteristic of homogeneity (of space) is combined and interwoven with the notion of continuity: the air is said to be a continuous, all-pervading unity.

Examples: níłch'i t'áá ałtsogo hólǫ́, "there is air present everywhere" (it is not going anywhere, any specific direction); Diyin t'áá ałtsogo hólǫ́, "God is everywhere, all-pervading"; tó t'áá íílį́, "water keeps flowing on continuously"; t'áá ałtsogo naaghá, "he walks in all directions."

Components: continuous/homogeneous; volumeness; extension; pluridimensional.

e) adeest'į́į́', 'as far as you can see'. The present expression (derived from adees, 'along the length of a path', and atiin, 'path, trail') characterizes the considerable length of a path or its longitudinal extension. The limit or border is the limit of one's eyesight.

Examples: diné bikéyah bikáágóó adeest'į́į́', "the Navajo reservation spreads out in the distance as far as you can see"; deigo adeest'íí, "as far as you can see in the sky" (beyond which you cannot see anything [Milky Way is considered border phenomenon]); yaago adeest'íí', "as far as you can see downward" (in a canyon, in the ocean, in a crater, etc.).

Components: continuous; path; border; all directions; extension (huge phenomena).

IV | Building a Model of Navajo Spatial Knowledge

Based on the material of the previous chapter and on the perspective outlined in Chapter II, I shall now proceed to build a model of the explicit and empirically checked spatial differentiations that have been elicited. I shall not repeat the necessary methodological and epistemological prerequisites for this construction; instead, I refer the reader to the exposition of this subject in Chapter II.

List of Navajo Spatial Notions

In this section I present a full list of the notions sought out in the Navajo cultural knowledge system. To reiterate, I did look carefully in order to find out whether the differentiations made in the UFOR entries were found in the Navajo knowledge system, and if so, how. This was done primarily through their explicit rendering in the set of terms and expressions, of which every notion was isolated, checked and cross-checked by Navajo consultants. Each semantically relevant notion points to a culture-specific differentiation of spatiality in the Navajo cultural knowledge system. The actual content of this relationship of "pointing" is made explicit in my analysis of the particular sets of Const. Hs and Const. Is that characterize the relationship. The total system of interrelations, between all notions involved, is graphically depicted; which offers a second and more synthetic view of the actual "system" of Navajo spatial differentiation. It may be called the "native model (or theory) of space" for the Navajo culture.

102. (Numbers 102, 202, and 302 of the UFOR): Nearness, Separateness, Contiguity

Near
This notion was handled extensively in an earlier section. It is sufficient to present the formulas of semantic relevance for it:
"Near"
Const. H: volumeness/planeness
Const. I: overlapping a and b, convergence/divergence, upon/under

Separate

The Navajo interpretation of this spatial notion emphasizes a relationship where two items (or one item and ego) are not easily accessible to one another. In particular expressions the relationship of nonreachability (or nonaccessibility) can be augmented or reduced, while in others the absolute, or the specific, or the culturally installed or accidentally manifested nonreachability is expressed.

"Separate"

Const. H: volumeness/planeness

Const. I: overlapping a and b, convergence/divergence, upon/under, path

Contiguous

With this notion (and the expressions and terms that render it) the emphasis is on the actual process or action of reaching, touching, being together, and the like in the Navajo context. The particular expressions stress the resulting structure, or the actual event of touching or any other aspect so that, again, only one constituent is constantly recurring in the semantic analysis of all of them:

"Contiguous"

Const. H: volumeness/planeness

Const. I: overlapping a and b, upon/under, path

103. (Numbers 103, 203, and 303 of the UFOR): Part/Whole

In Chapter I it is explained that part/whole distinctions, or at least the epistemic emphasis of segmentability that is typical of Western knowledge (of space, but also of time), are somewhat alien to the Navajo cultural knowledge system. The very dynamic aspect of the universe and everything in it in the Navajo tradition was pointed out as a possible explanation of the absence of the recurrence of objectlike, static, and multifariously segmented parts of space and/or time. In the course of the detailed questioning of bilingual and monolingual consultants on these issues, I came to a somewhat modified, but certainly consistent conclusion: a question about parts was invariably answered with a counterquestion, or with the suggestion that I asked about the way every bit or aspect of a system works together with every other to keep the system going. In general, a profoundly organismic view was implied by the answers, and the consultants often referred to the function of aspects within a broader setting (including at some stage the working or acting of the aspect [part ?] questioned). On the other hand, the system resulting from the cohesion of aspects would approach what would be the correlate of the question of the whole. No words for "part" and "whole" as such were elicited through the procedures. This does not mean, of course, that parts and englobing wholes were not perceptually distinguished or not actually used in manipulation. In my hypothesis, the situation rather reflects a specific cultural emphasis in the Navajo knowledge system: a system of cohesive actions is more to the point, and describes the fact more adequately than distinction of invariants at different levels of segmentation (parts, wholes).[1] In the following characterization, the organismic aspect is rendered in the constituent "function."

"Part/whole"

Const. H: volumeness/planeness, function

Const. I: border (ultimate); center; volumeness/planeness

104. (Numbers 104, 204, and 304 of the UFOR): Bounding, Bordering

I decided to distinguish, both on the basis of action and of linguistic observations, between two subcategories of "boundary" notions: "obstruction borders" and "ultimate borders." In the former case, actions have to be modified slightly since the boundary phenomena can be overcome by human agents. In the latter case, the space in which one is acting may change radically in implications of meaning and action beyond the boundary referred to, such that actions either have to be altered completely or abandoned altogether. Distinct terms and expressions are used to refer to situations of either sort.

Obstruction Boundary a

The space one is talking about or acting in is clearly continuous and its borders are transgressible through a modification of the action described or produced.

"Obstruction boundary"

Const. H: volumeness/planeness; motion; horizontal dimension or in/out

Const. I: inside/outer side; in/out; volumeness/planeness; angle/point [2]

Ultimate Boundary b

The space that is bounded in this sense is understood to be the culturally distinguishable (or explicitly culturally distinguished) action space, that is, a space that is clearly different from any other because of the cultural confinements that go with it. You are to act according to the Navajo tradition within it (since it is in a mythological sense, the Navajo World), and are subject to non-Navajo influences outside of it; within it the supernatural forces are active and influential on your deeds and thoughts, but not on the outside

---

1. Obviously, a car is dismantled and reassembled with the same manipulation of the same parts by the Navajo, but the very notion of part is different and does not have a cultural meaning (and certainly not the same use either) that it has in our tradition. Hence, it is not explicitly represented in the terminology of knowledge.

2. The seemingly "circular" definition that appears here need not bother the reader: a) it appears quite natural in everyday knowledge (as, indeed, it is inevitable in any epistemology), and b) it is "seemingly" circular, since no definition, strictly speaking, is produced.

(in the other space), and so forth. The culturally significant aspects of action are thus fundamentally altered in the transition from one space to the other, if such a transition is conceivable.

Apart from these connotations, the more general case of ultimate border applies as well (and is understood in the same sense); that beyond which there is nothing (which implies indeed a complete alteration of actions), or beyond which another type of action is required (e.g., swimming when you have been walking). In other words, these terms and expressions mark the distinction between two altogether different spaces (or spaces culturally distinguished as such).

"Ultimate boundary"

Const. H: volumeness/planeness; part/whole or plural items; order or specific dimension[3]

Const. I: inside/outside; in/out; volumeness/planeness; angle/point

105. (Numbers 105, 205, and 305 of the UFOR): Overlapping

As is the case with the notions of open and closed, the Navajo terminology on "overlapping" primarily pertains to an action that takes place or an event that continues throughout a certain period. In fact, both meanings are distinguishable in the analysis leading to the separate treatment (with separate and clearly distinct sets of terms and expressions for each subcategory):

Overlapping a: Active

Clearly means active involvement of material or spatial units, as rendered in English expressions like folding, stretching, and the like.

"Active overlapping"

Const. H: volumeness/planeness; near, contiguous, or border; horizontal[4]

Const. I: none

Overlapping b: Active or Passive

This notion (or subcategory) is different from meaning *a* in that the action of overlapping is not necessarily named distinctly. Rather, the permanence of the event is stressed: this situation (in Western understanding) can be characterized in Navajo as "keeping something or some spatial unit overlapping something else." The semantic description is quite different from case *a*.

"Active or passive overlapping"

---

3. The part/whole distinction appeared to play the same role or have the same function as the distinction in a plurality of items (the set and particular items); "order" is understood in a somewhat similar, but less specific sense than "dimension" (cf. section numbers 110 and, e.g., 115), which explains why they can to some degree figure as alternatives for each other.

4. The same substitutability that was seen to operate with inside/outside applies: contiguity and border are sometimes interchangeable.

Const. H: volumeness/planeness; border (almost always); horizontal (almost always)

Const. I: none

106. (Numbers 106, 206, and 306 of the UFOR): In/Out, Central/Peripheral

In/Out

Navajo terminology never confuses or equivocates in- and outward movements on the one hand, and inside and outside as spatial units on the other. There is a clear distinction between both (absent in English or most other European languages) that is indicated through the use of radically different expressions and terms in each case. I will distinguish between two subgroups within the in/out category, as follows:

In/Out a: This subcategory defines a spatial segment by the character of the volumeness or planeness of the instance (of spatiality) and by its accompanying constraints on behavior. A particular unit in space is singled out through the use of those expressions particularly recording its position with reference to another unit (e.g., someplace is the inside of something, or is inside with regard to another thing). Most of the time, moreover, special constraints on possible forms of appropriate behavior systematically and similarly differ: behavior that is appropriate in some aspect inside is not so outside, or is not possible outside, or vice versa.

"Inside/outside"

Const. H: volumeness/planeness; border

Const. I: border (ultimate and obstructive); angle

In/Out b: This subcategory specifies a transition between two clearly distinct spatial units that are implicitly characterized as having in/out *a* notions as codeterminants. In other words, the transition is recognized to take place between spaces which are identified as having opposite features on this semantic dimension: one is inside with regard to the other, while the other is outside.

"In/Out"

Const. H: volumeness/planeness; border; movement[5]

Const. I: border (ultimate and obstructive); angle

The only difference between these subcategories lies in the explicit value of movement as a constituent in one case, and of a "defining spatial unit" in the other.

---

5. In one particular case, ch'é'etiin, contiguity seems to replace border as a constituent. This "replacement" is feasible because of the psychological "nearness" of contiguity and "border" in Navajo: the topological test used as a testing device for semantic analysis showed considerable neglect of the distinction between both in perceptual recognition at least.

Central/Peripheral

These notions primarily characterize aspects of action, clearly constraints on its development, regarding the agent's initial spatial location or his final state, or indeed specify the basic frame within which the action must proceed (from center to periphery in a spiral, or in a straight line, or whatever). Also, and concomitant with this use, the notions serve as important minimal forms of order in social or physical settings.

"Central/peripheral"

Const. H: volumeness/planeness; part/whole; order

Const. I: convergence/divergence; cardinal points

107. (Numbers 107, 207, and 307 of the UFOR): Open/Closed

A peculiarity of the recognition and use of the open/closed notions in Navajo cultural knowledge is the fact that the distinction is not at all recognized as relevant, and is absent from the total series of topological test drawings presented on the topic. In other words, the set of drawings especially worked out to test openness and closedness was not seen as relevant to it. Other features were pointed out instead. This and similar observations led me to conclude that openness and closedness are insignificant concepts in the Navajo knowledge system. The set of expressions that deal with these characteristics, on the other hand, is limited and contains only terms and expressions that designate actions. No dominant position of this distinction in perception (as is the case with Western correlate notions, cf. Piaget and Inhelder, 1947) can be detected in the Navajo context. Consequently, the notions "open" and "closed" seem to be aspects of action (or movement) rather than mere perceptually spatial aspects. Generally, by the "act of opening (and closing, respectively)" a specific spatial constellation is described in Navajo.

"Open/closed"

Const. H: volumeness/planeness; movement/action

Const. I: none

108. (Numbers 108, 208, and 308 of the UFOR): Converging/Diverging

In the Navajo spatial system this pair of notions again has clearly dynamic connotations: the terms and expressions for them all refer to the movement of, or the event of coming to one center of plural items (the movement or event of expanding from one center of plural items).

"Convergence/divergence"

Const. H: center; near/separate/contiguous; plural; movement/action; horizontal

Const. I: none

109. (Numbers 109, 209, and 309 of the UFOR): Volumeness/Planeness

In preceding sections I said quite clearly that the notions of "volume-ness" and/or "planeness" are recognized in Navajo as basic or fundamental semantic codeterminants, that is, they (either one or both of them) constitute the meaning of a great number of expressions of spatial structure that I encountered.

In an oversimplified way we can say that Navajo categorizations of different types of planeness or volumeness describe, as it were, the basic Navajo ontology of objects.[6] It is difficult to accept this characterization since similarly oversimplified, one can say that "object" in the English (and every Indo-European) language and "thought system" primarily and necessarily conveys a meaning of "static entity."[7] And it is exactly this characteristic which is not shared by Navajo categories (cf. chap. I). A broadening of scope and a change of terminology is necessary. Moreover, what the Navajo categories seem to emphasize most of all is a praxiological aspect: categories of particulars of the external world are primarily delineated through the way in which the particulars of one category can be differently acted upon, manipulated, or acted in than those of a clearly distinct category. In still more general terms one can say that any particular of a category of volumeness or planeness implies specific modifications of actions and relations to it for any person, animal, plant, or "inanimate" item that is spatially defined with reference to the particular or category in question, These modifications are specific for that category and clearly identify all instances in it in a specific, praxiological way. The detailed analysis of the classificatory verb stems clarifies this point (cf. chap. III, section 109).

I distinguish between three sets of terms and expressions in the total set of expressions for the volumeness/planeness category. The first sub-category distinguishes between different types of spaces as delineated through the available expressions. The second subcategory differentiates qualitative types of "instances with spatial extension" in terms of the way these instances can be handled, manipulated, and so forth. The distinctions are often subtle and very unusual for Western knowledge, and determine spatial aspects of items or processes, rather than "units of space" (places, spaces). The third subcategory distinguishes still different spatial modifiers.

6. The important and fascinating article by Witherspoon (1971) on Navajo categories of "objects at rest" aims at reintroducing this issue (after the example of Hoijer, 1945). It falls short with reference to the point I consider essential in my exposition of Navajo natural philosophy, because not only is it rather hazardous to speak of objects "at rest" in Navajo (because of the dynamic nature of everything in the Navajo world), but the mere use of the term and category of "object" cuts off genuine interpretation of Navajo knowledge on this point. Therefore, I use "item" or "instance" throughout.

7. This idea is basic to the psychological interpretation of knowledge categories like "object" in work by Campbell (e.g., 1973) on "entitativity."

a) Units of Physical, Sociogeographical, and Cosmological Space

The distinction between the three levels of spatial extension follows that which is made in the section titles of the UFOR. The basic character of all terms and expressions listed in this section is identical: In each particular case a type of volumeness or planeness is identified by its characteristics (modification of possible actions or events) which differ from its background or environment. For instance, in the glosses and paraphrases offered by Navajo consultants on á'áán ('hole in the ground'), it is clear in which way this spatially specific phenomenon differs from (or even contrasts with) the surrounding environment, a fact which really makes the recognition of spatial phenomena of the category of á'áán possible.

Consequently, the recognition of volumeness and/or planeness as spatially basic distinctions is always taken for granted in Navajo, and remains implicit, while the type of volumeness or planeness is expressed through the recognition of other (and apparently less basic) spatial features like border, in/out, and so on. It is important to note that the categories are explicitly definable through the recognition of other spatial features (that is, other than volumeness/planeness). A certain circularity appears in the spatial representation system (volumeness defines x and x codefines volumeness).

"Volumeness/planeness"

Const. H: no single feature is always used to define or paraphrase particular volumeness/planeness categories, but border, part/whole, and dimension often occur.

Const. I: front/back; up/down; left/right; part/whole; upon/under; lateral; near/separate/contiguous; overlapping a and b; in/out a and b; border a and b; center; dimension; open/closed; order; multidimensional extension; angle; path.

b) Classificatory Verb Systems

The classificatory verb stems cannot be considered as spatial terms in themselves. However, their role in pointing to particular spatially delineated forms and formations is crucial for the Navajo agent and perceiver. Their use, in any particular case, delimits a range of phenomena by virtue of their spatial peculiarities. In the following paragraphs I give rough characterizations of the spatial units or prerogatives they codetermine. The same reasoning which I defended in the foregoing section applies: spatial types are pointed out merely through the use of the verb stems, while no single constituent can be abstracted for all the spatially characterized categories concerned (given in a new order):

1. si'ą́: single multidimensional item; solid,
2. sinil: plurality of multidimensional items; solid,
3. shijool: single multidimensional item; flexible,
4. sił̜tsooz (B): single or plural two dimensional item(s); flexible,
5. sitą́: single one dimensional item; stiff,
6. sikaad (A): single two dimensional item,

7. sikaad (B): single one dimensional item; no motion,
8. silá: single two dimensional item including position in a third dimension,
9. siyį́: mass (no item distinction); big,
10. siką́: plurality of multidimensional items or mass; in a bordered space (open container),
11. siłtsooz (A): plurality of multidimensional items within a bordered space (container).

c) Spatial Modifiers

These expressions and terms clarify the constraints which apply to spatial types without strictly determining the actual spatial categories (the actual volumeness and planeness instances) occurring.

"Spatial modifiers"

Const. H: part/whole; border; (others eventually)

Const. I: See above, section *a*

110. (Numbers 110, 210, and 310 of the UFOR): Ordering, Succeeding

In order to understand the Navajo category of "order," a minimally and an elaborately described notion must be distinguished: the latter is called "semiorder" while the former will be called "order."

Order

In our material linelike formations generally express the notion of order in a rather strong way, that is, organizing distinct units in an unambiguous way. The stress in Navajo then is on the regularity or smoothness of the pattern of a set of units or items that appears in perception and/or in action. Such expressions are translated with a dynamic connotation, resulting in meanings like: items exist in an orderly way, or a constellation of items has order. In some instances, a more agent-centered translation is appropriate: items form a constellation such that a smooth, repetitive action series is adequate to operate on them (e.g., with íít'í' and ałkéé'aníí'á).

"Order"

Const. H: volumeness/planeness; dimension (one dimension dominant or plural dimensions); plural/singular

Const. I: center; point; multidimensional extension

Semiorder

There is a set of Navajo expressions for semiorder. They refer to a position in or particularity of a pattern of apparently successively organized material (an order) without reference to the pattern or to the englobing order as such. In other words, any general order is implicit and/or hypothetical, while the explicit information states that at least that one (or those few) item(s) is (are) recognized in the specific relation to the bulk of all other (and undifferentiated) items.

"Semiorder"

Const. H: volumeness/planeness; dimension; plural/singular

Const. I: center

111. (Numbers 111, 211, and 311 of the UFOR): Preceding/ Following/In Front of/In Back of

This pair of notions refers to a situation isomorphic with the structure of the human body and to actions of the body. Both aspects are clearly distinct in Navajo language and behavior, that is, each aspect is dealt with separately, while the "dimension" as a whole is not rendered explicit in the language.

"Preceding/following"

Const. H: volumeness/planeness; movement/direction

Const. I: depth dimension

112. (Numbers 112, 212, and 312 of the UFOR): Perspective

This concept was found to be neither perceptually distinguished (through the topological test), nor referred to by any linguistic expression.

113. (Numbers 113, 213, and 313 of the UFOR): Deep, Far (Dimension of Depth)

The front-back or depth dimension itself is not expressed very explicitly in Navajo. The two expressions that approximate the general notion of depth both had to do with movement and/or direction in a more restricted sense (naaniigo and ákónaa, cf. chap. III, section 113). Still, from their use and from the manifest "knowledge" of the dimension in actual behavior and its products, I have arrived at a (provisional) semantic characterization:

"Dimension of depth"

Const. H: preceding (following); path; movement

Const. I: border (ultimate and obstructive); volumeness/planeness; angle; line; path[8]

114. (Numbers 114, 214, and 314 of the UFOR): Distance

The more or less sophisticated representation of metric front-back propositions (distance notions) is always expressed by reference to action or

8. For several of the notions in which "depth dimension" is a constituent, I found simply that the recognition of one or more dimensions in space is required (e.g., volume implies that things, items, etc., are recognized as having nonmetric extension on three dimensions). In Navajo knowledge (as in many cultural knowledge systems), the three dimensions are primarily recognized through reference to the structure of the human body.

movement in the Navajo spatial system. Locomotion of the human body is often taken as the implicit unit or "measuring rod"; objects and spaces between different objects are compared in distance by the use of this implicit rod. Most often a more qualitative (rather than a strictly quantitative) measurement or comparison is considered satisfactory: something is so far off that you walk up to it, or so far away that you can still see it, or so far that only marks can be distinguished, and so on.'

"Distance"

Cont. H: path; dimension

Const. I: none

115. (Numbers 115, 215, and 315 of the UFOR): Above/ Below; Upon/Under

Again, the englobing direction "from up to down, and vice versa" is not found in explicit form (cf. section 110). Moreover, a clear and unambiguous distinction in the Navajo vocabulary pertains to these notions; whereas the English word "up" is ambiguous in meaning (referring to a direction as well as a position), Navajo speech makes strict and unambiguous distinctions in this respect. One set of expressions refers to the direction ("upward, going up"), while a clearly distinct set of terms and expressions refers to the position ("up, upon, on top of"). No confusion is permitted, since two clearly distinct sets of expressions apply, and they have markedly different semantic constitutions.

Above/Below

All linguistic forms I found pertaining to this notion are related to movement or an aspect of movement (e.g., direction). Once again, the easiest and "more natural" reference is to the structure and locomotion of the human body.

"Above/below"

Const. H: Volumeness/planeness; movement and/or direction

Const. I: vertical dimension; height/deepness; volumeness/planeness; angle; line; path

Upon/Under

Typically, terms and expressions that I consider relevant in this subcategory all had to do with a relation of contiguity: all expressions that describe the location of something upon or under something else imply (1) that both items are different from each other (and distinguished in perception and/or action), and (2) that they are physically touching each other:

"Upon/under"

Const. H: volumeness/planeness; contiguity

Const. I: vertical dimension; height/deepness; volumeness/planeness; angle; line; path

116. (Numbers 116, 216, and 316 of the UFOR): Vertical (Dimension)

No expression of the vertical dimension (up-down dimension) could be gathered.

117. (Numbers 117, 217, and 317 of the UFOR): High/Deep (Metric)[9]

Again, the metric concepts under this heading have, as was the case with distance, an implicit or explicit reference to aspects of the human body which appears to be basic. However, it is not so much the locomotion of the body or the eyes that is considered the determining means to point out degrees of height or deepness. It is rather, the human body which is often implicitly taken as the standard unit or "measuring rod," and external objects and spaces are compared in height (or deepness) with this implicit and always available unit. Most often qualitative comparisons, rather than numerical ones (for e.g., x times the unit) are considered satisfactory (e.g., more or less extended than the unit).
"High/deep"
Const. H: volumeness/deepness; up/under; order
Const. I: none

118. (Numbers 118, 218, and 318 of the UFOR): Lateral; Next to

"Nextness" or laterality is rendered in Navajo (language and cultural knowledge system) primarily as specifications in terms of the basic distinctions of nearness, separateness, and contiguity. In all my analyses of concrete terms and expressions, I found one of these differentiations. Still, no ambiguity seems to occur between "nextness" expressions on the one hand and "nearness/separateness/contiguity" expressions on the other (except for two particular expressions, cf. chap. III, section 118). The former are more specific. They are often specified in several different ways by means of more complex semantic aspects (e.g., horizontal, overlapping), than the latter in the Navajo cognitive system.

Most often, a relationship between at least two items or processes is referred to with the next/lateral expressions. Occasionally a characteristic of a single instance or process is described in this way.
"Lateral, next to"
Const. H: volumeness/planeness; near/separate/contiguous
Const. I: horizontal dimension; width

9. "Deepness" is to be distinguished from "depth" (section 113). The former refers to the high/deep distinction and the latter deals with the preceding/following distinction.

119. (Numbers 119, 219, and 319 of the UFOR): Left/Right

Both notions are clearly recognized by Navajos through reference to sides of the human body: left and right hands have different connotations and serve as the main referents in this regard. Again, action on part of the human being is a most important determinant of these expressions' meaning (action of hands, feet).

"Left/right"
Const. H: lateral; volumeness/planeness; direction/motion
Const. I: horizontal dimension; width

120. (Numbers 120, 220, 320 of the UFOR): Horizontal (Dimension)

The identification of the horizontal dimension as such is derived from material that deals with the notion in an implicit (though clear and unmistakable) way; the dimension, however, is not expressed distinctly in a single Navajo term. Two expressions concerning types of spatial extension are considered closest to explicit recognition of horizontality. However, when I asked precise questions about the terminology of the notion of horizontality (in terms of horizontally extending lines, planes, or volumes), consultants gave no answer.

"Horizontal"
Const. H: volumeness/planeness; extension
Const. I: width; volumeness/planeness; angles; line; path

121. (Numbers 121, 221, and 321 of the UFOR): Wide, Broad (Metric)

The few notions I found that clearly express a qualitative (rather than a quantitative) measure of width are presented in Chapter III, section 121. In fact, the rough and imprecise mutual comparison of horizontal and vertical extension of items and places with the human observer is similar to the usual procedure for reaching decisions about the appropriateness of specific expressions of width of items and places. Navajos will call something wide if its width is considerably larger than its thickness or height, for example, rather than stating how many units (yards, inches, etc.) its extension actually is. So, again, I met with comparative visual decisions rather than exact measurements.

"Width"
Const. H: horizontal; planeness/volumeness; no strict measuring unit
Const. I: none

122. (Numbers 122, 222, and 322 of the UFOR): Cardinal Points, Cardinal Directions

In the Navajo lexicon and knowledge system it is more appropriate to speak of "cardinal directions" than of "cardinal points." The three main directions are defined in terms of the diurnal movement of the sun: East, South, and West are named after specific movements and directions of the sun in the Navajo lexicon. North is defined through reference to a major star constellation that can be seen near the Northern limit of the universe. Again, reference is to the movement of this constellation (turning around) rather than the mere figure itself.

Zenith and nadir are orthogonally defined in relation to these four. The stress is on the center notion in an upward and a downward phenomenon (the center of heaven and earth respectively).

Finally, all six directions can be combined in systems of two, four, or six directions, wherein specific processes of the cosmic order take place.

"Cardinal directions"
Const. H: direction; center; path; motion
Const. I: none

123. (Numbers 123, 223, and 323 of the UFOR): Coordinate Systems

This category needs no separate treatment since all relevant information is already given in section 122 (cardinal directions).

124. (Numbers 124, 224, and 324 of the UFOR): Multidimensionally Extended (Metric)

Notions of measurement of multidimensional spaces (two- or three-dimensional) are expressed primarily in qualitative terms, that is, by rough and imprecise comparison of expansion along different dimensions. No fixed or a priori unit of measurement is used, but the implicit or presupposed action of going about the action of comparing or measuring is decisive.

"Multidimensionally extended"
Const. H: volumeness/planeness; order (measure)
Const. I: point

125. (Numbers 125, 225, and 325 of the UFOR): Point

A correlate of the geometric notion of point cannot be found in the Navajo spatial knowledge system. A qualitative notion appears which is more specifically based on the qualitatively derived metric system that is used. Instead of defining a "point" as a basic concept (cf. Euclidean geometry), it is expressed as a two-dimensional extension which is very small. It does not play any significant role in Navajo geometry.

"Point"

Const. H: multidimensionally extended; order (smallest)

Const. I: none

126. (Numbers 126, 226, and 325 of the UFOR): Line, Straight Line

The notion of line is intelligible in terms of the notions of direction (and hence movement) and/or dimension in the Navajo spatial system. The specifications in glosses and paraphrases were minimal, but I was able to get substantial supplementary information through the use of the topological test and through the (unorthodox) use of Campbell's visual illusion test battery (Segal et al., 1966). The latter was used primarily as a system of cues, very much in the way the topological test was introduced: people were presented with the different drawings having to do with visual illusions and were asked to report on the line constructions in paraphrases, comments, metaphors, and comparisons with structures they employed in the external world. Basically, lines were recognized as paths of movement or direction, whatever their setting in the drawings presented. A strict distinction between straight and non-straight lines was not deemed highly relevant by the consultants.

"Line, straight line"

Const. H: direction/dimension

Const. I: none

127. (Numbers 127, 227, and 325 of the UFOR): Angular, Pointing, Parallel

It is important to keep in mind that angles and corners are predominantly considered to be volumes or surfaces in the Navajo knowledge system. Consequently, they were paraphrased as specifications of such basic spatial structures (aspects or instances of volumeness or planeness). Parallelism, on the other hand, is considered to be a visual or activity-linked condition of the relationship between two or more instances of volumeness (mountains, fences, walking persons exist parallel to each other). The metric element in these notions is again scarce, imprecise, and approximate. It is based on vision or behavioral comparison rather than on measurement with the standard unit.

"Parallelism"

Const. H: plural items; planeness/volumeness; dimensions; movement

Const. I: none

All points distinguished are types of volumeness, that is multidimensional structures that have a marked pointedness at one end. Different forms are distinguished within this set by the exclusive use of different terms for horizontally and vertically pointing structures, or by the use of an exclusive terminology for compactness and extension of the pointing structure (e.g., needle point versus razor blade).

"Pointing"
Const. H: volumeness; border; direction or dimension
Const. I: none
Angles and corners, again, are instances of volumeness (rather than linear structures as in Western geometrical notions). The topological test showed that the geometric notion of angle is nearly absent since obtuse angles did not match the Navajo notion covered by specific expressions, but were referred to as mere "lines." Only the spaces (volumeness instances) bordered by some clear limits and within such limits were considered relevant for some terms, while the outside angles were expressed wtih different terms.
"Angle, corner"
Const. H: volumeness; inside/outside; border; direction
Const. I: none

128. (Numbers 128 and 228 of the UFOR): Surface, Volume

The following types of surfaces and/or volumes (cf. basic characterization in the UFOR) were clearly distinguished in Navajo language and action:
a) ringlike, circular surface;
b) round, ball-like volume;
c) curved, wavelike volume;
d) cylindrical or barrellike volume.
These forms are clearly recognized and distinguished in the Navajo knowledge system with exclusive and distinct linguistic expressions and stems for each of them. However, no precise or metrically sophisticated paraphrases or definitions were found. Instead, vague and approximate circumscriptions of geometric surfaces and volumes were offered by consultants. The forms are supplementarily distinguished through the actions that can be performed on them (to roll, to wind around, etc.).

129. (Number 129 of the UFOR): Geometric Figures

Here again, no sufficient or adequate information could be gathered. In general the notions are distinguishable and seem to be constituted in terms of concrete actions and manipulations that can be performed. The consultants pointed to actions that should be performed to reach a visually satisfactory representation of a figure in question. The material is estimated to be too unsatisfactory to allow generalizations as yet.

130. (Numbers 130–133, 230, 332, 333, and 334 of the UFOR): Movement

The notions designating movement were not detailed enough in this fieldwork period. Although the notions of movement and direction have been shown to be highly important in the constitution of several other spatial notions in Navajo knowledge, I will not treat them in any systematic way in this semantic analysis (see however the information presented on this topic in chap. I).

134. (Number 134 of the UFOR): Spatially Random or Spatially Determining

This notion seeks to distinguish between the concepts of chaos and determinability (in space) in myths, language, and human behavior. It is certainly the case, as the material in Chapter I indicates, that Navajos do make these distinctions. Creation is constantly referred to as "putting things in place," the disturbance of the natural order is a bad thing, and so on. However, no single and straightforward attempt to make explicit the distinction and the two concepts involved was found.

229. (Number 229 of the UFOR): Map, Scale

The Navajo notion of map is known and expressed in terms of action, movement, and environmental information needed to perform a movement through the environment. Numerous temporal, culturally significant, and other not strictly spatial indices are taken into account when "construing" a map in the Navajo tradition. Graphic representation (approaching the idea of a printed map in our tradition) is known and occasionally used.

"Map"

Const. H: movement; volumeness/planeness; near/separate; path; nonspatial notions

Const. I: none

A rudimentary notion of scale is used, phrased basically in terms of actions: scale is only recognized in the sense of "scale model," that is, the spatially characterized reproduction of the original. The similarity between original and scale model is implied and pointed out where possible, but it is not defined or otherwise specified explicitly in a systematic way.

"Scale"

Const. H: movement; volumeness/planeness; making

Const. I: none

231. (Number 231 of the UFOR): Path; Orientation

Notions of path are construed in Navajo semantics by a reference to actual tracks of movement or action and/or by reference to a dimension (from ego out) along which the eventual movement is to take place. A path essentially links two places (instances of planeness or volumeness) or overlaps a spatial phenomenon (instance of volumeness or planeness) in the Navajo spatial system.

"Path"

Const. H: planeness (volumeness); contiguous/separate; movement; one dimension

Const. I: dimension; cardinal directions; distant/high/wide; map

"Orientation and navigation"

See section 232. Both represented the systems of information about actions and about the environment that is necessary for a person to reach the destination. Navajo consultants gave this general description when asked about these notions and went into minute details when pressed for concrete examples. Consequently, I conjecture that several (probably numerous) other spatial notions constitute navigation and orientation notions. Since no systematic and decisive propositions on the matter could be reached, I prefer not to enter these notions in a more detailed system of semantic characteristics as yet.

Global Spatial Characteristics (Numbers 140, 240, and 340 of the UFOR)

Explicit information on global spatial characteristics is only available for the notions of continuity and homogeneity (cf. chap. III). All other global aspects (boundedness, finiteness, and absoluteness/relativity of space) must be derived from the material gathered.

All terms and expressions relating to continuity/discontinuity express the continuous character of space in one way or another. So, discontinuity in space does not seem to have a meaning in Navajo knowledge. Moreover, continuity is conceptualized as a complex and sophisticated concept involving at least the recognition of movement and a notion of multidimensional extension. Different expressions are further differentiated by the emphasis they put on linelike, plane or voluminous forms, apart from other specifications.

"Continuous"

Const. H: extension; volumeness; movement; dimension

Homogeneity of space, or the notion that space at all times and at all points has the same regularity, the same basic structure, and the same "laws" is dealt with explicitly in only one expression: t'áá ałtsogo. Its characterization is not very sophisticated, but it stipulates the essential feature or requirement for any notion of homogeneity: all-pervasiveness. It is, however, difficult to decide if space has this characteristic in the Navajo knowledge system or not. It is attributed explicitly to air alone. Furthermore, the recognition of change in the rules of social and mythological order on leaving the space of

Navajo creation (going beyond the borders of Navajo territory) points to a restriction; within the confines of the Navajo world (in mythological speech), space is held to be homogeneous:

Const. H: extension; volumeness; pluridimensional

Const. I: none

Absolute/relative can be derived in somewhat the same way. The mythological information gathered on the global character of the Navajo world points to an "absolute space" notion: Mother Earth and Father Sky delimit and in fact define the World, forming moreover a genuine "container" wherein the Navajo way of life is possible and factually meaningful. Once in the outside world, there can be no genuine understanding of spatiality or worldliness whatsoever, as was made clear by consultants. When consultants are asked how they do in fact visualize or behave in the "world outside" (outside the confines of the Navajo world, that is), they tend to refer to it in terms of distant places linked through voyages. The latter might seem to express a relativistic notion of space (of the outside). However, the information is too scarce and unsystematic to warrant such a broad conclusion.

Finite/infinite. Upon a careful reading of the information presented in Chapter I, and in the material of Chapter III, certain conclusions are drawn concerning the concepts of finite/infinite. Under no circumstances are instances of infinity held relevant by Navajo consultants. Even the expressions of continuity clearly refer to processes or spatial phenomena that come to an end sooner or later. The exclusively spatial notion of finite is quite clear in the discussions relating to both the spatial extension and the temporal existence of the (Navajo) world: it is held together by the Earth and the Sky, and it will come to an end in a foreseeable future. Hence, finite can be agreed upon to be a genuine characteristic of the total space of Navajo world view.

Bounded/unbounded is a more difficult issue. It is never made quite explicit whether the Navajo space is bounded, although the phenomena mentioned (Sky and Earth) point in this direction. However, the holes in both of them may obscure strict boundedness. On the other hand, the absolutely basic status of "center" in the ordering and structuring of Navajo global space tends to hint at an absolute boundedness of Navajo space. However, in view of the slight ambiguity in material, no decisive and satisfactory conclusion can be reached.

Graphic Representation of All Navajo Spatial Notions

As was anticipated at the beginning of this chapter, the global representation of Navajo spatial knowledge aimed at is presented most clearly in a graphic form.

The information on the semantic character of spatial notions always

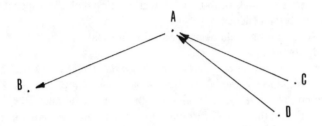

Fig. 2 Graphic representation of spatial notions.

consists of a double list of "constituents": a list of semantic constituents of a given notion (notions which codetermine the meaning of a given category) and a list of notions of which the particular category is a constituent.

The notions that codetermine the meaning of a given category are represented as incoming graphs (starting out from a particular notion and pointing in the direction of the notion determined). The notions that are determined by the category (or of which the category is a semantic constituent) are reached through an outgoing graph (starting in the determinant and ending in the determined). For example, for an imaginary situation like:

"A"

Const. H: C; D

Const. I: B

the graphic structure above is appropriate:

Each notion is represented as a node in the graphic structure, from which incoming and outgoing graphs are drawn. The picture becomes, of course, quite complex once several notions are mutually determining to some degree.

The general graphic structure represents all the information of the list of semantic characterizations (the first section of this chapter). In other words, the set of Const. H's and Const. I's of all the notions discussed graphically represents the semantic structure of Navajo space.[10]

This graphic scheme of the semantics of Navajo space suggests several conclusions:

1) In the first place, the topological test corroborated several remarkable results of the analysis, as shown in the diagram, such as:

a) the open/closed distinction does not determine anything else, which is compatible with the test result that none of the consultants considered the distinction relevant at all;

---

10. Some notions (e.g., scale, direction) have been left out, since information on them is considered to be too shallow.

b) the part/whole distinction is relatively unimportant (in contrast to the Western extensive dependence on it) both in the test and in the diagram;

c) volumeness/planeness instances are used in many descriptions, glosses, and paraphrases of other spatial notions. In the test, as in the semantic analysis, they appeared as important constituents of more sophisticated notions like "surface" and "volume," as well as of others.

2) In the second place, a "primitive" notion as used in several other semantic analyses (e.g., Katz, 1972) cannot be said to be revealed in this analysis of Navajo spatial knowledge. On the other hand, several notions play considerable roles and can thus be said to be more "basic" or more "fundamental" in the structure of Navajo space: for example, volumeness/planeness, movement, dimension.[11] Their relatively dominant role in spatial construction was reached only through empirical work, which illustrated the possibility, and indeed validity, of a synthetic approach to semantics. Moreover, their status can certainly not be that of "primitives" in the classical sense, since they are themselves constructed by means of other notions (they have constituents). This situation leads to the recognition of a certain degree of circularity in Navajo knowledge. This fact is interpreted as corroboration in defense of the approach adopted, since circularity (rather than a unilinear or strictly hierarchic structure) of knowledge systems is a well-known feature both of scientific and of natural knowledge systems (e.g., Hamlyn, 1970, chap. 1).

Adequacy of the Analysis

The present semantic approach still has to be tested for adequacy. The first criterion of adequacy requires an adequate and efficient description of the material under investigation (cf. the end of the third section of chap. II). This will be discussed now. The second criterion has been treated in Chapter V.

The first criterion of adequacy is satisfied, I argue, because

1) All terms and expressions of the spatial representation of Navajos have been placed unambiguously in the model. That is to say, not only is the semantic characterization of the Navajo concrete terms and expressions such that ambiguity or arbitrary substitution is impossible within this model (cf. data in chap. III), but this is also true at the regional and global level, where the notions or categories of Navajo spatial knowledge are sorted out. More concretely, all notions are clearly distinguished in the analysis and in the ensuing model, and, moreover, their representation is such that their peculiarities

---

11. The attempt to present the complex interrelationships in a graph automatically led to the abstraction of these three notions and to their position at the top of the graph. In this way, the graphic diagram helps clarify their superior position. However, more notions have a more dominant role as can be seen and, secondly, a three-or-more-dimensional representation may give another picture, probably more appropriate to this body for the sake of data.

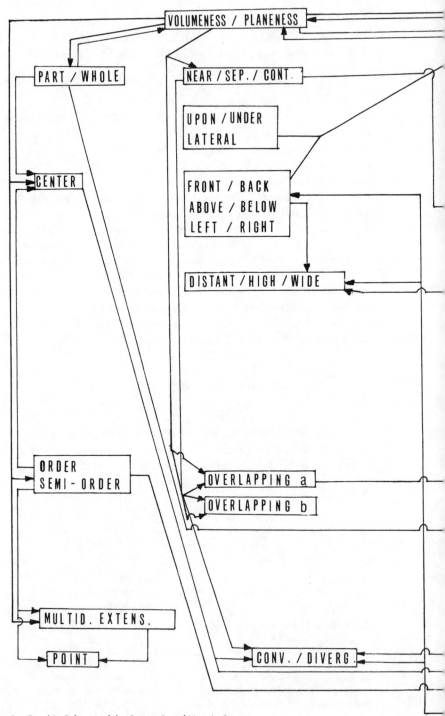

Fig. 3   Graphic Scheme of the Semantics of Navajo Space.

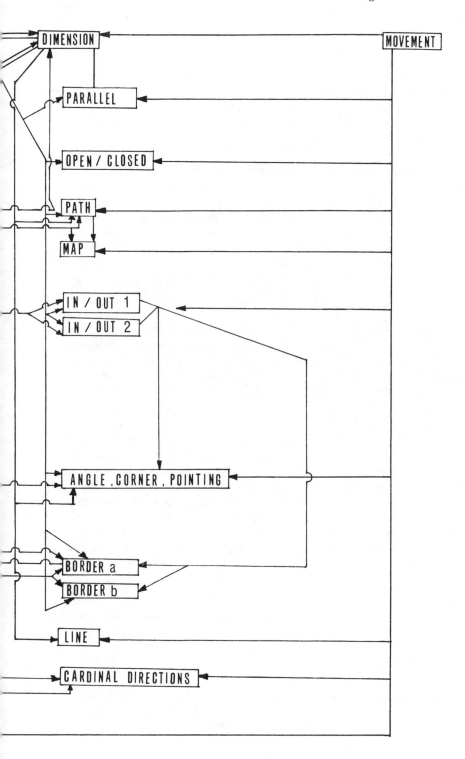

as well as (and most of all) their interrelationships come out clearly. In practice, this situation is reached through the determination of the combined sets of Const. H's and Const. I's that define the semantic character of each notion in itself and by its interrelationships with any other relevant notion. Above all the total sequence of procedures (apart from the drawing of a graphic representation of the complete system) is continuously and systematically based on field work, with the consultants' complete collaboration.

2) The second argument of adequacy is provided by the fact that the native character of the spatial representation in the Navajo world view is in effect safeguarded, not only in the detailed analyses (the local and regional analyses), but even at the global level of the model. Not only was the basic natural philosophy of Navajos not betrayed in the analysis, but it is consistently represented. I feel that two basic characteristics of the Navajo world view and mentality, as expressed in the explications concerning natural philosophy (chap. I) and in the different analyses of language and world view that already existed,[12] draw particular attention here: the dynamic character of the world (as expressed in Navajo ontology) and the action-oriented or even the praxiological nature of several basic notions.

The dynamic character of the world implies, as stated also in Chapter I, that segmentability of the world is rather secondary, not to say unlikely. The semantic analysis and the model presented above point to the same conclusion: part/whole distinctions, which are so basic in Western thought,[13] are practically absent in the Navajo semantic characterization of space. At the same time and concomitant with this feature a general (although not exclusive) tendency toward action-directed or genuinely praxiological interpretation of spatial phenomena is apparent: spatial units are not characterized through mere formal features, but are recognized instead in terms of what can be done with them, what manipulation they induce or prohibit, what types of actions need to be performed in order to know or handle them. The list of "classificatory verb stems" is of course a clear example, since in a way several praxiological alternatives are offered for the description of what would basically be aspects of the verb "to be" in the Western interpretation. Most of the differentiations within the volumeness/planeness category have this peculiarity, as has also the interpretation of the notion of dimensions. The fact that these notions all have a basic status in the system, that is, that they, to a considerable degree, codetermine the meaning of a host of other notions, only

12. Cf. Young and Morgan (1942, and again 1980) point to the "phraselike" character of Navajo verbs and translate in a behavioral sense most of the time; the same point is followed up in Hoijer (1974).

13. The part/whole distinction is so basic to Western thought that Piaget's description of space, but also of mathematics, logic, and world picture in general, in fact stresses the one main operator that must be acquired and handled properly by children in order to become efficient adults in the West: conservation (that is, the recognition of a whole, or of parts as separate wholes with particular extension) (Piaget, 1947 and Inhelder and Piaget, 1966 on logic). Other psychologists of concepts go as far (e.g., Bruner, Goodnow, and Austin, 1956).

enlarges the relevance of this point. The predominant role of the notion of movement in several semantic characterizations certainly does strengthen this point. The general point I aim to make with this emphasis is that the model is able to describe this situation, whereas an object- or percept-dominated model of semantic representation (Katz's 1972 model or any other static space model, e.g., Rosh, 1976) is not. Moreover, the description and representation along these lines claim to be consistent, since they match the information on Navajo natural philosophy completely (cf. chap. I, but also Wyman, 1975, and Witherspoon, 1977).

3) Finally, the model and the analysis are effective since they enable me to interpret and eventually anticipate or predict several aspects of factually occurring behavior on the part of the Navajos. In some crucial matters of "failure to understand," it can point to reasons and maybe even causes of such failure. In the first place, I think of the two historical events which were told by very disappointed Navajo consultants (corroborated by E. T. Hall's memories as well). The first instance concerns fencing: although fences are generally respected by Navajos, a latent feeling of inappropriateness is held toward them, which occasionally gives way to endless and tremendously lasting trials in cases of disagreement about concrete territories (corroborated by Oswald Werner). One way to understand both negative reactions in the case of fences (the latent uneasiness about them and the litigious effect), and one that was explained to me by several consultants, is that the earth, the soil, and the space in general within the Navajo world cannot really "be cut up like that." In other words, the segmentability of space is not taken for granted (and is in fact imposed for traffic security reasons). These reactions are confirmed, then, in the present analysis by my insistence on both the dynamic and the unsegmentable nature of space and (to a much less decisive extent) by the relative unimportance of border notions in the Navajo spatial representation.[14]

A second example is an even more dramatic and highly emphasized event in Navajo history: the livestock reduction on the reservation at the end of the Second World War. It was, and still is, incomprehensible to many that through any act of genuine reasoning (such as that which the government in ordering the stock reduction claimed to follow) one would effect the reduction in a drastic way of the lifegiving source, the social and cultural symbol of well-being: the livestock. One of the factors I can point out in light of the present analysis is the fundamentally different, and indeed incommensurable, ideas each party had and still has (government and Navajos) about land and its "objectifiability" (in consequent use). Other factors could certainly play a role. The awareness and the better knowledge of the representation of this idea in both parties may have helped, however, to bridge the evident gap of

14. This may be a matter of degree: borders seem to be predominantly important in Chinese myth and daily life of certain periods (Granet, 1935), and may be less so in Navajo culture.

mutual understanding and may have helped to secure communication between the two parties.

A third example concerns the failure of present-day education in the sciences (which is the point that interested me primarily in this study), that I learned about in talks with numerous Navajos, school teachers, and others. This example is treated in Chapter V.

Conclusions

In the foregoing sections a different, fundamentally synthetic approach to semantics was presented. From micro- to macrolevels of meaning (or in my terminology: from local to regional to global levels), the different semantic characterizations were worked out on the basis of fieldwork data. Indeed, on all levels except the highest level of abstraction, the consultants were systematically involved in the determination of meaning, in the recognition of relevance and adequacy of presented categories and in the elimination or rephrasing of unwarranted translations. The categories described in the universal or culture-free UFOR (cf. Appendix B) served as the main guides of heuristic and intuitive value to both ethnographers and consultants in the process. The result of the total sequence of procedures is a synthetic picture of Navajo spatial semantics.

Fundamental characteristics of such a semantic model were: the determination of meaningful characteristics exclusively on the basis of empirical analysis (a nonaprioristic approach), the combined use of purely linguistic and extralinguistic analyses (the topological test, the reference to behavioral and material culture), and the search for compatibility between the spatial, representational notions and broad, natural philosophical notions.

The criteria of adequacy, that were defined to defend the present approach (end of the third section), were twofold: in the first place it was required that the model give an adequate and efficient description of the lexicon, and in the second place it was required that the model pay off in the form of directions for a better education and a viable bridging of the "untranslatability" gap between Navajo and Western categories. The first criterion has been discussed. The second one is dealt with separately in the final chapter of this volume (chap. V).

V | Applications in the Teaching of Mathematics and the Sciences[1]

From the outset of this study I continuously searched for possible applications of its results in a useful and beneficial way for the Navajo people. The first and foremost domain of application was found in the education of young Navajo Indians (and maybe other groups of people of non-Western origin), particularly regarding instruction in disciplines that involve spatial conceptualization and representation.

Statement of the Problem

When reading the works of Piaget, Bruner, and others on genetic psychology and ensuing educational procedures, one is compelled to reconsider the premises of these authors. In general terms it can be stated that all the authors agree on the genetic primacy of some kind of part/whole distinction, of some kind of "qualitative geometry" (or, more precisely, topology), and of some definite notions of order (conservation principles in Piaget, for example). With this preschool knowledge in a more or less developed form, the child enters the organized instruction in mathematics, geography, history (as well as a more systematic study of the environment). The fact that Piagetian strategies and insights are generally applied in Western European schools now, and that the so-called "new mathematics" (set theory mathematics) has conquered the West by now, is evidence in favor of the applicability—even successful applicability—of the theory.[2]

When looking for possible applications of similar insights in the same disciplinary instruction on the Navajo reservation (even in the best schools that are to be found there), one is struck by the utter ineffectualness, not to say the total inappropriateness of the same material, the same psychological convictions and findings in this different cultural setting. What has happened? Why is there this difference between the two types of education? In my view these questions will be answered if we look at the presupposed conditions of

1. I am grateful to Professors Leo Apostel and Fernand Vandamme, who discussed many of the problems that are dealt with in this chapter, particularly the philosophical and more technical problems.

2. It is impossible at this point to go into this matter. However, numerous publications on the topic exist. The publications by the Genevan school of thought offer ample examples.

knowledgeability that are required. The fact must be mentioned that my questioning of instructors/teachers, both Navajos and whites, on these matters and on their individual understandings of the problems yielded very little useful information. Very different outlooks of the educational task and setting are realized. The school at Rock Point is quite free or "progressive" in educational and social matters, while the school at, for example, Round Rock is rather classical, a Bureau of Indian Affairs (BIA)-dominated school with low aspirations and rather poor results. Still, teachers from both schools, particularly the Navajo teachers I talked to, showed a very poor understanding of the difference in outlook, system, preconceptions, and actual notions between the so-called Western (e.g., Piagetian) and the Navajo way of talking about, manipulating, acting upon, and actual formalization building of spatial differentiations in both cultural knowledge systems. Only one Navajo consultant was really able to shift consciously and swiftly between both "systems" (BB).[3] He started a deep discussion on the differences he saw between both spatial systems and the way "intranslatability" is felt when one looks at one from the perspective of the other, and vice versa. He encouraged me to go about the present study, and I can only hope that I have reached a sensible result, one that will bridge the gap of untranslatability and promote mutual understanding. Most of the teachers (Navajos as well as white teachers, eventually) occasionally told me about concrete instances of "misunderstanding"; the spatial interpretation of time in English ("before/after in time" was generally considered to be a very difficult distinction for Navajo teachers and children alike) and the varying interpretations of the presumably "evident" part/whole distinctions in English.[4]

These experiences convince me that the widespread feeling of ineffectiveness of schooling may be due—among other, more social and cultural factors—to the fundamental and poorly understood lack of commensurability of Western and Navajo knowledge systems, since they already exist and play a role in further, formal education within the school settings. The success of Piagetian approaches in education must at least partly be explained by the fact that, for example in geometry, they are founded on and built up from logically satisfying and closely "similar" or "naturally presupposed" preschool notions. In other words, the preschool knowledge is highly appropriate to and compatible with the contents of instruction in school. Further, our culture has built on a spatial systematization that has clearly continuous and smoothly developing stages that stretch from the natural environment (indeed the "carpentered world" Campbell, 1964, is talking about) and its conceptualization,

---

3. BB, a brilliant young Navajo man, reacted to the idea of studying Navajo spatial knowledge by saying: "The moment I heard of your study, I thought you would run into great and highly complicated problems. Space is a deep notion and poorly understood in the Navajo studies."

4. One consultant, LB, told me about a test on taxonomic classification that was carried out for some time. Although consultants followed the instructions and filled in the test, they confessed not to have understood what was "known" from them in this way: they simply would not work in this manner on their own. The principle did not really apply.

all the way to more abstract and complex geometries. This seeming relativization of Piagetian notions is not new: both at the center at Geneva (e.g., Bovet, 1974) and elsewhere (e.g., Pinxten, 1976a) this critique on the Western biases in Piaget's theory of intellectual development has been heard. The problem with Navajo education (and with any education in non-Western cultures) can then be summarized as follows: apart from other factors (social, emotional, etc.), the impact and precise content of preschool native knowledge is different in the Navajo culture than it is in ours, and consequently the curriculum and its actual implementation in the Navajo situation should be adjusted in order to reach a smooth, understandable, really integrated development in the knowledge acquired at school. Most certainly, in order to prevent a merely "schizoid" situation (like the one that exists currently, where Navajos obtain some knowledge from their tradition, some woefully incomplete knowledge from the Western tradition, and few and badly worked out means of comparing, transforming, shifting, or translating from one to the other), it is very necessary to gain a better understanding of the differences between both cultural systems. The possibility, then, of building formal schooling on the Navajo natural knowledge background acquired in the preschool age, can be pursued. It is this task that I confront when I consider the value of the present study[5] for education.

The Problem with Spatial Representations

I shall present a sketch of the problem of spatial and mathematical preschool conceptualization conveyed to Navajo and Western children to indicate the range and depth of the problem under discussion, for which I propose a solution. The presentation is a "sketch" in the sense that only some basic notions will be highlighted, whereas the more sophisticated or derived ones will be omitted from consideration.

The Western Case

I see three main points in the description of Western psychological development of formal and mathematical thought that are developing in a mutually exclusive way in Navajo thought:

1) The Specific Hierarchy

In his explanation on the child's construction of space, Piaget (with others like Bruner, Furth, Goodnow, etc.) gives a detailed analysis of the way

5. The lack of understanding of the incommensurability between the two cultural knowledge systems (Western and Navajo) that is so apparent in discussions with teachers and students on this matter is not difficult to grasp. It is a well-known fact that Kant considered Euclidean geometry to be innate/evident, the only possible geometry of the outside world, and that

more sophisticated notions are linearly deduced or construed in a systematic one-to-one progression from notions acquired earlier. (Piaget and Inhelder, 1947; cf. also in schematic form: Pinxten 1976a). The notion of "distinctness" is built upon (or deduced from) that of "neighborhood." The notion of "order" is built upon those of "neighborhood" and "distinctness." The notion of "border" is built upon that of "order," and so on until all more sophisticated notions (the projective geometric and the Euclidean notions) are integrated in the total conception by similar, quite linear and systematically progressing procedures. It is pertinent to emphasize that these notions and the system of progressive acquisition is not at all meant as a mere external or formal interpretation, but aims to describe the genetic progression that is actually taking place in the child's mind over the years. In my semantic terms of meaningful spatial representation, it can be said that the progression of Const. H's and Const. I's follows a quite systematic and nearly necessary progression of the following type:

Near: Const. H: none; Distinct: Const. H: near; Order: Const. H: Near, distinct; and so on.[6]

One fundamental feature of the model of the Western development can thus be summarized as follows: it is a hierarchical progression in the sense that each "higher" (more complex) notion necessarily and exclusively implies "lower" (less sophisticated and earlier acquired) notions as constituents. In practice, the Euclidean notions are clearly constructed from topological notions, while all topological notions in turn have only one basic or "primitive" notion in common, that is, "neighborhood."

The educational consequences of this description are straightforward: since children start with topological spatial preschool notions, the curriculum can take these for granted (in a specific order of acquisition) and construe the logically and genetically "subsequent" notions quite naturally on top of and on the basis of these topological notions. The success of this procedure in actual schooling has been accepted as corroboration of the theory. The hierarchy has validated itself in practice.

2) The Part/Whole Distinction Is Omnipresent

A certain atomism is obviously characteristic of the current Western style of thought. The "objectification" of the environment is taken for granted in the sciences (situations, static entities can be abstracted from their environ-

---

thinkers until the first half of this century (including Frege and Husserl) could not really cope with the non-Euclidean geometries worked out by Riemann and Lobachevsky in the nineteenth century. The latter seemed mere "faits divers," counterintuitive products that could not really claim compatibility with anything in the physical world, until they did show it (Einstein, 1949, discusses this point). The matter is not yet fully ingrained in our education, let alone the more basic "shifts" through topology (cf. Reichenbach, 1958; Thom, 1977).

6. The progression does not always present itself in that rigid form, but the idea of a systematic and clearly hierarchical progression certainly holds for the total system of spatial representation.

ment for a certain time) and in school instruction (we study particular animals, places, objects in themselves). A particularly powerful aspect of this approach, it seems, is the segmentability of objects (and of space and time as aspects of objects). The physical and, to some degree, the psychic and cultural world is considered to be sliced, segmented into smaller parts, which can be studied in themselves in greater detail.[7] It is not surprising that genetic psychologists and cognitive psychologists have in general been concerned most of all with this perspective when they wanted to study thought and the development of thought.[8] Neither is it surprising that modern mathematics, which is meant to have more natural links with the Western child's preschool knowledge, is essentially set theory, that is, a formal system that basically deals with and operates in wholes of which the initial entity is but a part. In all disciplines taught at primary and other school levels, the types and characteristics of segmentation of part/whole systems are of central importance, since indeed this atomistic perspective is basic to our cultural knowledge. Consequently, one should emphasize that in order to successfully approach or learn the more systematic presentation of Western knowledge (as is attempted in the school setting), a clear and common understanding of part/whole notions is absolutely required.

3) The Static World

A very general and possibly somewhat metaphysical sounding characteristic of Western knowledge, as it is practiced and taught, is the static interpretation: The outside world is primarily interpreted as a composition of situations, objects, transitions between situations, and so forth, and not as a composite of processes and actions. Physics, biology, and the social sciences decide on constants and thus turn to the most static characterizations of static phenomena in the first place (e.g., taxonomies in biology: see Raven et al., 1971), only to introduce dynamic phenomena in the range of study at a later stage of development (a most typical and well-known case occurs again in biology: Darwinism comes up in the middle of the nineteenth century). The perspective is most clearly detectable again in discussions on the philosophy of science: after numerous generations sought for sense data, atoms, minimal characteristics, and so on, it is only in very recent years that attempts at praxiology and theories of event and change are discussed fully.[9]

Space and time are construed orthogonally, that is, aspects of the

7. See the discussions in philosophy of science: Russell (1921) sought sense data, Goodman (1977) seeks for "qualia as atoms." Cf. also Quine (1969), "Speaking of Objects."

8. See the summary up to 1970 in Pinxten (1972). Cf. also Bruner, Goodnow, and Austin (1956), Bourne (1975): they always deal with the recognition of wholes and parts in the experimental setting as criteria for concept acquisition.

9. Even there, the "static" paradigm remains strongly defended. See Care and Landesman (1968), von Wright (1963), and others where "action" is essentially taken to be a transformation between two situations: starting and finishing with static phenomena. This owes a lot to Apostel and Vandamme, who try to construct a genuinely dynamic theory of action.

world (objects, situations) are characterized in a three dimensional space upon which, as it were, time is defined. Time is, in its turn, most often represented as segmentably spatialized, cut up in identical units (atoms so to speak), which is similarly an attempt to make it manageable in a static framework (cf. Grunbaum, 1964; Einstein, 1949, particularly emphasizes this problem as one of his main points; Smart, 1964). The present outline may appear far-fetched in regard to the problems at hand; this may be because of the conciseness of the discussion offered here.[10] However, the relevance of the point will become clear when I deal with the "Navajo correlates" to these fundamental aspects of knowledge.

Some more down-to-earth arguments may illustrate the point as well. Geography, from the primary school level and on, deals with segmented and segmentable units of land ("continent" is a constant, "state" is a static unit, mountains, prairies, and even agricultural land and cities are conceived of as surfaces, lines, and points, that is as static aspects). Natural sciences speak about the different species, families, and individuals as static units that are distinguishable in constant interrelationships; teaching about the human body emphasizes the part/whole relationships, together with the constancy of the body and its organs (it is not the continuous and never-ceasing processes of metabolism, of destruction or reconstruction that are emphasized, but rather the constant forms, the morphology of it all).

In a general way, I would like to emphasize that Western schooling (and Western knowledge for that matter) looks at the world, first and foremost in terms of objects, states, situations, constant aspects of phenomena, and that dynamic aspects are introduced in a lesser and at least secondary way. The discipline of geometry is evidence of this point: topology, and most certainly Euclidean geometry as it is taught in Western schools, concern themselves with points, lines, volumes, sets, and the like as static units. Dynamic aspects of spatial phenomena are seldom, if at all, introduced in these curricula. The appearance of this emphasis in geometry and other disciplines is considered to be compatible, indeed quite consistent, with the view of the general emphasis on static aspects of phenomena, on form, on structure, and on segmentability in both the Westerner's natural and his learned knowledge.[11]

The Navajo Case

As has become clear in the two preceding chapters, the Navajo conceptualization of the external world differs from the Western one on fundamental points. I shall take up the three correlated characteristics in Navajo to

10. The interested reader is referred to the works cited. I have made a detailed analysis on these points elsewhere (Pinxten, 1975).

11. I am quite aware of the fact that this characterization is an oversimplification, and that it tends to draw a somewhat one-sided picture of the topic. Still, my general conviction seems to be justified (cf. references to philosophers of science), while the one-sidedness is meant to give the point extra emphasis.

bring out the difference, on the basis of which the educational implications can be outlined:

1. The Specific Hierarchy

In contrast to the neatly regular hierarchical structure and, development that were shown in the Western space conceptualization, Navajo space (according to our semantic analysis) appears to be founded on at least three equally important "basic" notions (movement, volumeness/planeness, dimensions). All three are topological in character. Moreover, none of them are really "primitive" in the sense that the (Piagetian) Western notions are: They are clearly composites themselves, and have spatial notions as their constituents; they codetermine themselves. Hence, they exhibit a certain circularity. Finally, they cannot, in any strict sense, be said to be the sole "basic constituents" since they have this status by virtue of the fact that they were selected as the notions involved in the constitution of most other notions. If this is a criterion of "basicality" (and no other criterion could be defended by such strong arguments), it is certainly weaker than the deducibility criterion Piaget forwarded.[12]

Hence, the hierarchical structure or, more generally, the organizational structure in Navajo spatial knowledge is not of the type that was found by Piaget in Western children. Consequently, the educational procedures that would be appropriate and satisfactory for the teaching of spatial notions in Navajo cultural settings cannot take the Western hierarchical spatial structure for granted.

2. The Part/Whole Distinction Is Secondary

The part/whole distinctions that proved so important in Western thought and knowledge systems play a minor role in Navajo knowledge. Navajos tend to speak of the world in terms of process, event, and fluxes, rather than parts and wholes or clearly distinguishable static entities. The emphasis is on continuous changes rather than on atomistic structure. This becomes more understandable when one envisions the world as constituted of dynamic "things," forces, changes, actions, and interactions: it is then not quite so obvious (as it is in a static world, a world of objects and constant forms) to try to segment perceptual and actional aspects, to distinguish parts in the continuous flux as a first and self-evident characterization. The difference is crucial, I feel, and it must be made totally explicit: "objects" cannot be defined in the same way, "form" cannot be understood in quite the same way as in the Western outlook, since all aspects of reality in Navajo knowledge are process-like

---

12. Hence the point is not that Navajos are shown to think more primitively or "prelogically," but rather that the same type of notions and the same operations are used in different ways (cf. the concurring position on the use of logical operators by Kpelle in Cole et al., 1971).

and not thing-like. In the first place, processes or fluxes should not be "cut up" and considered as (statically defined) combinations of (statically defined) chunks of processes or fluxes. This point is important: even in Thom's "dynamic topology" (1977, pp. 1–10), the dynamic phenomena are rendered understandable and manageable by petrifying them, that is, by defining them as changes between initial and final states. In other words, a dynamic phenomenon can be grasped in the Western outlook primarily by defining it as a transformation of a static phenomenon (state, situation) since it can then be segmented. This is the primary (though not exclusive) way of approaching reality in the Western atomistic outlook. This approach is generally alien, inappropriate, and unnatural to the Navajo eye, both at the level of practical manipulation (you cannot divide land and fence it off because by doing so you would then miss the essential character of land as a living, changing aspect), and at the theoretical level (you cannot speak sensibly of the parts of the human body; the complete phenomenon of a human being is a highly solid system).

The foregoing analysis does not mean that Navajos do not distinguish obviously distinct forms, bodies, objects, and the like in their environment. First, the foregoing is an analysis of the interpretation of (partially) similar percepts in Navajo and Western world knowledge, not of the percepts themselves. Second, and this is the most important point, Navajos react to the outside world as if it were primarily constituted of regular phenomena, of presumably patterned or "constant instances" (objects) of processes or fluxes. Consequently this means that if a notion of "object" is introduced to describe these constancies of processes,[13] this notion has but a minor kinship with the Western notion of "object." The Navajo emphasis is clearly on process in form instead of form as such.

The relevance of all this to educational strategies must be demonstrated: reference to point, line, atom, and other part/whole instances is obvious, for instance, in teaching geometry and the sciences in the Western cultural context. Even when starting out with presumably the most general spatial notions of topology in education, the central importance of the notions of point, line, surface, and volume in a clearly segmentational (indeed set theoretic) sense is noncontroversial (cf. e.g., Thom, 1977, starting with "form," chap. 2; Arnold, 1962). After that, distinctly Euclidean notions can be taught and actually construed on their basis, since they consist of similar (though more specific) notions of point, and so forth. This entry into the construction of geometric notions and models is inapplicable in an arithmetic sense to the Navajo students. Rather, a genuinely dynamic topological entry—as yet I have failed to find such a thing worked out in the literature—is required: clearly a formal system of "dynamic volumes," "dynamic dimen-

---

13. Thom (1977, pp. 10–11) tries to develop a more or less dynamic notion of "object," which contrasts only with the percept-dominated notion. His notion is not applicable here since it starts off from states and construes "object" as the result of transitions between stable states.

sions," and "dynamic interpretations of movement" (cf. the results of foregoing chapters), which will translate the Navajo natural knowledge notions of space efficiently. From there, further metric notions should be worked out as refinements of this genuine basis of Navajo spatial knowledge. I will suggest a detailed solution to this problem in following paragraphs. In any event, work should be started, beginning with a topology and following with a system of geometry that emphasizes segmentability and atomism to a lesser degree than contemporary approaches do.

3. The Dynamic World

In earlier sections it was pointed out that the Navajo world view stresses the dynamic rather than the static aspects of reality. Although it cannot be said that these two terms are used in any exclusive sense in either the Navajo or the Western representation system, the primacy of one is obvious for each.

Space and time orthogonality are present to a certain degree in Navajo knowledge, although the clear "dynamization" of spatial phenomena obscures this fact. Indeed, some aspects of time in Western thought (notably the time aspect of change, "existence in time," and the like) are not distinguished in Navajo: rather, spatial phenomena are considered to possess these qualities inherently (that is, in a Westerner's terms). Other aspects of time (e.g., the notions of "generation" and "linear progression of time") are held as separate and "genuinely temporal," features (cf. chap. I). Consequently, to a certain extent one can speak of "timespace" in the Navajo world view (cf. Whorf, 1956), referring to the relatively "time-laden" identity of space. In other words, spatial phenomena always have this special dynamic aspect, which—from a Western viewpoint—makes them different, less strictly or purely "spatial" than, for example, Euclidean geometrical notions.[14] Again, the instruction in a system of purely static spatial representations as is currently practiced in Navajo schools easily leads to miscomprehension.

How Can the Problem of Cultural Alienation Be Met within Education?

I distinguish among three possible approaches:

1. Teach the Western System

In the present school situation, even where the Navajo view on reality receives due attention, I have seen the question resolved in the wrong way.

14. Throughout, as will be clear, "dynamic aspect" cannot be identified with "movement" or displacement through space. The latter category has relevance both in Navajo and Western systems, but is alien to the "static/dynamic" dichotomy.

The Navajo knowledge input was tolerated or even encouraged in matters of traditional moral and social concern, but was considered completely irrelevant or, even worse, nonexistent in other matters. To the teacher trained in Western schools, it appears obvious that the Navajos (or, for that matter, any other non-Western people) have nothing really to say or to think, within the confines of their cultural knowledge, on subject matter that is considered in the realm of the sciences. The argument goes as follows: Sometime during the Classical age a few people started a completely new way of thinking and nothing of the other peoples' knowledge has any real value as compared to that. This attitude is understandable when one reckons the technological explosion that is linked with this type of thinking, the "scientific thought" that conquers huge domains of nature and society wherever it is implanted. However, as I explained above, the problem of the input of other peoples is more delicate and makes itself felt at another level. The two following alternative approaches will make this clear. Meanwhile, the effect of the present approach is, as illustrated in previous paragraphs, that the "victims" of Westernized education, in this case the Navajo Indians, gain a hybrid and badly integrated knowledge. That is, they end up being not really knowledgeable in their own tradition and having another distinct, separately organized, and definitely incomplete second system of knowledge, the Western system. They are often unable to give good and valuable information on their traditional system, and also unable to discuss and question critically some of the aspects of the schooled knowledge. Moreover, the integration and the degree of translatability or even substitutability of elements of one system in the other, and vice versa, is most often alarmingly poor. Such were my experiences, at least, when I talked to and questioned children and schooled adults in this situation. In other words, the net result is the gain of a partial and relatively unintegrated knowledge of both systems (a bad example of "biculturalism" according to Fishman, 1979), and an alienation from the relevance and mutual relationships of both systems.

2. Elaborate the Navajo System

The second possibility I envision would take the Navajo spatial distinctions as genuinely qualitative material for the teaching of geometry and would work toward the usual Western geometric notions from its Euclidean foundation onward. In practice, I found, this approach would amount to the translation, translating the basic Navajo notions and the relationships between all notions distinguished in the course of the present semantic analysis into existing formal notations and an existing formal theory.

To realize this strategy, the different Navajo spatial notions require a notation system that a) deals with or is appropriate for representing the more or less qualitative (rather than strictly metric) interpretation of spatial distinctions in Navajo and that b) has the capacity to emphasize the dynamic aspect (rather than the static character that is conveyed by most geometric systems).

The only formal approach available that to some extent honors this type of interpretation of space is the dynamic topology or catastrophe theory as worked out mainly by Thom (e.g., 1977).

In general terms, Thom set out to construct a formal theory that would account for several dynamic aspects like change, alternation, ceasure, wave-like movement, and so on. He sought applications of a model in several sciences, including social sciences (mainly linguistics). Waiving details of his theory, it can be stated that he presents an approach to dynamic aspects according to which they are changes between two states (initial and final state), and a formal characterization of types, features, regularity, and so forth of such changes. His theory is a topological theory, dealing with presumably the most general characteristics of space (or those that are common to different sophisticated spaces like Euclidean space, non-Euclidean spaces, and so on). Topology, as is well known, offers at least the advantage of speaking about the foundations of spatial models (e.g., the Euclidean model), and therefore dynamic topology could be tried out as a candidate for a general and foundational approach to geometries, specifically starting out with dynamic spatial aspects. It is this type of program, I feel, that should be tried out with Navajo spatial differentiation.

The problem with the Thom approach, though, is that there is no easy and thoroughgoing introductory text of the theory, as we have for general (static) topology (e.g., Arnold, 1962; Sauvy and Sauvy, 1972, is a guide for application in the classroom). It may be hoped that mathematicians may find something valuable in the present explanation and thus be encouraged to work out a teacher's guide.

The procedure would run as follows: Western geometries can be reduced to their foundations and expressed in topology. Navajo spatial conceptualizations could be formulated in a like manner (emphasizing dynamic topology) and could thus be reduced to a particular system of topological propositions.[15] In a second stage, the "Western" and the "Navajo" system of topological premises, axioms, and statements should then be compared. Finally, exact adaptation procedures should be devised in order to ease the transition from the "Navajo" statements to the "Western" system and the related "Western" geometry.

This strategy will have the tremendous advantage that the transition into "Western" biased geometrical notions is understood and explicitly taken into account, while in the former strategy it was bluntly imposed without consideration for the Navajo native categories. Indeed, starting from the presumably more basic formulations and notions of topological aspects in both cases would offer the opportunity to compare both systems of spatial structuring (the Western and the Navajo system) as alternatives to each other. Further, it

---

15. I am aware that there would be considerable technical problems involved: for example, the emphasis on "volumeness" in the Navajo system is difficult to render in any existing topological notation system or formal theory, since most (if not all) topologies work with "points" as the basic unit.

would make an adaptation or "guided transitions" possible for the Navajo child. It would start with the differences between the child's notion and the Western ones and train the transition between the two explicitly and purposefully, in order to carefully convey the detailed and difficult "pitfalls" (from the point of view of the "Westernizing" teaching) that confront the child because of the difference in outlook of the systems. In further development of geometric thinking, the "Western" basis could then safely be taken as a point of reference since it was instructed in the proper way.

Since this strategy has the tremendous advantage in that at least the gap of translatability has been taken into account, it alone could improve schooling. However, it has two serious drawbacks. In the first place, it unquestionably endorses a reductionist frame. Statements and outlooks described in the representation are always reduced to topological phrasings within a formal system. Since, as I mentioned, existing formats (as far as I know) would cause a very serious reduction of the Navajo conceptual content (with no alternative for "Navajo volume," i.e., without the notion of "point," and numerous difficulties with the hierarchical and not strictly interrelated notions), the drawback may outweigh the advantage in the case of Navajo space. A decisive balance can only be made when the detailed mathematical "translation" in a dynamic topological model of the semiformal spatial representation model of Chapter IV is completed. A second drawback, and one that is plain without complex argument, has to do with the employment of topological phrasings in grade school processes. The procedure, as outlined, aims at integrating the Navajo conceptualization into a general set of spatial differentiations. The inevitable upshot would be that Navajo children and teachers would have a better grasp and in fact a better entry into the field of geometry since they would be able to understand the basic, foundational link it has with topology and thus with their specific "topological system." However, all this is but an avenue to Western knowledge and thus a "Westernization" of communication and interaction in schools.

So, although the second alternative would offer a better understanding of the link between Navajo thought and Western thought (at least in some fields), it rests on the same implicit conviction that all is well as long as the West expands its hegemony. Not only is it morally and politically a very questionable position to hold, but moreover it could lead to an ensuing disastrous uniformity in the world. Indeed, it does not take too vast an imagination to understand that the investment of all survival dependence on one, presumably "true," outlook on the world in every detail is in fact an incredible risk; the risk is so much greater because only very limited areas of the world, in which we have to survive, can be said to be reasonably well understood by this outlook. Nevertheless, that is the gamble we are actually engaging in by the present attempts at colonial and semicolonial institutional "development" of all non-Western peoples, be they Navajo Indians or others. Good intentions are certainly not lacking, but consciousness of the payoff in risks is.

3. Integrate the Western System

An alternative consists of the integration of the Western outlook within the Navajo model and in terms of the Navajo spatial model. The net result of this strategy would lead to the integration of Navajo and Western thought in a Navajo-biased frame, with both politically and educationally justified ends.[16]

I intend to use the model of spatial notions (as presented in chap. IV) in two ways: in the first place, the model should facilitate an unambiguous and clearly explicit education in the Navajo knowledge; in the second place, it should facilitate the introduction of Navajos to a cognitive context of foreign notions (i.e., Western notions or any other) which they learn in school. Further, these notions should be translated into the native system of knowledge as much as possible. In a way, then, this strategy is comparable to that of the foregoing section, the result being exactly the inverse of the previous one: Instead of reducing Navajo knowledge to Western knowledge, I rather defend the opposite. The general political or sociocultural reason for this maneuver is quite straightforward. In view of the impossibility (for the time being) of any clearly englobing metasystem approach (there is no adequate metalanguage and no rules of correspondence and translation that I know of), I try to safeguard as much as possible the typically native frame at the cost of the imported one, because its survival will enrich us and actual communication between cultural knowledge systems is certainly at the cost of the native one at the present time.

Education in the Native (Navajo) Spatial Knowledge

I conjecture that in education the explicit treatment of the Navajo spatial knowledge in schools, in geometry courses, and also in other parts of the curriculum (cf. below) would change the present unhappy situation dramatically. Consonant with the results of Cole and his coworkers on schooling and literacy, I argue that the explicit treatment of this material in a classroom setting would improve teacher's and pupil's understandings of spatial notions (Cole, 1979). I propose the following scheme, based on the results of the semantic analysis:

Postulates

1) Space (in Navajo knowledge) is finite, bounded, and absolute. This can be demonstrated through the model of the world that is held: every exist-

---

16. At first it was my intention to try to build a parallel development of Western and Navajo spatial organization. However, I would need a metalanguage that would at least be able to describe simultaneously and adequately both the static and the dynamic outlook. No formal sophistication whatever could be reached in this outlook, landing us with mere vague and analogous comparisons. The actual search for "correlations" between both systems of spatial representation thus became highly hazardous, leaving no possibility of describing the correlations in any significantly clear and unambiguous way. In view of all these drawbacks I decided to abandon this pro-

ing thing is contained in a saucerlike grand structure, which assigns a definite place to any imaginable entity. (One need not identify this structure with the Earth between the four Mountains, as long as the idea of an absolute, finite, and bounded space is rendered.)

2) Space, like the entities or objects within it, is dynamic. That is, all "entities," "objects," or similar units of action and perception must be considered as units that are engaged in continuous processes. In the same way, spatial units and spatial relationships are "qualitative" in this same sense and cannot be considered to be clearly defined, readily quantifiable and static in essence.

Elaborations: while the preceding "postulates" should be explored and demonstrated through numerous, indirect examples and can draw directly on the meanings in Navajo terminology and phrases, the elaborations of all specific notions should be more rigidly governed in the classroom.

In practice, all notions that were isolated from the Navajo vocabulary in Chapter I and Chapter III can be taught systematically, starting at whatever point one chooses. Perhaps the most convenient entry would be the more basic notions like "volumeness," "dimension," and "movement." In any event, a practical and pedagogical approach seems fairly easy, as, for example, "volumeness."

The following procedure can be followed step by step in order to convey the abstract notion of "volumeness":

1) The teacher has his pupils play with different types of objects, sets of objects, and the like, so as to cover all instances of volumeness encountered in the Navajo lexicon. In the first place, all different classificatory verbs in a way define different types of nonrandom objects, and other terms and expressions complete this picture.

2) Throughout the process, and at several different stages of this conscious and explicit exploration of the Navajo world of objects, grows the more abstract and englobing notion that all these phenomena are but instances of "volumeness" (a Navajo correlate to this noun is needed, as is the case for all technical and noncommon notions). Particular exercises to train the acquisition of the notion of "volumeness" can be introduced. The difference between this notion and notions like "movement" can be trained by a thorough and explicit comparison of instances of both notions.

Subsequently, all other notions of the Navajo spatial knowledge system can be taught in similar ways. Once the more basic (and less constituted) notions are acquired, one can introduce more sophisticated notions, that is, those that show several "constituents" in their semantic paraphrases. For example, let me explain:

---

gram and concentrate on a pedagogically feasible alternative. I acknowledge Dirk Batens' insights and advice on these points.

"Distance," a more or less metric notion that is acquired by Western children in a full and systematic way as late as the fourth or fifth year of schooling (cf. ten years of age, Piaget and Inhelder, 1947), can be introduced through the following processes of learning:

1) The teacher has the children play with rods, displacements of volumes, and so on, and tries to make the notion of "spatial distance" clear. It is treated as a more sophisticated and highly abstract form of "separateness" (which was acquired earlier because it is less sophisticated).

2) In a subsequent phase it is made clear in the same way (by trial and search with volumes, objects, sticks, or steps between them, etc.) that at least "something or someone" must be at a distance from "something or someone else," introducing in this way the constituent character of "volumeness" (object or ego) in the notion of distance; distance exists between instances of volumeness.

3) In similar ways the other constituents are introduced as necessary (but insufficient) components of "distance." In the end, at least the semantic characterization of "distance" (given in the semantic analysis of chap. IV) is acquired. It should be borne in mind, at all times, that the schooling process aims at acquiring the abstractions. Concrete instances as well as names for these instances can only serve as examples at the beginning of the procedure (of each attempt to get at each specific notion), but cannot hold as the definitions or abstractions themselves.[17]

This procedure can be followed until all notions of the semantic model given at the end of Chapter IV are taught in their specific characterization, that is, in their double role of having constituents and being constituents (for other notions). In this way, the Navajo notions of space and the total structure of Navajo spatial knowledge can be taught explicitly and with proper pedagogical means.

I scarcely elaborate on the actual and detailed educational means and devices that can be used in this process. I am confident that they would be somewhat similar to those used in the modern play-and-learn schools of the West, although proper and quite different strategies may be defensible. However, this is outside the domain of the present study. These questions are technical in nature and may well be delegated to the educational services and the specialists in those fields, who have insights into the practical matters of learning in a school setting. I am satisfied to have provided a general outline and hopefully to have demonstrated that a proper teaching of the Navajo spatial knowledge in (modern) schools is sensible, desirable, and indeed possible. It is up to the specialists in the curriculum services to try to implement this information in the proper pedagogical ways.

17. English, like most European languages, is ambiguous in this sense: the same word is used for the abstract notion and the geometric notion (most of the time) that is used to denote the concrete instance. The noun plays a double role, at two levels of thought.

Education in the Western Spatial System

Once a fully developed and well-trained knowledge of the Navajo spatial system is acquired, the (more or less corresponding) Western spatial knowledge can be instructed. Again, in order to avoid a blind and misunderstood training in a completely "foreign" knowledge system and, on the other hand, to restrict the reduction ultimately of the native categories to a Western-biased education, I propose to teach the Western notions against the fully conscious and explicit background of Navajo knowledge. If reduction need be, it will then be on the part of Western notions. I thus propose to teach the Western alternative at a later age, as a specific and differential elaboration on the same basic problems of interaction with the outside world, somewhat in the way the non-Western approaches to problems are, to a certain degree at least, taught to Western children once they have reached an age of understanding in a Western cultural context.

Consider the following postulates:

1) Space (in the Western knowledge system) is infinite, bounded and relative. This perspective, that so drastically differs from the Navajo view, can be taught in similar ways through reference to the basic scientific model of the world and can be visualized through substractions from the Navajo view: imagine a never ending line, imagine a circle as a continuous movement along its contour, imagine the characteristics of a ball (in fact very much the same way we were taught about the characteristics of these phenomena); imagine a relativistic point of view working with mere relations between things and nothing more—the Leibniz description, almost to the word, in his discussions against Newtonian absolute space (cf. Smart, 1964).

2) Space is static, just as the objects and entities within it are static. This may be teachable through the idea that Western space takes account of "snapshots," momentary pictures of Navajo spatial phenomena and acts upon them "as if" they were the things or phenomena (in a Navajo sense) themselves.

Elaborations: some training is, of course, required in order to instruct the above postulates, so that reasoning within such a world view becomes feasible to some degree. (I experienced difficulty in switching frames during fieldwork and I do not intend to minimize the difficulty of such an acquisition.)

From this point on, then, several Western notions of space, in fact geometrical systems can be instructed, always securing the delicate "translations" that were shown to be presupposed.[18]

18. I propose to start with notions that are generally closer to the Navajo native system than, for example, point (which was shown to be lacking completely). Whitehead (1953), in a brilliant little book, demonstrates that geometry and all geometrical theses can be built with equal validity and equal strength, starting alternatively from "point," or "volume," or "surface" as primitive notions. Starting from the primitive "volume," one can subsequently satisfactorily define "surface" and any other geometric notion, ending with "point" as the most detailed and complex notion of the whole system. In other words, the approach is possible with equal validity

For "volume," the following procedure can be followed:

1) In rehearsing the Navajo notion of volumeness, the ways in which (Western) geometric notions of volume are similar to and at variance with the former notion can easily be pointed out. A major difference that is easily clarified concerns the static-dynamic dichotomy. Again, the volume notion is special in the sense that it results in a "snapshot" view or a momentary slice of the dynamic volumeness instances known in Navajo. Besides such features, the strictly metric nature can be explained in a similar way (for instance, segmentability and respecting of constancy of form is basic and easily instructed by drawing on the work of Piaget). Instances of volumeness can be reduced or manipulated, in practice as well as theoretically, to result in the type of regular and highly symmetrical forms that Westerners deal with as volumes. A high degree of similarity, if not identity, between Western and Navajo volumeness lies in the fact that volumes can be manipulated, perceived, classified, reconstructed, and so on in the same way as instances of volumeness can. The difference between the notions is a set of supplementary, and therefore highly refined, features.

Similar explorations of differences and likenesses between Navajo and Western concepts can be performed, both at a practical (active, concrete) level and at a theoretical level. A supplementary and more difficult task is the teaching and systematically explicit analysis of the difference in relational definitions (or semantic characterizations) between pairs of notions. This theoretical work, that is, construing the appropriate sets of relations and definitions, is most often done through contrasts with the corresponding structural information in the Navajo spatial knowledge system. I propose that this level of reasoning, which informs the actual axiomatic way of relating and structuring that is typical of all sophisticated Western knowledge, be introduced through drills or through a detailed analysis of the use of logical rules in the Western system. The latter are easily linked with native Navajo logical rules that are, no doubt, much the same as the Western ones (cf. examples in analysis and field material): consistency, coherence, and logical operators are stressed in explaining and teaching the Western (absolutely crucial) dependence on them in the elaborated form of geometrical reasoning.

But let me, for the sake of clarity and strength of argument, point out in very general terms what procedure can be followed to introduce the basic notions of Western geometry starting from "volume."

2) In a second step, the notion of "line" can be introduced: whenever two concrete volumes (in the above sense) touch each other at several points in a row, the structure that can be seen, drawn or "walked" (eventually) through all these points, by passing and touching each point once, constitutes

---

and strength from a multitude of perspectives. It is this idea that I would like to refer to here (in a less strict and less sophisticated way, to be sure). I consequently propose to introduce volume first in the instruction of Navajos, eventually ending up with other notions of more "primitive" status, but at a much later stage.

a line. Visually, the connection between sky and heaven is such a line. As well as the connection between two "volumes," a concatenation of places where both touch each other, like a mountain and a river, is seen as an ever-progressing concatenation.

3) Whenever two volumes touch or overlap with one "side," the notion of "surface" can be reached.

4) Whenever two volumes touch or overlap in such a way that their place of being together is but one and cannot be seen or visualized or made to progress in any direction, but to be always the same place, we have a point. And so on.

The descriptive sophistication of these steps can be improved greatly. Again, I refer those interested to the brilliant work of Whitehead on these topics to get an idea of a much more appropriate (i.e., less intuitive and "logically" messy) version of this line of thought. What I intend to do here is merely to point out a possible way of communication between the two systems, without worrying about the appropriateness of the steps and notions implied. It is up to a well-trained pedagogue or psychologist to "translate," as it were, Whitehead's suggestions into the proper and correct form that would suit the instruction of Navajos. The general nature of such translations should have become clear from this exposition.

Elaboration of Other Materials along These Lines

The preceding type of instruction is not restricted, of course, to mathematical (or, more strictly still, geometrical) reasoning alone. Similar "programs" can, and should, be worked out for other domains of the curriculum where space is implied.

Geography obviously employs plenty of spatial representation. It would be quite interesting to develop a geographical segment of a social studies curriculum that would take into account the dynamic and holistic perspective of Navajo space. For example:

a) A mountain or a valley should not necessarily be introduced the way "objects" are in the Western context, but should rather be represented as a complex unit of mutual interaction, where valley and mountain aspects change status over the years. The dynamic interactive relationship between the two is what counts most in the teaching.

b) The earth should not be subdivided easily into states, but should primarily be seen as a relatively constant body surrounded by water, wherein different life-circles or territories are identified, that is, the cities, the spaces of peoples, the communities, and so on. These life-circles exhibit a relatively dense pattern of interaction with each other (some more, some less) and have a dense inner scheme of interaction; they have a certain amount of growth, decay, change, and so on.

This approach to geography can, of course, be worked out in full detail and may yield very interesting results. The approach is not at all outlandish, since the so-called New Geographers have tried to work upon Western geographical notions in somewhat similar (but less radically elaborated) ways: see Gould and White (1974) and the pioneering work by Lynch (1960). On the other hand, the beautiful book on Ifugao geography by Conklin (1980) could be used as an example of this approach in other cultures.

Natural sciences can, obviously, be recast in a similar way. The organismic view of persons and animals as "systems that were placed to work in specific ways" can easily be emphasized in education, instead of the objective and segmentability-centered approach of contemporary Western teaching. Again, this alternative is not so alien to modern perspectives in the life sciences: Waddington (1977, chaps. 1, 2) stresses the importance of an alternative, dynamic, and even organismic approach in these disciplines today. Nature seen as a symbiotic system with ecosystems and relatively autonomous biological systems (man, animals, plants) can be a rewarding outlook.

Even in disciplines such as history, social science, and linguistics, a similar approach can yield important results. In each of these, the systemic and diachronic outlook of Navajo knowledge could be worked into the syllabus.

What Is the Use of All This?

It will have become clear that I push toward a genuinely native approach to aspects of knowledge that seem to be rather "established" in the Western context. The general question that arises against such a laborious and painstaking reorientation of parts of knowledge and schooling will be: what is the use of all this? or, why engage in such a hazardous and unwarranted enterprise instead of sticking to established data and disciplines?

I have a number of different and important (not to say universally relevant) reasons for proposing such a complicated approach:

1) The Navajo reason: in the very first place, there is today the phenomenon of the totally inappropriate education, leading to misunderstanding and sociocultural and psychological alienation of Navajo children and adults. With its almost complete lack of consideration for the authentic Navajo world view, the school curriculum is scarcely integrated into the native context. The result is that people at some point have to choose between their native system of knowledge and the Western alternative. Most people never choose and come to live and think in a "divided world," partly Navajo and partly Western. Nobody deserves this second-rate treatment in a democratic society. The alternative, as I emphasized earlier in this chapter, is a redesign of the curriculum in terms of the native frame. This is precisely what I have tried to accomplish in this third alternative. I know of some institutions that try to work in this fashion, notably the Division for Curriculum Services at Albuquerque, the community schools at Rock Point and Rough Rock, and some individual workers. It is hoped that the present work can be helpful for them in the domains that have been treated here.

2) The epistemological reason from a Western point of view: it is fascinating and theoretically rewarding to try to work out alternatives to the his-

torically and culturally specific outlook that predominates nowadays. The challenge of bridging the tremendous gap of quasi-intranslatability and incommensurability between Western and non-Western outlooks is a most rewarding and important task for any (Western) scientist who claims to work toward universal truths. The formal and interpretational intricacies of such a program codetermine the adequacy of a particular proposition. So, apart from the political and social dimensions of this and similar researches, I want to emphasize the epistemological relevance.

3) The evolutionary reason: finally, and from the most general point of view, an evolutionary argument appears compelling. Through a systematic superimposition of the world view and thought system of the West on traditional non-Western systems of thought and action all over the world, a tremendous uniformization is taking hold. In the past, inputs from other cultures into the Western pool of thought have proved significant and at some points even crucial (e.g., the impact of some Chinese concepts via Leibniz's transformation of modern mathematics and physics), while the orderly communication and interaction with Western ideas proves beneficial to other cultures at some points. However, through the systematic extinction of other systems of knowledge that is now taking place, the original "pool of responses" (a metaphor, of course) is dramatically reduced and eventually ends up being identical with the Western pool. The risks we take on a worldwide scale, and the impoverishment we witness is—evolutionarily speaking—quite frightening. As long as science cannot pretend to have valid answers to all basic questions (as is the case in our contemporary situation, because only some aspects of nature and social life can be treated with satisfactory validity and confidence in the still-incomplete scientific system), it is foolish to exterminate all other, so-called primitive, prescientific, or otherwise foreign approaches to world questions.

One does not have to believe with J. Needham (1956) that Chinese models are appropriate for the (Western) life sciences where the native (Western) outlook fails to apply in a satisfactory way. However, mutual inspiration and interaction at a fundamental level of epistemology and ontology (natural philosophy, strictly speaking) will probably always be rewarding and illuminating in all instances. In view of this general appreciation of the possible relevance for survival and the value of a multitude of perspectives (rather than the unique approach at the cost of all others or whatever culturally biased perspective one may cherish), I mean to defend the sensibility and the possible power of the conscious and full-fledged elaboration of native knowledge (e.g., the Navajo system). This should be maintained to the extent where comparison and mutual influences can be mapped, or even planned, in an egalitarian way. As a concretization of this general strategy I propose, for example, that it may be very inspiring for a mathematician to try to construe an axiomatization of dynamic topology, in a broader and less confined way than Thom has tried to do, starting with the insights of Navajo spatial knowledge. The elementary and intuitive inspiration that springs from the confrontation with a system of thought that differs on such basic levels cannot be measured beforehand, that is, without full consciousness and primary consideration of the spatial knowledge system as such.

The foregoing arguments unite in a general appreciation of the strength and validity of particular theories and models of science, converging to the position held by Don Campbell (1973, 1979). All human beings confront the world in much the same way, notwithstanding their particular cultures, and deal with almost identical questions, even if they receive somewhat different elaborations. If an evolutionary model of science and truth has validity, as I agree with Campbell that it does, then the variability and the multitude of perspectives is valuable, certainly in areas where the validity and strength of presumed scientific models and theories are so weak as to prohibit valid prediction. I share the conviction that inability in this aspect is characteristic of a lot of disciplinary knowledge today, and I therefore defend the thesis that as many rational approaches as possible should be supported and elaborated to serve as a comprehensive analysis of life questions at some later point. The Navajo thought system certainly is rational in several aspects and can therefore, when it is fully elaborated, illuminate the Western system at some points, and vice versa. It is the task of philosophers of science and anthropologists to try to elaborate more adequate criteria of rationality (a task currently being undertaken by several scholars) and to organize an effective and nonalienating communication with, and interaction between, non-Western cultural knowledge systems that are not extinguished, through a confrontation with foundational propositions of the modern sciences.

VI | General Conclusions

In the present investigation I intended a comprehensive exposition and analysis of Navajo spatial knowledge. My general view is most closely related to that of cognitive anthropologists, although I attempted to give a somewhat different and improved model of semantic analysis and representation, as well as a substantially more elaborate philosophical treatment of Navajo knowledge than is known to us in the ethnoscientific and cognitive anthropological literature to date.

All the material necessary for a better understanding of the analyses presented in the preceding chapters is brought together in two parts: Chapter III contains the information on Navajo spatial terminology while "The Device" (Appendix B) details the main device (the UFOR) used throughout the fieldwork, the recording, and the analysis of material.

The aim of the study was achieved in three steps and the results can likewise be summed up in three main points:

1) An alternative approach to semantic analysis is defended, which claims solely to use and recognize only synthetic or nonaprioristic information in the actual analysis of verbal and nonverbal material of a system of cultural knowledge (the spatial knowledge of the Navajos) and in the construction of an adequate and efficient semantic model of this domain of knowledge. In this respect the difficult and tremendously detailed differentiation of spatial recognition and conceptualization in Navajo language and action offered an extremely fruitful and promising case for study. The importance and factual feasibility of a synthetic approach was demonstrated in the most concrete way through the possibility of designing programs of action or directives for application in the curricula of primary and other grade courses in Navajo schools. Indeed, the subtle, but quite important and basic, differences in preschool knowledge of Navajo and Western children could be taken into account in a systematic and unbiased way by adopting this approach. The range and impact of the differences was made clear with appropriate "corrections" the least, and alternative strategies for teaching matters, dealing with and building upon these preschool conceptions, the most discernible, through the systematic avoidance of aprioristic elements in the modeling and application of differentiations in meaning. Consequently, it is contended that the possibility of nonaprioristic semantic analysis has been demonstrated sufficiently in this study, both at the level of fieldwork and at that of "data"

analysis. Together with this theoretical point, it needs to be emphasized that the consequent directives for educational planning and reorientation of school curricula toward a genuine development of a people's natural knowledge is one of the most urgent aims of this study. I hope that the possibility of a truly democratic-minded educational focus, with unmitigated respect for the native knowledge, may gain some benefit from the work done here. The problem can no longer be stated as naïvely as it was before, when native knowledge was but a collection of "faits divers" and "things," so to speak, and when education was to provide the necessary and evidently Western network of relationships. Even this, already somewhat respectful treatment, is demonstrated to be naïve. Instead, the possibility, the worldwide necessity, and the actual production of instruments for the implementation of a curriculum that would actively build on the native knowledge provided by different peoples (i.e., the Navajos) should be brought into focus. Since knowledge acquisition ought not to alienate, the author of this study hopes to have provided some insights (and a preliminary outline of a course of action) to avoid this effect. Beyond this, the hope is to have paved the way toward the genuine development of other (than Western) knowledges to the highest levels of explicitness.

2) The study demonstrates analysis and recording of the deep sense of native philosophical insights. I emphasized the natural philosophical ideas I found, and integrated them in several questions of spatial semantics at different levels of abstractness. It needs to be reiterated that this was done in accord with the golden rule of cognitive anthropology, where the native consultants are continuously and necessarily involved in any process of investigation of their cultural knowledge. The result underscored the fact that such philosophical insights play a role, or at least are relevant, for several less sophisticated notions (space semantics).

The basic attitude I learned in using and applying these philosophical insights in other domains of Navajo knowledge was to systematically search for a consistent and coherent interpretation of reality. Navajo consultants showed me the way in this respect, a way that I followed with some hesitation in the beginning, but with full enthusiasm toward the end. Apart from the matter actually discussed here I learned to take seriously what Western philosophers like Carnap (1958) agree to call "proper thinking," particularly regarding the Navajo thinker and Navajo knowledge. The point implied, but not fully worked out in this investigation, is that there are various "levels" of thought in any community, including the thought of non-Western peoples. Only a few people were able to talk freely and thoroughly about highly abstract relationships between more commonsense items of knowledge. However, those few who did talk dealt with them in a thoroughly systematic, critical, and sophisticated way. Most people I encountered knew something in a more or less practical way about the proper relationships between aspects of reality. Apart from these "domains" or "levels" of thought, clearly esoteric knowledge was reserved for some specialists. The latter type of notion seemed at first to relate to philosophical thought, but with clear extrapolations and "applications" in ceremonial behavior. This general characterization deserves more exploration. A fact that emerges in no uncertain terms from the present line of research is that anthropologists and laymen alike should, in the future, be more careful when talking about "*the* Navajo" or "*the* so and so," in order to avoid the inherent ambiguity of the nomenclature, especially where knowledge is concerned.

3) The study demonstrated the usefulness of the "Universal Frame of Reference" approach for the analysis of spatial knowledge and spatial language of other cultures. As was pointed out, in the course of the investigation the UFOR was used at each level of data eliciting, semantic identification, and model building. It was set up to provide subtlety and breadth of elicitation on the one hand, and a sensitive control of the role of intuition and fantasy on the part of the investigator (anthropologist) on the other. In my judgment it served its purpose very well, particularly in the investigation of so vast (and almost unmanageable) a domain as the differentiations in language and behavior of space. A genuine advantage of the present domain of study (Navajo spatial knowledge) was the feedback information I got from the field: indeed, as was anticipated where I pointed out the dialectic status of the UFOR, the Navajo information on space necessitated adaptations in some respects (introduction of the Convergence/Divergence entry and modification of entries in minor respects). Since universality, concomitant with the general view of semantics, can be reached only a posteriori, this result was indeed enthusiastically received. The UFOR showed its strength both in coping with the bulk of Navajo material and in its adaptability on specific points; the multiplication of the same form in studies of other cultural knowledge systems may finally enable me to achieve a more solidly and amply amended version, ending (in the tradition of the Munsell card for color analysis) with a strictly aposterioristic Universal Frame of Reference.

Appendix A

List of Consultants

A final word is due the people who helped throughout the present investigation with intellectual, moral, and sometimes material means. Oswald Werner, Ed Garrison, Allan Manning, and John Farella were among the white "consultants." Most of all, the beautiful and everlasting attention and help of the Navajos should be remembered. I hope to have been able to come up to the standards of a great people by bringing to them something that can serve them.

Navajo Consultants

All consultants listed below worked with us at different times and places, some throughout the period of fieldwork, some more occasionally.

FH: Frank Harvey, main consultant and interpreter, age 66, Naakai clan, Lukachukai.

CM: Curly Mustache, consultant, monolingual, wise man, age 104, Tsaile.

TB: Tabaahah Begay, consultant, monolingual, Tabaahah clan, age 53, Sweetwater and Rock Point.

M-AL: Mary-Ann Lee, monolingual, consultant, age 65, Bitter Water clan, Lukachukai.

LB: Lorraine Boomer, bilingual interpreter, age 30, Black Sheep clan, Crystal.

AD: Agnes Dodge, consultant, monolingual, age 75, Black Sheep clan, Crystal.

BB: Ben Barney, consultant, bilingual, age 34, Rock Point.

LT: Leroy Tsineginnie, consultant, bilingual, age 35, Many Goats clan, Rock Point.

RB: Rita Begay, interpreter, bilingual, age 26, Rock Point.

HT: Harold Tsoh, consultant, monolingual, age 50, Sweetwater.

DH: Dolly Harvey, consultant, bilingual, age 65, Bitter Water clan, Lukachukai.

BW: Ben Williams, consultant, bilingual, age 58, Cow Springs.

KB: Kenneth Begishe, consultant, bilingual, age 40, Shonto.

Appendix B

"The Device": A Synoptic and Revised Edition of the
Universal Frame of Reference for Spatial Analysis

The analytic tool used throughout this work is called the Universal
Frame of Reference for spatial analysis (UFOR). A previous version was
worked out in a dissertation (Pinxten, 1975). Some modifications seemed necessary. I shall present here the UFOR in full, but in a concise form, so as both
to inform the present work and to offer any interested researcher its use as
applied to any other culture.

The Status of the Frame

When first approaching it, a UFOR can be understood as an alternative
to a field manual. In the first place, through the use of the UFOR, a limited
area of human experience is focused on, in this case, spatial differentiations.
In the second place, a genuinely universalist pretension is typical. Whereas
field manuals shun involvement in the universalist-relativist issue, the UFOR
approach presupposes degrees of universality in the area under investigation.
That is, it is a framework, the presentation of which has to be compatible with
the study of any particular culture one may encounter. Consequently, universality cannot and will not be ascribed a priori: it can only result from numerous detailed analyses in the field.

The present UFOR was tested on the Dogon of Mali (on the basis of
written and printed material, not of fieldwork) and was put to test in the field
with the Navajos of Arizona. It was changed and modified in some aspects
after each "test" so as to gain further universal strength from the detailed empirical studies. A second criterion of universality is manifested in the actual
formulas and presentation arrangements of the present UFOR. It will be dealt
with later in this appendix. It can be mentioned here that the same demand for
empirical testing is upheld for each of the formulas introduced.

The frame was initially inspired by a close acquaintance with the
Munsell card, as used in Berlin and Kay (1969) and with the Goodenough
(1970) program. Berlin and Kay's analysis of semantic categorization of color
discriminations works with the physiologically defined set of color differentiations presented in the Munsell card. In this way they visualized the extent
of the psychologically and perceptually relevant domain of color differentiation for the consultants. Goodenough could not work with perceptual or other-

wise directly ostensive or denotable entities since he worked on kinship characteristics. He constructs a general set of criteria or underlying properties that play a role in the organization of kin relations in any culture (language), starting with the extensive series of kinship studies that we have at our disposal after a tradition of more than a hundred years. It is important to note that his criteria ("components" in Goodenough's terminology) are purely theoretical in nature and have no direct psychological or physiological correlates.

It is to these forerunners in the anthropological literature that the present UFOR refers. However, this reference is not blind and implies several ramifications. Color and space are two qualitatively different physical phenomena which are processed in perhaps cognitively different ways. I have the impression that color can be expressed by means of a physical continuum precisely because there is only one (or at least one dominant) physical "quality" of color, so to speak. It can be measured in a uniform way by means of a unique set of criteria (i.e., a measure on the dimensions of hue, brightness, and saturation). Human beings tend to cope with this physical phenomenon in a way which is particular to the cultural tradition they are raised in. The term or category of "space," however, has a different status. In some specific instances there is a direct link between a cultural or semantic unit (e.g., volume, hole) and some unit in the phenomenal world (e.g., a box, a hole in the ground). In these cases, spatial phenomena can be compared, to a considerable degree, with color instances in that they can be pointed at or experientially discriminated from background aspects by an agent: a red object can be pointed to in one's environment, just as a box (or voluminous object) can. In both cases the color aspect or the spatial aspect can be known through direct reference to something which exhibits this facet. However, most spatial characteristics do not have this simple featurelike status: overlapping, being near, being distant, and so on are all relationshps between phenomenal instances. Being homogeneous, being discontinuous, and the like are features which specify relationships in space or other spatial features. It is clear that spatial notions have a variety of levels of abstraction and cannot be mapped out in a uniform and standardized format like the one we find in the Munsell card for color differentiation.

Furthermore, the abstract concept of "space" covers a vast domain of physically and semantically disparate features. One could distinguish at least three qualitatively different "spaces" in the Western knowledge system: topological, projective and Euclidean spaces, noting that the characteristics of each of them are not reducible in any strict sense to those of the other two. It is, for all these reasons, difficult and dangerous to strive for too strong a uniformity in the construction of the UFOR. I chose to develop the framework from a central perspective on knowledge building, which seems warranted at the present stage of cross-cultural knowledge (Lloyd, 1972): all human beings are agents and perceivers and it is through perception of and interaction with the environment that they build up knowledge. Consequently, the minimal paraphrases of the UFOR entries stress the praxiological character of the focussed spatial notions. That is to say, the ethnographer approaches the consultant with a set of notions which express, as much as possible, body motions, and features of action and interaction with the environment, as well as perceptual characteristics inherent to the spatial phenomena discussed. It is necessary to start here, rather than with abstract or fully processed cognitive features of the spatial notions themselves as found in the ethnographer's or consultant's cultural knowledge system. This is a major rule of uniformity in the present UFOR.

In the second place, I tried to construct each entry as an autonomous unit of the frame, that is, I tried to avoid relationships of definition or of hierarchy between particular entries as much as possible. This rule of uniformity was aimed at, without actually applying it in each instance. The meaning and impact of the second rule is clear: Piaget described the spatial system of the Western child as a logical and hierarchical structure (Piaget and Inhelder, 1947: each notion is logically deduced from a simpler one), ending up with one least and one most complex spatial notion. It is by no means obvious that this structure (provided it is adequate to picture the Western spatial knowledge system) is universal. A first glance at the Navajo spatial model in the present model (chap. IV) or at the spatial knowledge of other cultures (e.g., Pinxten, 1976a) immediately makes clear that neither the strict logical structures nor the hierarchical ordering of notions, need to be present in non-Western systems. Therefore, the relationships between each and every notion of space cannot be presupposed by the researcher. Consequently, the device to reach knowledge of the spatial system of another culture, the UFOR, cannot be biased on this point. It is in light of these arguments that I chose to introduce each entry of the UFOR as a minimally connected or maximally autonomous nucleus. Reasons of intelligibility forced me to drop this rule from time to time (e.g., it is cumbersome or next to impossible to introduce horizontality without using some notion of dimension), but the rule was safeguarded to the fullest possible limit.

The experiential aspect of space in behavior and perception is important to the anthropologist, but an approach which would focus on this aspect exclusively cannot capture the metaphorical and social use of spatial representations and segmentations. Since the latter is equally important to the anthropologist, three possible approaches remain open to me:

1) A detailed set of spatial concepts of one particular culture could be used as a UFOR for all cultural knowledge. Data may be found which are satisfying and agreeable for that purpose in the ethnographic material of some particular cultures (the Dogon or the Tewa, for example). However, the comparability of data is a priori, so highly biased by this approach that it seems uneconomical to adapt this perspective if one wants to guarantee at least some universality.

2) The set of Western spatial concepts could be taken as a frame for cultural analysis. At an initial stage, I took this approach to be rewarding, since our knowledge of this specific outlook on space is indeed extensive by now (Pinxten, 1976a). However, the bias of one particular cultural outlook, namely the Western, remains a strong hindrance to comparison.

3) A maximally general and scientifically defined set of spatial terms and concepts can be proposed as a neutral and sufficiently flexible UFOR. This alternative is chosen here. It implies that I had to construe an artifact, an especially constructed frame that is likely to function as a guide within any particular culture (to guarantee universality a posteriori) and still pose enough constraints to avoid truism. The precise character of the present frame is made clear through its structural features.

The Structure of the UFOR

The generality of the frame is guaranteed at this level by three prerequisites:

1) The terms that can serve as entries in the UFOR represent the set of spatially relevant characteristics and distinctions, in our, as well as in any, conceivable language or cultural knowledge system. They match the set of terms and expressions that can be found in a thesaurus of Western common-sense knowledge (e.g., Roget's Thesaurus) and are, furthermore, generalized by the application of material from non-Western cultural knowledge systems. Each term represents a set of specific perceptual, actional, and representational spatial differentiations. It is defined—in a minimal way—in neutral, that is, scientifically viable and action-directed statements. Information from different disciplines (physics, geography, cosmology, architecture, urban studies, philosophy, psychology of perception and action, anthropology) is used and rendered in as general a form as possible, in praxiological (action-directed) paraphrases.

2) The entries are ill-defined. This feature is most pronounced in, and made prominent through, an attempt to reduce the interdependency of the spatial aspects introduced. In the Western spatial system—most strikingly in geometry, of course—all spatial differentiations are interrelated with one another in a more or less strictly deductive network of relationships. This "system" is too specific for the purpose of cross-cultural application of the UFOR. The bias of a particular cultural system in the actual UFOR is only avoided when the interrelatedness of the entries of the frame is maximally reduced. Indeed, the specific way of defining, construing, and interrelating separate spatial differentiations in a given culture is guaranteed, provided the framework one uses to approach that culture allows for as many alternative ways of systematizing or constructing as possible. This prerequisite is fulfilled by the present UFOR through the avoidance of clear and binding links or definitional relationships between separate entries. It is in this sense that the entries in the UFOR are badly defended: they tend to blur or altogether neglect relationships with other entries in the specific definitions or paraphrases offered.

3) The entries are defined in a standardized way, as much as possible.

The Use of the UFOR

In actual use each and every entry of the UFOR are handled as if they were "primitives" to the native system of differentiation and segmentation: that is, any set of basic spatial characteristics can only be agreed upon by the consultants themselves, and not by the bias or the philosophical or cultural preference of the investigator. It is only through the detailed and painstaking analysis of the relationships between all native differentiations, carried out with the help of native consultants, that the more basic notions will be distinguished from "derived" ones.

The ethnographer and the consultant use the same UFOR entries as a common ground for mutual understanding, and as a mutual control on the correct understanding of the native categories being discovered. Both at the level of eliciting information and at that of model building of the native spatial knowledge, the same UFOR can be used as a guiding device by native consultant and ethnographer alike.

With the detection of native-specific differentiations, the initial formulations of the UFOR entries are abandoned and native correlates or alternatives are introduced. Both, the specific paraphrases of and the actual differentiations in entries of the UFOR can be corrected in the field experience. The particular formulation of each of them is most certainly neglected in the process of constructing the specific native semantic domains mapped out with the gradual comprehension of the native terminology and behavioral differentiations of space. Thus, while the more or less neutral device of the UFOR is used most thoroughly in the process of detection and exploration (by native consultant and ethnographer) of the native knowledge, it is not to be referred to in any literal sense for the actual construction of native paraphrases or semantic domains. On the other hand, the UFOR entries themselves can be refined and reconsidered through the information gathered in another cultural knowledge system. So while the UFOR plays an important role in the detection phase of the investigation, it cannot determine the resulting emic descriptions. On the other hand, the emic descriptions in culture X or Y will have a feedback on the paraphrases and distinctions of the UFOR later on.

Divisions in the UFOR[1]

By virtue of universally acceptable divisions of action and perceptual experience of the external world in terms of varying ranges of magni-

---

1. With the Navajo field experience it proved necessary to introduce a supplementary pair of distinctions in the original UFOR: convergence/divergence had to be taken into account as a separate entry in its present, modified form.

tude, it seems reasonable to sort out three different "spaces" in semantic representations:

1) The physical space (also termed object space) ranges over all those characteristics of space or of spatial phenomena that human beings can manipulate, handle, look upon as a whole, move in totality, and so on. It sorts out those aspects of spatial phenomena that are treated as wholes by the human agent-perceiver. As such, only comparatively small phenomena, and those moreover having an objectlike appearance, fall into this category. Humans cannot manipulate a house or a mountain as they can a dog or a wooden pole, for example.

2) The sociogeographical space is comprised of all those aspects of space that are ascribed to phenomena of larger magnitude than object space. That is, it concerns those spatial phenomena that human beings can only be confronted with or locate themselves *in*, without being able to genuinely manipulate them. Man cannot see or manipulate the spatial phenomena of this range in an objectlike way. Human beings cannot be said to move or act upon the totality of a house, for instance, whereas they can enter that space or confront it. The same holds true for acres, countries, and so forth.

3) The cosmological space is comprised of all phenomena of a still larger range of magnitude, for example, the sun, the universe, and the like. Here again, a different way of experiencing is an important criterion: human beings know about cosmological phenomena only in indirect ways, generally limited to observation at a distance. No other means of contact is possible (except in very recent developments in the West, of course). Here one finds the earth as a whole, and also the celestial phenomena.

| UFOR for Spatial Analysis
List of Entries

100. Physical or object space
101. Spatial aspects
102. Near, separate, contiguous
103. Part/whole
104. Bordering, bounding
105. Overlapping
106. Internal/external; central/peripheral
107. Open/closed
108. Converging/diverging
109. Volumeness/planeness
110. Succeeding; ordering
111. Preceding/following (in front of, in back of)
112. In perspective
113. Deep, far (dimension of depth)
114. Distant (metric)
115. Upon/under; above/below
116. Vertical, upright (dimension)

117. High; deep (metric)
118. Lateral; next to
119. Left/right
120. Horizontal (dimension)
121. Wide; broad (metric)
122. Cardinal points, cardinal directions
123. Coordinate systems
124. Multidimensionally extended (metric)
125. Geometric point
126. Geometrically linear, straight
127. Geometrically pointing, parallel, being an angle
128. Geometrically being a volume, a surface
129. Geometric figures
130. Resting, moving
131. Moving along one dimension
132. Moving linearly; curving; rotating; spiraling
133. Having a direction in movement
134. Being spatially random/spatially determinable
140. Global spatial characteristics
141. Absolute/relative
142. Finite/infinite
143. Bounded/unbounded
144. Continuous/discontinuous
145. Homogeneous/heterogeneous
200. Sociogeographical space
201. Spatial aspects
202. Near, separate, contiguous
203. Part/whole
204. Bordering, bounding
205. Overlapping
206. Internal/external; central/peripheral
207. Open/closed
208. Converging/diverging
209. Volumeness/planeness
211. Preceding/following (in front of, in back of)
213. Deep, far (dimension of depth)
214. Distant (metric)
215. Upon/under; above/below
216. Vertical, upright (dimension)
217. High/deep (metric)
218. Lateral; next to
219. Left/right
220. Horizontal (dimension)
221. Wide, broad (metric)
222. Cardinal points, cardinal directions
223. Coordinate systems

224. Multidimensionally extended (metric)
225. Geometric notions
226. Geometrically linear, straight
227. Geometrically pointing, parallel, being an angle
228. Geoso: surface, volume in sociogeographical space
229. Map, scale
230. Resting; moving
231. Being (on) a path; orienting
232. Navigating
233. Having a direction in movement
240. Global characteristics of sociogeographic space
241. Absolute/relative
242. Finite/infinite
243. Bounded/unbounded
244. Continuous/discontinuous
245. Homogeneous/heterogeneous
300. Cosmological space
301. Aspects of space
302. Near, separate, contiguous
303. Part/whole
304. Bordering, bounding
305. Overlapping
306. Internal/external; central/peripheral
307. Open/closed
308. Converging/diverging
309. Volumeness, planeness
311. Preceding/following (in front of, in back of)
313. Deep, far (dimension of depth)
314. Distant (metric)
315. Upon/under; above/below
316. Vertical, upright (dimension)
317. High, deep (metric)
318. Lateral; next to
319. Left/right
320. Horizontal (dimension)
321. Wide; broad (metric)
322. Cardinal points, cardinal directions
323. Coordinate systems
324. Multidimensionally extended (metric)
325. Geometric notions
326. Earth
327. Moon
329. Planets
330. Stars, constellations, universe
331. Comets, meteors, and meteorites
332. Rotation of celestial units (including earth)

333. Movements of earth-sky (constellations)
334. Movements of the universe
335. Relations between earth-sun, earth-moon, planets-earth, planets-sun
336. Phenomenal space versus real space
340. Global characteristics of cosmological space
341. Absolute/relative
342. Finite/infinite
343. Bounded/unbounded
344. Continuous/discontinuous
345. Homogeneous/heterogeneous

The Function of the UFOR

It is important to remind oneself of the philosophical positions one tends to take, even if one is not fully conscious of them. The use of a UFOR approach cannot be neutral with respect to the universalist-relativist discussion in anthropology and linguistics. I should therefore like to clarify the implications of the present position.

My position accepts it as a fact that different perspectives of the world are possible and are actually expressed in different, culture-specific knowledge systems throughout the world. This position has been termed cultural relativism (Herskovits, Whorf) and is more broadly covered in epistemological relativism (Campbell, 1977). If universalism were guaranteed a priori, there would be no need to construe a device like the UFOR: it would be adequate to stick to the one generally accepted true version of knowledge. Since I favor the possibility of universals a posteriori, a device like the UFOR suggests itself as a possible and indeed necessary research tool.

On the other hand, I tend to sympathize with ontological realism (rather than ontological relativism or "nihilism," cf. Campbell, 1979), which claims that there is one world and one universal source of information for whatever possible cultural outlook one may come across. The relativism, if any, is epistemological and not ontological. In any event it remains to be seen in what ways and to what degree relativism is valid regarding the latter, and the UFOR may serve to clarify matters in this respect, but I conjecture that reality is unique and uniform for all human perceivers/agents.

The UFOR, in its optimal form, serves as a minimal ontology, so to speak. That is, it simulates the set of phenomena and features of the "external world" for such widely differing perspectives on nature and reality as those of Western researchers and non-Western consultants. They use the UFOR entries as a common ground, on "what is there" in the external world that is represented in some way in each cultural knowledge system. In this respect, the UFOR acts again as a heuristic and intuition-controlling device.

Given this interpretation of the UFOR, one problem arises: why are its entries described in terms of human actions and human perceptions? I propose to solve it the following way. Honoring both the validity of ontological realism and of epistemological relativism, I claim that man's only chance to say anything true and sensible about the external world (its ontological character) is by drawing on his experience of constraints imposed by the external world on his knowledge of that world. In other words, since the constraints exercised on human behavior (action) and perception by the phenomena which human beings want to know about are the only source of his actual knowledge of the "real phenomena" (aspects of reality), these constraints are tantamount to the building of a (tentative) ontology. It is for this reason that all entries of the UFOR are phrased in terms of the features of perception and action that human beings tend to employ to assimilate knowledge of the world. The specific interpretations and emphases of particular percepts and actions or results of actions are in the realm of specific knowledge systems.

Obviously I do not hold any divine knowledge as to the validity of the ontological perspective presented. I will have to reconsider entries and their paraphrases during the process of applying the UFOR.

Entries of the UFOR

102. Near, Separate, Contiguous

Aspects, things, phenomena, movements, and so forth, anything that can be perceived, handled, or otherwise experienced by human beings, are said to be in a relationship of nearness or proximity to each other (and/or to the observing subject), if the observer handles them in a mutually non-differential way. He sees them as a set, or acts upon them as if they were one thing rather than a series of them, and so on. In the experience of the Western child, as studied by Piaget and Inhelder (1947; 1972, p. 15), the surrounding space is primarily structured through the identification of groupings of phenomena in various locations on the experiential field: each grouping is handled as a unit and is considered distinct from any other. However, each grouping can comprise several objects that are not mutually distinguished for the sake of the primary structuring of space in the child.

More generally, then, the paraphrase of nearness can be given as follows:[2]

a) Anything experienced in the human being and termed x can be considered near anything else, termed y, provided y is near x also, and

b) The given x and y are near, provided, moreover, that they are distin-

---

2. In this paraphrase and in the following, the agent/perceiver himself can be one of the items of physical space dealt with and thus may be conceived as a substitute for an x or a y on occasion. This relativistic interpretation need not be dealt with separately, since the same formal criteria obtain in both specific cases.

guishable in action or perception for the human being, but are handled in a mutually nondifferential way, in contrast to the agent's manipulation of any z (where z is experienced to be in a similar relation to both x and y and to the "unit" x and y).

Separateness can be defined in a similar way, with specific variations in the type of relationship that is focused on. Again, a symmetrical relationship between two or more items of physical space obtains, but this time the one who experiences distinguishes both (or all) items on the criterion of their not being a unit, so to speak. In perception they are looked upon as so clearly distinct and dislocated from one another that the space between them is perceived as separating them. In action, the agent can only handle one at a time, or conceives of them as unreachable or not influenceable through direct action.

Paraphrasing separateness more generally, I conclude that

a) Anything experienced by the human being and termed x can be considered separate from anything else, termed y, provided y is separate from x also, and

b) The given x and y are separate provided, moreover, that they are mutually distinguishable in action or perception to the human perceiver or agent, and are handled in a differential way.

Contiguity is a somewhat different notion. It describes the relation between two or more items in space that are touching, linked, or otherwise coming in contact with each other. Again this relation can be concluded from perceptual and/or actional information.[3]

Paraphrasing contiguity in more general terms, I conclude:

a) Anything experienced by a human being and termed x is considered contiguous to anything else termed y, provided y is contiguous to x as well, and

b) Moreover, the given x and y are contiguous to each other, provided they are mutually distinguishable in action and perception for the human being, but such that an act on (or the perception of) one will have an effect on (or imply the perception of) some part of the other one, and vice versa.

202 and 302. Near, Separate, Contiguous in Sociogeographical and Cosmological Space

The same concepts are introduced with these entries, modified only with respect to the type of spatially specified items. The relationships hold between pairs of sociogeographical and cosmological items respectively.

103. Part/Whole

Through the formal theory of part-whole relationships, known as "mereology" (Tarski, 1956; Kotarbinski, 1964; tracing its origins to Lesni-

---

3. The importance of the relationships of contiguity in the psychology of perception is well known. Examples are therefore superfluous.

ewski), an approach to all spatial distinctions on the sole basis of part-whole differentiations has been established. It remains to be demonstrated that the approach has firmer ground in more than one particular knowledge system (the Western system), which has served as a source of background information to the philosophers engaged in the endeavor. The authors in this dimension work with formalized concepts, which is inappropriate to ethnographic work on these topics for the time being. I will have to approach the notions in a somewhat less sophisticated way in order to ensure usefulness in ethnographic and cross-cultural research. Dieterlen (1950) gives a good example of cultural part-whole relations: the Dogon conceive of the structure of the house in analogy with the human body (head = kitchen, doorway = penis, etc.). Particular actions correspond to particular parts, e.g., man sleeps in doorway, woman works in kitchen/head, social interaction takes place in the big room/belly, etc.)

The minimal requirement necessary with reference to part-whole distinctions is understood in the following way: if x is a part of y, then x can be handled, acted upon, or perceived without having to imply y systematically in any of these manipulations. On the contrary, in the same constellation, any action on or perception of y will always imply a similar manipulation of x (provided x and y are differentially treated and mutually distinguished). Until I reach a more elaborated and still universally useful characterization of the part-whole distinction, I will have to work with the present one.

Obviously x and y, as in the previous paragraphs, are understood as items that have physical spatial relevance, and that can be specified further through differentiations in physical space.

203 and 303. Part/Whole in Sociogeographical and Cosmological Space

The same characterization holds, provided the relationships pertain to sociogeographical and cosmological items respectively.

104. Bordering, Bounding

Any spatial characteristic of items of physical space like border, edge, or contour, of any imaginable form or appearance should be entered under the present heading. A pointer to the way in which this peculiarity could be paraphrased is to be found in Zusne's work on perception of form:

> An object's edge . . . is a sudden change in colour, texture, or the direction of lines, . . . An edge here signifies the end of a surface, hence passage to another surface or simply the end of an object. An edge stands out against another surface or some other colour, texture, etc. . . . or simply against the air. (1970, p. 17.)

It is clear immediately that two types of borders (at least) can be profitably distinguished: the "end" border (where the object ends), and the intermediate border (where surfaces, colors, etc., change).

Generalizing Zusne's information in order to make it match with actional ways of exploring and experiencing the world, I can say that borders, edges, and the like are entering the knowledge system of human beings through the fact that they are the cause of sudden changes in action, of adaptations in the direction of action or of minor or major modifications in the type of action carried through.

The paraphrase[4] of entry 104 then comes out as follows: a given item x has a border with y which is another item, or the rest of the world of experience (background, air), provided x and y are distinct in the experience of the human being, and provided, moreover, that the border indicates that a discontinuity in action upon or perception of item x is recognized. Or: v borders or bounds item x provided v triggers off a discontinuity in a human being's action upon or perception of item x (y can be another item or, indeed, the background, the air, etc.; v in this latter paraphrase is an aspect of the item x, the ultimate or intermediate border).

204 and 304. Bordering, Bounding in Sociogeographical and Cosmological Space

The same paraphrase holds good, with the modification that borders are described and recognized in the spaces of another magnitude.

105. Overlapping

Perceptually, the relation of overlapping is most clearly manifested in situations where one thing or phenomenon "covers" another one, thus abstracting the latter one from the visual field, partially or fully. A more abstract instance of overlapping can be seen in the mere process of "taking up space": an object, a shadow, a person can occupy a certain amount of space at any particular moment, thus overlapping a surface or a volume in space in a definite way. Finally, an agent can perform the act of covering something (eventually his own spatially determinable body), thus producing another instance of the relation of "overlapping" between the item covering and the one covered.

Again, different cultural knowledge systems will be specific on differential treatments of the notion of "overlapping": the Dogon have a word for shadow that conveys the meaning rather physically (cf. Pinxten, 1975): "blocking something from sight by casting darkness over it." The common English meaning of "overlapping," would point rather to "sharing identical elements" in two or more objects or sets of elements.

---

4. Formally, the distinction between intermediate and ultimate borders need not be made here. Both forms are but sophisticated differentiations of the identical spatial kernel notion treated in the paraphrase.

Paraphrasing the general meaning I am aiming at, I arrive at the statement: phenomenon x overlaps phenomenon y in space, provided x and y are clearly distinct for the perceiver or agent involved, and provided y cannot be fully perceived or acted upon without manipulating x in some parts.

205 and 305. Overlapping in Sociogeographical and Cosmological Space

I propose again to safeguard the main characteristics of the notion of "overlapping" as presented in entry 105, and to modify the paraphrase in such a way that it speaks of sociogeographical or cosmological space.

106. Internal/External; Central/Peripheral

In children these basic distinctions, at a topological level, occur early in development: rooms, houses, bodies, and so forth are subdivided according to what is in and what is out, what holds a central position in the visual and actional fields and what is "far out of reach" (Sauvy and Sauvy, 1972). According to Kagame (1956), in Rwanda thought the in/out distinction is basic in the conceptualization of a human body (and hence the outside world by analogy). The Dogon speaks about life forces "wandering around" inside the human body (Pinxten, 1975). Numerous examples could be given.

A useful approach to the characterization of the in/out pair was given by Greimas (1974, vol. 3), who deals with architectural space in terms of two basic pairs of notions: near/separate (cf. section 102 above) and "englobé/englobant." The advantage of this outlook is that paraphrasing in terms of border (separating inside from outside) is but a specific case, a mere sophisticated version of the general notion of "being englobed," taken up inside something else, and "englobing." I will present a tentative paraphrase along these lines:

X is an item of physical space which is recognized to be "englobed" in, and internal to y, which is another item. This is the condition when, in order to act on x, one has first to perform some actions on y (one has to run through, jump past, etc., y in order to reach x), or provided one has to perceptually scan y whenever one would like to perceive any aspect of x. External, then, is the inverse relationship.

"Central" and "peripheral" are taken to be specifications of the internal/external relationship. Indeed, the center can be most conveniently perceived as the item that is most "internal" with respect to any other possible item of a set that is perceived. Evidently, a very thin, disembodied notion (so to speak) of internalness is used here, leaving open any specifications desired for actual ethnographic concerns. It is, however, precisely this skeletal notion that enables me to understand the meaning of center as well.

206 and 306. Internal/External; Central/Peripheral in Sociogeographical and Cosmological Space

Again, similar paraphrases obtain as for entry 106, modifying the statements so as to purport to sociogeographical and cosmological spatial phenomena, rather than physical spatial ones.

107. Open, Closed

In topological treatises (cf. e.g., the Sauvys), opening and closing are basic operators. In perceptual psychology, most strikingly in Gestalt psychology, they take an eminent place in the explanations of results. Finally, in nontraditional perceptual psychology, they are again dealt with in great detail. Gibson's description in this latter tradition can be pointed out in order to introduce a quasi-psychophysiological definition for the differentiation: "the specification for a hole in the world, an aperture, window, or space between obstacles, is that it 'opens up' on an optically denser array" (1968, p. 206).

A typical characteristic of the paraphrases of "open" and "closed" one finds in the relevant literature (and Gibson may suffice as an example on this point) is the emphasis on contrast in texture, accessibility, optical, or actional constraints in the instance that is described as "open" or "closed." Openness then connotes the way by means of which interaction is possible: for example, the Dogon define doors and windows by means of the verb for interaction (Calame-Griaule, 1968).

I draw on this particularity and generalize it to result in the following paraphrase for the present UFOR:

A spatially specified phenomenon is said to be "open" (or have an "opening") provided the phenomenon x has, through experience (perceptual or behavioral), a uniformly structured appearance that allows no contact or transgression toward a clearly distinct phenomenon y, but for one specific and delineated part of the phenomenon x. Any contact, or transgression, from y to x or vice versa is to take place by means of this nonuniformly structured part. In other words, an otherwise uniformly structured phenomenon x can be acted upon, or can come into interaction with any other phenomenon y solely and specifically through one aspect of x. This one aspect has the characteristic of being "open" (i.e., the opening from x to y). Y can be any other phenomenon that is actually perceived or otherwise experienced to have interaction with x, be it an object, a human being, the environment, air, or light, and so on.

If a spatially specified phenomenon does not show any such "channel" of interaction or communication, it is known to be "closed."

The above paraphrase may appear to be rather cryptic. However, in order to guarantee the most general use possible (in ethnographic description), it should be kept that way. Indeed, a relativistic interpretation of "open" and "closed" with respect to specific phenomena is necessary: x can be a solid body that is "closed" to y, where y is another solid body. Or x is "open" to y, providing the latter is a gas or a spirit (cf. Navajo beliefs that "spirits" enter and leave the body at certain moments). Moreover, specific entries can be distinguished in folk knowledge for specific types of interaction (e.g., smoke enters the head through the skull in Navajo belief, while food passes through the mouth, etc.). To secure the possible detection and phrasing of all intricate differentiations in particular cultures, a most general paraphrase is justified.

207 and 307. "Open" and "Closed" in Sociogeographical and Cosmological Space

Similar paraphrases can be introduced here, modifying the original one in order to apply it to sociogeographical and cosmological phenomena.

108. Converging/Diverging

The image of a root growing from the stem outward in ever widening expansion conveys the idea of divergence. The perceptual and behavioral pattern of continuously increasing activity, traffic, and population density as shown in a map that gives information on the surroundings of a big city and approaches the center of the town provides a possible example of convergence (cf. e.g., Amedeo and Colledge's graphic representation in terms of minor, tertiary, secondary, and primary nodes for suburban . . . and city complexes in geography, 1975, p. 394). The perceptual concurring of a set of elements (people, animals, wars, anything) from different directions toward one central point illustrates convergence.

It must thus be clear that both specific types of configuration and specific complex movements can have the characteristic (indeed both characteristics, convergence or divergence). It is a feature typical in both its structural and dynamic instances that interests me here.

Paraphrasing this information, I conclude:

Phenomena x and y (where x and y are experienced as clearly distinct in the person's knowledge system) are said to be "converging," provided they are perceived as elements (or acted upon as elements) in a structure that appears denser in the vicinity of x and y than in other parts of that structure. The diverging relationship holds if the opposite characteristic exists (less density).[5]

208 and 308. Converging/Diverging in Sociogeographical and Cosmological Space

The same paraphrase is presented, modified to such a degree that it speaks of sociogeographical and cosmological spatial phenomena.

---

5. Density can be conceived of in terms of the number of elements per spatial unit or the degree to which elements fill space (blocking further perception or making interaction impossible).

109. Volumeness, Planeness

Through manipulation, contact, and perception, human beings can determine whether and in what way phenomena of the outside world (and the human body itself) are extended. When extension, without further specification as to measures, specific shapes, or spatial peculiarities are grasped, we are dealing with either the volumeness or planeness of the phenomenon examined. Phenomena that have extension in a flat planelike form tend to be handled and seen differently from those that are experienced as bulky or roundish or having an extension "in all directions." For example, a flat form may be folded or broken into pieces in order to move it, while an instance of volumeness may have to be grabbed on all sides in order to move it. It is at this basic level of recognition of forms and spatial aspects that the notions of "volumeness" and "planeness" bear relevance.

The perceptional psychologist Vernon taught us that, "in fact, from early childhood we are aware of a three-dimensional spatial continuum of objects, extending away in all directions from ourselves" (1970, p. 81).

The notion of "dimensionality" mentioned clearly has a meaning that is much less specific or more sophisticated than the Cartesian one, as the specific phrase "in all directions" explains. Zusne dwells on the same point, working on a problem in perception theory: "Form is never experienced alone, in two dimensions. It is objects that have form, and objects are three-dimensional, hence form is always form-in-depth" (1970, p. 145).

I experienced, both in Dogon and in Navajo cultural knowledge, that the aspect of "form-in-depth" was definitely attributed to phenomena, while "flatwise extending phenomena" were distinguished as belonging to a separate group. Within each of these sets multiple distinctions were made, detailing subsets of forms that were felt to be genuine classes in view of their specific requirements in terms of actions and/or perceptions for the human being. As such, the mere distinctions at the level of "volumeness"/"planeness" characteristics sometimes took the place of a basic ontology in particular knowledge systems: phenomena are grouped according to the way they are undifferentially manipulated or perceived, in contrast to another group that puts slightly different requirements of action or perception on the human being. No elaborate spatial characteristics can be pointed out. Rather, the bulkiness or roundishness, the flatness or elongatedness, and similar distinctions between types of volumeness or planeness are the core of the matter.

In general then, it is the differentiation of extendedness in a nonmetric characterization that is aimed at in this entry.

The paraphrase that is offered is as follows:

A phenomenon x is recognized as an instance of volumeness, provided x is manipulated or perceived as an aspect of the world with extensions in more than two directions of action or perception, each one orthogonally defined with respect to each two of the others.

A phenomenon x is recognized as an instance of planeness, provided x is manipulated or perceived as an aspect of the world with extensions in two directions of action or perception, where each direction is mutually orthogonally defined.

209 and 309. Volumeness, Planeness in Sociogeographical and Cosmological Space

The same paraphrase is applicable, modified to such a degree that it speaks of sociogeographical and cosmological spatial phenomena.

110. Succeeding; Ordering

Spatial succession is nothing more than the strictly spatial specification of the general relationship of order. Again, it is one of these abstract notions in spatial organization that is either introduced implicitly in most disciplinary discussions on spatial characteristics, or entered through a reference to a temporal sequence. An example of the latter procedure is given in Arnold's topological definition of a path through the use of the succession concept: "A path in a network is a sequence of different arcs that can be traversed continuously without retracing any arc" (1962, p. 32). Typically, Arnold's reference is to a temporarily characterized action (traversing) and a vague structural phenomenon (network): the relation thus "defined" is that of nodes and arcs succeeding one another.

A convenient example of succession, without specification of any particular direction, is given in the well-known drawing game for children: points are given in apparently scattered and unordered constellations on a sheet. They are ordered by giving them numbers (e.g., 1 to 16 in the drawing below). The task is to detect and draw (explicitly, so to speak) the relationship of succession that is defined through the numbering.

I propose to introduce succession as a specific form of order. I first present the generally known formal paraphrase of "order" (e.g., Carnap, 1958):[6]

A relation of (spatial) order exists between all elements of a set that is perceived or acted upon, provided all elements of the set are recognized as being clearly distinct from one another and such that they can be located and/or relocated in space at will, without ambiguity as to the clearly differential position (in space) of each of them.

The relation can be modified, and weakened in a sense, to allow for semiorder (where two or more elements can occupy the same space, i.e., are undifferentiated from each other in space).

---

6. The present paraphrase differs from Carnap's definition in several ways: no restriction to linear order is withheld, no definition in terms of arithmetical order is given, but the more general and spatially relevant notion of order is extracted from Carnap's more sophisticated presentation (cf. Carnap, 1958, p. 122ff.).

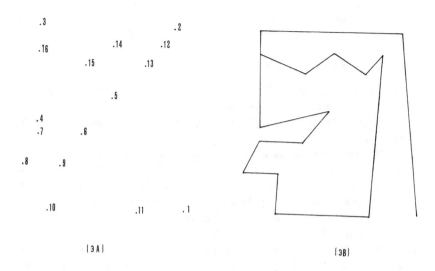

.3   .2
.16   .14   .12
        .15   .13
            .5
.4
.7   .6
.8   .9

.10   .11   .1

[3 A]   [3B]

Fig. 4   Connect the Dots Schema.

Succession, then, is a specific type of order relation, in that the former requirements are kept up, but a supplementary criterion is introduced as well: it is recognized in the knowledge system of any culture, provided the order relationship holds between elements of a space set and provided, moreover, that the order is such that one can traverse through the whole set by going from one to the other without ever having to cross any elements twice (cf. Arnold's definition).

111. Preceding/Following (in Front of, in Back of)

Beck (1967, p. 18) states that these two aspects form a pair and are a part of the six main directions in the world of perception and movement of the human being. Their fundamental character is illustrated by the fact that in treatises on natural philosophical bases of physical theory they are not dealt with explicitly, but rather are taken for granted in the more sophisticated parts of analysis (e.g., Feather, 1974, section 2.3). In their psychophysiological treatise Howard and Templeton (1966, p. 274) propose to use the implicit reference to body structure as a means of differentiating the basic directions: "[we start from] that center, fixed with reference to the body, from which absolute directions are judged, such as straight ahead, to the left, to the right, upwards and downwards."

Further information is gathered from observations of behavior in people recovering from operations to correct blindness. Von Senden, in his important work, states:

the impression of objects in visual space as located at varying depths seems here also to be given at once, as soon as the patient's vision has become capable of separate attention to individual colour-patches, as distinct from others. (1960, p. 252).

Similar observations concerning the relative position of preceding and following (of two objects with respect to each other, and not to the observer himself) can be found in the reports on the use of the Ames room (cf. Ittelson, 1968, p. 26).

Paraphrasing the above information with emphasis on a priori awareness of the frame of the body, I arrive at the following:

A phenomenon x (being spatially relevant) is recognized as being in front of or preceding another phenomenon y, provided both are clearly distinguishable in their spatial location (order), and provided x is recognized in a relationship to y that is experienced as analogous to the relationship that exists between the breast or the eyes and the neck or the back in the human body. The relationship of "following" exists, provided the inverse relationship between body parts is recognized.[7]

112. In Perspective

Panofsky (1960) has it that perspective was "invented" in the West during the Renaissance. The construction and drawing of perspectival configurations has probably been invented, unless future data from non-Western cultures will correct this statement. Nevertheless, there is something to the spatial phenomenon that can readily be observed in open planes and is thus liable to come up in a specific form in one cultural knowledge system or another. It is this aspect that Panofsky refers to when speaking of "discovering" rather than "invention": "it was discovered that all orthogonals, and not only those located in one plane, had to converge: in one 'vanishing point' which thus established the 'general horizon' of the picture . . ." (1956, pp. 603–4).

A philosophical anthropological treatment (one not restricted to paintings) is available in the specialized book by Graumann (1960): "In seiner Doppelfunktion von Eingrenzung und Über-sich-hinaus-Verweisen enthüllte er die horizontale Verweizung als Kriterium perspektivischer Ganzheit" (p. 178).

Graumann stresses the "signaling" aspect of the experiential notion of perspective. A primary conclusion should be that perspective is indeed only relevant as a perceptual characteristic and cannot be generalized to include praxiological (behavioral) means of experiencing the world. I will consequently emphasize this particularity and present a rather "fallacious" paraphrase that may cope with the phenomenon to some degree:[8]

---

7. Again, one of the phenomena mentioned (x or y) can be the observer.

8. I agree that the following paraphrase is far from ideal (following our requirements for a UFOR entry). However, no more satisfying paraphrase seems possible at present, to my knowledge.

A set of phenomena (with spatial relevance) is said to realize an instantiation of perspective to the perceiver, provided they are in a relationship of order to one another, and provided the set is experienced as extending toward one remote element (n) in space in front of the observer where density is the highest and the ordering relationship between elements is no longer perceivable.

113. Deep, Far (Dimension of Depth)

This section deals with the specific "dimension" that is realized through a systematic recognition and/or manipulation of preceding and following relationships. Consequently, and in tune with positions expressed by other scholars on this point (Bourdieu, 1972, Howard and Templeton, 1966, among others), I propose to paraphrase the dimension with reference to the body knowledge that is presupposed in any individual observer and actor:

Phenomena *x* and *y* (both having spatial relevance) are recognized as being ordered, one with respect to the other in depth, provided that they are recognized in a relationship that is analogous to the one that exists between the face-breast-belly-side and the neck-back-bottom-side of the human body.

213 and 313. Far (Dimension of Depth) in Sociogeographical and Cosmological Space

The same paraphrase is defended, modifying it to such a degree that the analogy is recognized between body parts and phenomena in sociogeographical and cosmological space.

114. Distant (Metric Deep, Metric Far)

The high degree of sophistication that is acquired through time in the Western tradition of measurement cannot be expected in other cultural knowledge systems.[9] Some more basic characteristics of measurement can be selected to be used for the present purposes. Reichenbach (1958) helps out in this instance. The basic criterion for measurement is the use of a (physically or otherwise realized) conventional rod that remains invariable throughout the process of measurement. Furthermore, this conventional rod is used as the exclusive means of measuring. Reichenbach specifies the use of the rod in terms of actions to be performed: "If the measuring rod is laid down, its length is compared only to that part of a body, say a wall, which it covers at

---

9. Feather (1974, section 2.4) specifies that a strictly conventional instance of the perfect (or ideally constructed) measuring rod for a basic distance in the West, the meter, is kept under specific atmospheric circumstances in Paris (the standard international meter). He further mentions that recently (since 1960) a redefinition has been carried through, providing a standard international meter realized in light rays. All this specific handling of the conventional unit (most of all in the latter case) is not to be found in any other culture, although the basic principle of a conventional rod (as explained below) might be.

the moment. If two separate parts of the wall are to be compared, the measuring rod will have to be transported" (p. 16).

The rod will be laid down in consecutive, concatenated actions alongside the body to be measured until it has covered the total extension of the body in this way. In the ethnographic literature, examples of this notion of measuring abound: Dogon cloths are cut according to measures of armlength (Griaule, 1938), while Hall worked out a system to grasp the culture-specific fine points of using distance in conversation (Hall, 1968).

Phenomena x and y (with spatial relevance) are said to be distant (at a distance) from each other, provided they are in a relationship of preceding/following one another, and provided this relationship can be further specified by the actor/perceiver through the displacement of a conventional rod along the path between x and y as many times in a row as is necessary and sufficient to cover the space between them.

In this paraphrase x and y can be two random phenomena, or one of them can be the observer/actor, or they can be aspects of one and the same phenomenon (with an extension on the depth dimension).

214 and 314. Distant in Sociogeographical and in Cosmological Space

The same paraphrase holds, modifying it so that it speaks of sociogeographical and cosmological spatial phenomena.

115. Up/Under; Above/Below

The fundamental position of these distinctions in any spatial knowledge system is advocated by authors from different disciplines: Feather (1974, section 2.3) mentions them as equally important (and indeed implicit) in physical knowledge as the preceding/following couple, while Piaget and Inhelder (1947) point to its basic presence in the psychological genetic development of space notions in Western children. Finally, the importance in non-Western cultural knowledge systems is illustrated, for example, in Tan's description of the cosmology of South Bali: the place (South Bali) is seen by natives as the center of the cosmos that expands according to a set of pairs of axes of diverse nature, above/below being one of the pairs (1967, p. 444). Lévi-Strauss (1958) based several of his discussions of binary structures on the appearance of "upper" and "lower" moieties in clans and villages throughout the world.

The distinction between the two pairs introduced under this heading is quite clear: both speak of the same general orientation, but the former implies some relation of contiguity as well (x is "sticking to" y when x is said to be "over" or "under" y), while the latter is indifferent to this criterion.

The construction—within the confines of this framework—of the distinction is similar to that of the "preceding/following" pair in that the analogy with bodily peculiarities is essential for their understanding. In general then, the relationship between, for example, head and shoulders could be seen to illustrate the "over/under" pair, while the general relationship between head and feet in a human being is characteristic of the description of the "above/below" pair.

The paraphrase is then easily constructed:

Phenomena x and y (with spatial relevance) are recognized to be in a relationship of "above, below" (or over, under) with one another, provided the relationship of the former with the latter is analogous to the one between the human head and human feet.

An "absolute" reference can be made in narrower terms where the object of reference (the human body) is explicitly recognized and used as a referent: things are above when level with the head or when they go further above the head; below, when they are level or below the feet. As always, we consider the human body standing erect.

116. Vertical, Upright (Dimension)

The dimensional notion is derived from the basic distinction between above and below, and is constructed as a concept that expresses the systematic and abstracted recognition or manipulation of above/below relationships. Consequently, it can be paraphrased with reference to the body knowledge of human perceivers and actors:

Phenomena x and y (both having spatial relevance) are recognized as being ordered, one with respect to the other, provided they are recognized in a relationship that is analogous to the one that exists between the head and the feet of an observer/actor or of the human body in general.

216 and 316. Vertical, Upright (Dimension) in Sociogeographical and Cosmological Space

The same paraphrase is withheld, modifying it to such a degree that the analogy between parts of the body (head/feet) and phenomena in sociogeographical and cosmological spaces respectively, is recognized. It may be mentioned that this analogy is often recognized explicitly in particular cultures (e.g., the human body as a frame of reference in the structure of the village in Dogon; Pinxten, 1976a).

117. High, Deep (Metric)

In this section I have to consider the more or less metrical uses of statements on the extension of phenomena on the vertical dimension. The procedure is similar to the one adopted in the case of distance: metrics enters the knowledge system once people respect the use of a conventional rod to determine the magnitude of a phenomenon. The rod can be (and often is in cultural knowledge) the human body itself; that is, the height of an adult human being can be used as a particular measure to determine the height of buildings, trees, and so on. In the latter case, all requirements are fulfilled: by convention the length of an average adult is used as a rod, which is then matched against the phenomenon to be measured one or more times. The rod is not very precise (since persons tend to differ on this feature), but in general the procedure and specific means of measuring are respected uniformly.

The paraphrase is as follows:

The height or depth between x and y can be known, provided x and y are ordered as being above/below one another, and provided that that relationship can be specified by a human agent through the displacement of a conventional rod vertically between x and y as many times in a row as is sufficient and necessary to cover the space between x and y completely.

Again in this paraphrase, x and y can be random phenomena, or one of them can be the observer/agent, or they can be aspects of one and the same phenomenon.

217 and 317. High, Deep (Metric) in Sociogeographical and Cosmological Space

The same paraphrase holds good, with a modification of the actual statements to a degree such that it speaks of sociogeographical and cosmological spatial phenomena instead.

118. Lateral, Next to

The general topological notion of nextness (e.g., Goodman in his revised edition of 1968) is matched to some degree with the experiential knowledge of the division of the world through the body: the world is divided sideways in two parts that are incomparable (since neither of them can be seen or acted upon together with the other one), and the actual position of the limbs and of certain receptors (ears, for example) emphasize this division. This general scheme is reflected in the cognitive positioning of things "next" to each other. The relationship of nextness or laterality is further characterized through its symmetry: when x is next to y, y is also next to x. This characteristic is in contrast with the more specific left/right dichotomy (cf. below).

Starting from this psychophysiologically founded information, I can easily (through body analogy) arrive at a paraphrase:

Phenomena x and y are recognized in a relation of nextness (or laterality) to one another, provided their perception or manipulation produces spatial positioning which is analogous to that in which the two eyes, or the two legs, or the two ears of a human body are situated with respect to each other.

119. Left/Right

In anthropological literature considerable information is available on the recognition and use of the left/right distinction, both in the actual manipulation of phenomena and in ritual and social expressions. The reader is reminded of such important overview works as Douglas (1974), Needham (1974), and Kourilsky and Grapin (1968). Finally, the distinction has been studied thoroughly in perceptual psychology, both at the level of physiological processes and that of cognitive structuring (e.g., Gibson, 1968). From all these studies it is known that the righthand side is, for most people, the naturally dominant side, as expressed in writing habits, greeting prescriptions, and so on. Within any particular culture, a preference for one of the sides can be gathered from ritualistic contexts, from mythological associations that go with the one or the other hand, and from preferences in everyday usage. So, whatever the specific connotations that go with either hand in any particular culture (be it the dominant or preferred or usual, or any other position that one hand holds over the other in the particular cultural knowledge system), I can always work with the actual recognition in some sense or other of the difference and status of both hands on a differential level in all cultures. Consequently, this information can be used in the paraphrase I propose for the left/right distinction:

Phenomena (with spatial relevance) x and y are recognized to be on the left or right side of one another (x is to the left of y, and then y is to the right of x), provided they are perceived or acted upon as distinct from each other, and provided they are handled as being in a spatial relationship to one another that is analogous to that of the dominant or preferred hand of a human being toward the other hand (or the other way around, depending on the cultural information available).[10]

120. Horizontal (Dimension)

In agreement with the former paraphrases, horizontality can be constructed as the dimension or the systematic system of ordering of phenomena in keeping with the nextness or left/right relationships that are perceived between them.

Paraphrase:

Phenomena x and y (both having spatial relevance) are recognized as being ordered, one with respect to the other, provided they are recognized (through perception or action) in a relationship that is analogous to the one that exists between the left and the right hand or between both eyes or both ears in the human body. They are then said to be horizontal.

220 and 320. Horizontal (Dimension) in Sociogeographical and Cosmological Space

The same paraphrase holds true, modified to a degree that the analogy is recognized between the particular body parts and the phenomena of sociogeographical and cosmological space, respectively.

10. The universal fact of the neurological difference of one hemisphere over the other (Pribram, 1971, pp. 360–65) may suffice for the UFOR, but one should allow for culturally different interpretations of this fact.

121. Wide; Broad (Metric)

The metrical extension of bodies and/or phenomena with spatial relevance along the horizontal dimension is often expressed in terms of the span of parts of the body (the span between two fingers, or between two legs, the thickness of the thumb, and so on). The procedure for formulating a paraphrase has been similar to the one adopted for height and for distance. Again, the rod can be an aspect of the human body or of any other natural phenomenon. A notion of width is acquired, provided that it is used in a conventional way and alongside the horizontal extension to be measured in the prescribed way.

I propose the following paraphrase:

The width or breadth between two phenomena x and y may be known provided x and y are horizontally ordered with respect to each other and provided that the relation between x and y can be specified by a human agent, through the displacement of a conventional rod horizontally between x and y as many times in a row as is sufficient and necessary to cover the space between x and y completely. In this paraphrase, x and y can be random phenomena or one of them can be the observer/agent, or they can be aspects (horizontal extremes) of one phenomenon.

221 and 321. Wide, Broad (Metric), in Sociogeographical and Cosmological Space

The same paraphrase is obtained, the actual statement being modified to such a degree that it speaks of sociogeographical and cosmological spatial phenomena.

122. Cardinal Points, Cardinal Directions

The distinction of different cardinal directions (or points) seems to be a universal characteristic of cultural knowledge systems. Numerous examples have come to us through detailed ethnographic reports on this topic. However, where the topic is universal, its elaboration in particular cultural systems can vary tremendously. Again, it is not so much the directions themselves that vary (indeed, every culture one knows of has four directions in a horizontal plane), but the actual meaning and folk definition that they acquire that is subject to variation. For example in Chinese culture, according to Granet (1935), cardinal directions are defined through colors, seasons, and other nonspatial characteristics. In Dogon culture, their impact is felt in the actual organization of daily life and the structuring of space and material properties in the home, and in mythical contexts (Griaule and Dieterlen, 1965).

Generally, the different positions of the sun during a diurnal period can be used to construct a neutral framework concerning the cardinal directions: at the least these directions are natural in the sense that they are not manmade and are perceived and acknowledged by human beings in all different cultures.

The places where the sun rises and sets are recognized as two main directions throughout the world: East and West. The zenith position of the sun is to the South in the Northern hemisphere, and to the North in the Southern hemisphere. It is halfway in either direction for the people living near the Equator. Extensions of space in any of these directions according to or contradicting any of the movements of the sun during its daily cycle are taken to be expressions of the relevant directions. Eventually, the actual perceptual locations through which the sun travels at particular points in the daily cycle can be considered the cardinal points (cf. e.g., Navajo perception of the sun's positions vis-à-vis the Sacred Mountains that bound the Navajo world). Cultural knowledge systems may tend to describe either the cardinal points or the cardinal directions, or eventually a combination of both. Actual folk definitions, if any, may stress the movements of the celestial body or the perceptual phenomena that accompany it, or anything else considered important in this context.

The paraphrase I build stresses the analogy between directions of human action and directions of the sun's movement:

Cardinal directions (and cardinal points) are recognized, provided human beings organize their actions, their ways of moving, their constructions, or anything in the actional world in such a way that they are located in space as analogous to the different positions of the sun in the sky, from rising to zenith to setting places. The fourth direction is analogous to the one "where the sun never comes."

222 and 322. Cardinal Points/Cardinal Directions in Sociogeographical and Cosmological Space

The same analysis is relevant here, provided that in this case sociogeographical and cosmological phenomena are ordered or spatially interpreted by means of this notion, rather than physical phenomena.

123. Coordinate Systems

The Cartesian coordinate system for three-dimensional space is a fairly specific version of the general and "natural" coordinate system that is formed by the mere structure of the human body: "a hierarchy of bone directions, hinged together, relative to the vertebral long axis of the body (the cephalo-caudal) and the two shorter axes (the dorso-ventral and the right-left)" (Gibson, 1968, p. 120). It is not the Cartesian system as such that is very different, but the way in which one tackles the task of defining the system in terms of abstractions.

Differences in culture-specific recognition can occur along several lines: the three-dimensional space can be mapped in a coordinate system that is represented and consists of mere lines, or the coordinate system can consist of planes or even volumes in a certain cultural tradition. For example, Whorf gives the following view of the Hopi world structure (1950):

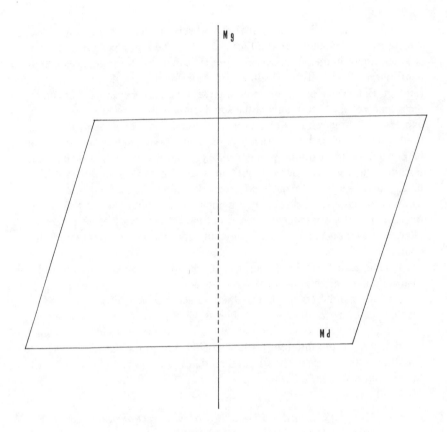

Fig. 5 Whorf's Model of the Hopi Universe.

The horizontal plane Md (everything "manifested") is cut by an orthogonal vertical axis Mg (everything "manifesting"). Both aspects of this coordinate system have a temporal facet: the horizontal plane consists of all things that have grown into existence in the Hopi world and belong at present to the set of things "manifested," that is, the set of things past. The vertical axis has a vitalistic aspect: the axis goes from the zenith through the heart of a man into the earth of the Hopis. It symbolizes the coming into existence and the short life of everything that manifests itself at a particular moment. The point where the axis cuts the horizontal plane is the world at present (the here and now). A bit away from the axis are situated things that have passed by already. The combination of a plane and a line in this diagram, and the configuration of static and processual aspects in the semantic field of this diagram, express the particular Hopi version of a coordinate system.

On the other hand, a coordinate system can be understood to consist of three intersecting planes. Thus, Howard and Templeton (1966, p. 7). are convinced that the Westerner conceives of a space as a complex of three planes, roughly corresponding to the three dimensions the human body can differentiate: along the vertical dimension runs the "middle transversal plane" which cuts the body from left to right in halves, along the horizontal dimension runs the "middle plane" which cuts the body in half at the navel, and along the depth dimension runs the "middle frontal plane" which cuts the body in half dividing left from right.

It is obvious that a similar coordinate system can be constructed, consisting of three-dimensional spaces instead of lines or planes. In the latter case, each of these "spaces" can be defined as the area of action for the human body (Bourdieu, 1972): the "depth space" is defined as that space in which going forward and backward is possible, while the "horizontal space" is the one in which sideways movement or rotation are possible, and the "vertical space" is the one that is defined by up-down or tumbling movements.

The paraphrase I propose is as follows:

A spatial coordinate system is a system that allows the ordering of a phenomenon through actions and perceptions in such a way that x is ordered in an unambiguous way, by means of the positions x has on several mutually orthogonal dimensions at the same time.

223 and 323. Coordinate Systems in Sociogeographical and Cosmological Space

The same reasoning is applicable, modifying the magnitude of the spaces referred to, to such an extent that sociogeographical and cosmological spatial phenomena can be ordered in the coordinate systems proposed.

124. Multidimensionally Extended (Metric)

Physical phenomena or objects can be long, broad, or high, but they can be measured in two- or three-dimensional ways also. Surfaces may be measured with "conventional rods" that have a definite extension on two dimensions, while volumes can be measured by means of conventional, standard-type volumes. The same principles are used that were discussed when dealing with one-dimensional measuring (high, far, etc.).[11]

We can paraphrase the notion as follows:

A phenomenon x is said to be multidimensionally extended provided it is recognized as an instance of volumeness (or planeness), and provided it is specified further through the displacement of a conventional unit.

The measuring can be more or less precise and accurate and may be performed factually or mentally. The human body can be used as a measuring

---

11. Commonsense terminology for multidimensional extensions is vague and ambiguous: big, vast, slim, thin, narrow, etc., can be used in this respect, but may sometimes apply to one-dimensional instances as well. Therefore, the more general label "multidimensionally extended" will be used.

unit (conventional instance of volumeness), or can be subject to measurement itself.

224 and 324. Multidimensionally Extended in Sociogeographical and Cosmological Space

The same paraphrase obtains, modified so that it speaks of sociogeographical or cosmological spatial phenomena.

125. Geometric Point

In the tradition of Western natural philosophy and geometry, a thorough approach to the problems of the construction of point notions is obvious. A well-known example is Whitehead's, where point is defined in a perceptualistic approach: it is that which is without extension, without parts (indivisible), which is still perceivable and has a definite position in space (Whitehead, 1920, pp. 91–97). In this sense a foundational notion of point is introduced emphasizing the physical aspects of it rather than the mere geometric ones. This I consider to be a positive point in the case for the UFOR, since the physical circumscription will undoubtedly have a more acceptable status in ethnographic contexts than a specific geometric definition.

The problem, with the above characterization by Whitehead, is its exclusive dependence on "perceptualistic" features. How can a praxiological interpretation of the same phenomenon be carried out? I propose an indirect approach: something is considered to be located in or at a point provided that the slightest displacement of this something will affect its location such that it is not recognized in or at that point anymore.

The paraphrase I propose is as follows:

X is recognized as a (spatial) point, provided it is perceivable in space and appears without extension, and provided something (y) that is located in or at that point x cannot be displaced in however minimal a sense without it losing that relationship with the point.[12]

126. Geometrically Linear, Straight

To reach a suitably general description of the entry "line," I may favorably start with specific characteristics of specific types of human action, namely aspects of the visual perception of lines. Zusne (1970, p. 16) gives a hint: "objects producing superimposed retinal images for a given position of the eye are judged to be in alignment." Already, Zusne refers to actions (positions—and thus positionings—of the eye) and to instruments of action

---

12. The paraphrase is not praxiological in any general sense since only a specific type of actions is focused, viz., displacement. This is as far as I can get in these terms at present. Future modifications may generalize the construction still more.

(the eye). The description is too specific in the sense that it speaks only of lines in depth perception since there is no such mechanism which produces horizontal lines.

A requirement one could introduce for action of a linelike constellation is that it ought to enable (or maybe oblige) continuous repetition of uniform action on all aspects or parts of a series, never coming to the same aspect or part twice in a row. Indeed, "continuous" is not enough in itself, since points could satisfy this requirement. Eventually, moreover, the agent can perform his action on the same "piece of line" (the same point, part of the configuration, etc.) he acted upon before, otherwise a circle or a loop would not qualify as a line (which they most certainly should in order to avoid odd interpretations). I consider the adoption of these two requirements to be sufficient to enable a minimal definition of a praxiological "line" notion.

I paraphrase accordingly:

A phenomenon x (with spatial relevance) is recognized to be a line provided it is the result (or path) of actions upon phenomena (set $a \ldots n$) There can be no two actions in a row on a, without their first acting upon at least one b.

Specific actions (like perceptions) can be performed rather than walking, drawing, and so on.

A straight line, then, is that line between phenomena x and y (with spatial relevance) which requires the shortest measurement between x and y, that is, where the invariant conventional rod has to be displaced the least number of times. (It is a metric notion, and we have to return to the former paraphrases of distant, deep/high, or wide/broad to construct it).

127. Geometrically Pointing, Parallel, Being an Angle

Here again, I am faced with clearly metric concepts. I thus have to work with notions paraphrased in former sections and combine them in a new paraphrase that pertains to the aspect under consideration.

The most straightforward paraphrase is possible for pointing phenomena. Indeed, phenomena are said to be pointing if they are recognized as being instrumental in, or acting in such a way that they can pierce, cut, or divide other phenomena. In other words, pointing phenomena are those that are recognized to be suitable or required for a very specific and delineated set of actions. There is no strictly geometrical connotation implied here.

Angles are crossing lines, with the restriction that they cross each other at just one point. This notion is again easily transferable into praxiological language, using the notion of "line" as basic information.

I derive the following paraphrase:

Given the situation where two lines are constructed independently (through mutually independent actions), an angle is obtained if and only if the actions have to be performed on the same part or aspect of phenomena at a certain moment in the concatenations of actions, and provided this event takes place only once. (If the event were allowed to take place more than once, we would have to consider loops, circles, and any recurrent structure of lines in this sense as angles.)

Parallels are constructed along the same lines of thought, specifying this time that it may never occur that two independently set up action series will act on the same part or aspect of phenomena (where the phenomena are clearly distinct from one another).

128. Geometrically Being a Volume, a Surface

Surfaces in Euclidean geometry are defined through the rotation or displacement of a line around one point, or through the systematic overlapping of all points of one line by a second and clearly distinct line. All lines involved are straight lines.

A more general paraphrase would imply the same procedure with lines of any form, not specifying them as straight lines (cf. Swinburne, 1968, pp. 116–17).

Rephrasing this notion in praxiological terms, I arrive at the following:

A phenomenon x (with spatial relevance) is recognized as a surface provided it can be constructed or worked upon by human beings in such a way that an ideally unlimited (and a practically limited) number of lines can be constructed in it, in at most two dimensions, that would cover the space of the surface completely.

The paraphrase of a volume is quite similar, but this time surfaces (or one surface and one line) constitute the constructing material.

129. Geometric Figures

Under this heading all specifically geometric figures can be treated. At least figures like a triangle, a square, a rectangle, a circle, a cube, a prism, a pyramid, and a sphere have proved cross-culturally relevant. Since in Western (Euclidean) geometry, as in the native geometries we may analyze, they prove to be constructed by means of notions that were defined in the previous sections, I will not give any paraphrases here. The mere presentation or display of these figures (in drawing, three-dimensional constructions, or any other form) will generally suffice to elicit the folk definitions and folk paraphrases that may exist for them.

225 and 325. Geometric Notions in Sociogeographical and Cosmological Space

The notions treated in entries 125 through 129 are reintroduced, safeguarding the paraphrases offered and modifying them only to the extent that they speak of sociogeographical and cosmological spatial phenomena.

130. Resting, Moving

The perceptual aspect of rest and movement is more difficult to demonstrate in empirical description than in praxiological foundation. Indeed, in physical theory (e.g., Feather, 1974, p. 47) as in perceptual theory (e.g., Minnaert, 1968, p. 172), the construction of a referent (the human body, the eye) with respect to which rest or movement must be evaluated is a delicate theoretical undertaking.

Rest and movement can more readily, one may say more "naturally," be constructed in a praxiological outlook. Indeed, it is the agent who moves or remains at rest, and who can judge the rest or movement of other phenomena in the world in analogy with the body's conditions.

I thus paraphrase the phenomena along these lines:

A phenomenon x (with spatial relevance) is recognized to be at rest by an agent/perceiver, provided x stays throughout some length of time in a position that is analogous to the position the agent is in, when acting in such a way as not to alter or change perceptibly.[13]

A phenomenon y is recognized to be moving by an agent/perceiver, provided it is acted upon by the agent or by anything else in the outside world (including the phenomenon itself) in such a way that y changes its spatial position throughout a certain period of time. The change is recognized as analogous to any change of relationship occurring between the agent and the environment (when moving), caused by the agent, in a certain period of time.

230. Resting, Moving in Sociogeographical Space

The same paraphrases obtain, modified to such a degree that they speak of sociogeographical space.

333 and 334. Movements Earth-Sky (Constellations) and Movements of the Universe

The same paraphrases obtain, being restricted and specified for the cosmological spatial units referred to.

131. Moving along One Dimension

A delineated set of movements can be selected and described in more detail. Since most of the human and phenomenal movements are of this type, they must be characterized separately.

Indeed, human beings tend to move most of the time in one specific dimension: they can either go up or down, to the left or to the right, or come closer or go further away from a referent. Some movements imply displacements in a multidimensional field, and they will be dealt with in a subsequent action.

---

13. Since I am interested only in spatial rest and movement, I center the paraphrase correspondingly.

The paraphrase goes as follows:

A phenomenon x is recognized to be moving along one dimension by an agent/perceiver, provided it is acted upon in such a way that it changes its relationship with the environment over a certain period of time, in a systematic way with respect to one dimension. The change is recognized as analogous with the change in the agent's relationship with the environment when he causes a systematic change by acting on his position on the horizontal, the vertical, or the depth dimension. The agent can either move back and forth, or sideways, or up and down.

132. Moving Linearly; Curving; Rotating; Spiraling

The linear progression or displacement of an object or a body is specified by a very specific type of "change of relationship" with the environment. The change is such that a line can be drawn through the different positions that are occupied over a period of time and the distance between initial and final positions can be measured. Its paraphrase thus has to draw on metric notions that were discussed previously:

An agent or a phenomenon x being acted upon (with spatial relevance) is recognized to be moving linearly, provided the distance between the position in environment displayed by him/it when the action (change) started and when the action ended along one dimension has changed.

The unit of measurement can be of various sorts. What comes most easily to the mind, of course, are the human "rods" that are often used for these measurements: foot, step, armlength, and so on.

Curving can be understood as the change in relationship with the environment that implies some degree of alternating between movements along first one and then another dimension. Wavelike movements, turning, winding, and the like can be understood in this sense.

Rotating is a very specific type of movement in that all relationships with the environment but one are changed: indeed, the rotating body or person keeps one relationship with the world constant (the point or place of rotation) and changes all others. It is said to be moving around an axis, pointing specifically to the one constant point (turning in place, tumbling).

Spiraling is a complex phenomenon. The spiral can be realized through an agent in a plane, thus stressing the center-periphery movement in two dimensions. It can be performed in a three-dimensional space, where either the spiral expands from a central point outward (or the other way around) or the spiral progresses along one dimension with no change in amplitude in the center-periphery relationship. Any of these notions can be described in great detail with the sole use of the notions introduced formerly.[14] For exam-

14. Because these paraphrases take considerable space and because they are of no use for the analysis of the Navajo materials, I must suffice by referring the interested reader to Pinxten, forthcoming.

ple, the Dogon distinguish between several of these notions of spiral in their complex mythology (Griaule and Dieterlen, 1965).

332. Rotation of Celestial Units (Including Earth)

The paraphrase is similar to the one in 132, but restricted to celestial bodies.

133. Having a Direction in Movement

The direction of a movement is intuitively felt to be the spatial result of it, in comparison to the initial position of the agent or the objects being moved. This cryptic statement is in urgent need of clarification.

I conceive of an agent primarily as somebody who is aiming at a goal. When interested in spatial aspects of his act, I thus visualize his goal as the spatially specific configuration he has been working toward. This turns out to be an insufficient characterization, since "direction" in natural language refers more to the perceived or acted upon relationship between initial and final positions in space, before and after the movement takes place. Thus, if anything, "direction" should be understood in the global spatial structuring of the world in which an agent performs. I will favor this most general view on "direction," eventually narrowing it down as and when the dictates of ethnographic material demand.

Paraphrase:

The direction of a movement of phenomenon x is that aspect of action in space of the agent/perceiver, which deals with the specific way of organizing the action before and during movement (changing of the relationship with the environment) to the extent that, upon achievement of the action, the agent or phenomenon will be located in the specific spatial configuration in which he set out to perform the action (movement). Formally: given SC_1 at t_1 (spatial configuration at time of initiation of action) and SC_2 at t_2, with ($SC_1 \neq SC_2$, and $t_1 \neq t_2$), then direction is that aspect of the transformation through action from SC_1 to SC_2 over a period of time, that describes the spatial relationship between SC_1 and SC_2 at t_2, and that is realized by the agent when progressing from t_1 to t_2.

Direction specifically speaks of the spatial peculiarities of the gap between the initial spatial configuration of the agent-environment relationship and the final one. This relationship guides and serves as a frame for the agent's conception of space while performing his action/movement.

233. Having a Direction in Movement in Sociogeographical Space

The same paraphrase obtains, modified to such an extent that it speaks of movement in social space.

134. Being Spatially Random/Spatially Determinable

The inspiration for this particular entry came from the study of creation myths. Time and again the distinction between chaos and order, between randomness of processes and phenomena and "placedness" is emphasized. Long (1969, p. 114), treating this distinction in creation myths, states, ". . . the stuff from which creation finally arises has always existed. Even in its indeterminate form of chaos, the possibilities of a cosmos were always present."

I now focus on "spatial" randomness and determinability. Objects, aspects of space and the world can be spatially random in that they cannot be distinguished, specified, or known in their spatial characteristics through action and/or perception of any human being. If they can be known or distinguished, even to a small extent, then they are spatially determinable to the cultural knowledge system involved.

228. Geoso: Surface, Volume in Sociogeographical Space

Specific and delineated aspects of physical or object space were distinguished and treated under a separate heading (Geometrically Being a Volume, a Surface, number 128). A similar, though somewhat less sophisticated approach to units of sociogeographical space is due. I call the resulting units of spatial extension "geosos." Several different characteristics of geosos can be pointed at in the material that came to me from anthropology and geography:

a) Specific units of social space can be distinguished through their differing economic or social functions (cf. Spreiregen, 1965, p. 129). This means that some regions are designated as agricultural areas, while others will be dedicated to habitation, and still others for ceremonial purposes.

b) Units are mutually marked off through "qualitative borders" or through paths and networks that cut across them: Stea (1970, p. 39) defends an ethological approach whereby the power or influence of a person is mapped in several concentric areas, with high power in the immediate vicinity of the person and decreasing degrees of power in ever-widening circular areas around him. This idea of territoriality has been used in different settings and with varying parameters in the study of socially or culturally delineated areas for tribes, clans, and peoples in all parts of the world. A very interesting study about the way people divide and reconstruct their sociogeographical world is found in Conklin's ethnographic atlas (1980).

Lynch (1960, p. 47) is one of the pioneers in geography to conceive of cities in a similar way: the network of roads and blocks assert (so to speak) social units, neighborhoods, and racial areas that mark clearly distinct lifestyles and social organizational forms.

As to the qualitative and structural characterization of geosos, in highly organized sociogeographical units (from houses to states), a complete set of requirements can be worked out spelling out the characteristics which should be found in any geoso in order to be considered a real "house geoso" or "state geoso," and so on. Some semiologists (e.g., the group around Greimas) and geographers (e.g., Gould, 1972) have been working in this direction, specifying several typical geosos in such ways.

What is striking in all the approaches presented above is the emphasis on some criterial or presuppositional elaboration of the minimal paraphrases of geosos. It is not merely instances of sociogeographical volumeness or planeness that are described. Aspects of space are also clearly and unambiguously defined or delineated through (most of all) qualitative requirements that are shared by all actors who use or occupy the spatial units indicated. The paraphrase I can introduce to capture the minimally necessary meaning that "geosos" convey has to be much more specific or sophisticated than the one proposed for "volumeness/planeness." Moreover, the "requirements" spoken of, can most easily be construed as constraints on types or ranges of action: specific types of action are appropriate within the confines of one or a few geosos, while they would be unacceptable or in some other way "out of place" in another geoso. In this way, for instance, part of the meaning of "hooghan" ('house, family dwelling' for the Navajos) is seen to consist of the rules for behavior: you do not shout or speak loudly or be unsocial within the "hooghan," while quite the opposite is allowed outside of it. Other examples can be given in anthropological literature (cf. again Pinxten, forthcoming).

The paraphrase then comes out as follows:

A geoso is a unit in sociogeographical space that can be handled or interacted with in specific ways by human groups. It is a spatial unit that puts specific constraints on the actions of the group, and is recognized and contrasted with other geosos through the set of action constraints that is conveyed by it. The geosos are mutually distinguished through the changes of action requirements that rule the behavior of groups, and these are often (though not necessarily) marked spatially by borders, alteration in texture or form, and other strictly spatial features.

229. Map, Scale

The study of different types of maps has had a good deal of attention in recent years. Recent developments in geography have led to the construction of "alternative" maps. It is not the physical characteristics of territorial units (or, not these exclusively) that determine how a map is built up, but the subjective or action-bound aspects. That is, the reachability or lack of it, the degree of preference for one place rather than another, the degree of familiarity with places, all these factors are considered to be of importance nowadays in geographical representation, and in the building of action and interaction schemes for particular regions.[15] In the same sense, architectural maps can be redrawn from the action-centered point of view: architectural spaces

15. Cf. for example, the reactions of Lowenthal (1972, p. 241): "The memorable geographies are not compendious texts but interpretative studies embodying a strong personal slant."

that are made to enable or to refrain from certain types of interaction, to emphasize social closedness of the group from the outside world or the other way around, and so on. (Cf. for example, Bourdieu's brilliant analysis of the Berber house in terms of social rules and cosmological beliefs, 1972.)

A map, then, is an expression of interaction and communication regulations as much as it is a guiding device for actual, material construction of a space. In both senses, it is a praxiological device. The paraphrase then goes as follows:

A map is the picturing device in any sense (drawing, building, etc.) of a sociogeographical space with constant reference in the representation to the action constraints, the types and modes of interaction or communication in the "real world" depicted in the device.

The notion of scale has been closely linked to that of map in Western tradition. This need not be the case, of course, as is shown by the Navajo examples (cf. chap. III). In Western tradition, as discussed by Boudon (1971, p. 63), the emphasis has been on the "congruent" representation of real space in a drawing or artifact, moreover, magnifying or diminishing the real world "measures" in a consistent way. In geographical maps, the scale always reduces the real sizes considerably (one inch on the map is ten miles in reality, etc.), while in some microanalysis the reverse occurs. The essential characteristic of the device produced is that all structural relationships in the real world are safeguarded in the representation, but drawn in much smaller size. To generalize the paraphrase of Boudon, I propose to stress the more general characteristics, that is, those that are not restricted to clearly metric approaches to space.

I conclude: A sociogeographical space is represented and reproduced in a scale model, provided the geoso and its model are produced or perceived by human beings as homeomorphous to one another and the reproduction of representation consists of the reduplication of all relevant structural relationships in both the geoso and the scale model. The size can eventually vary between model and geoso.

231. Being (on) a Path; Orienting

This entry may be found under the sociogeographical spatial entries. It is too specific to be treated merely as a special case of any physical space entry.

Gladwin (1973) studied the complex systems of navigation among the Puluwat of Micronesia. He states:

> When a Puluwatan speaks of the ocean the words he uses refer, not to an amorphous expanse of water, but rather to the assemblage of seaways that constitute the ocean he knows and understands. Seen in this way Puluwat ceases to be a solitary spot of dry land; it takes its place in a familiar constellation of islands linked together by pathways on the ocean (p. 133).

Lynch, in his study of the American city, studied the type of spatial analysis that is characteristic of modern city dwellers when seeking their way in the partly blurring experience of a big town. Typically, a highly similar appreciation in terms of action and movement of aspects of the structure of the modern city appears in the following quotation: "Paths are the channels along which the observer customarily, occasionally, or potentially moves" (1960, p. 47).

The picture that emerges from these examples (which could be greatly amplified) is that of a path, a way along which action is to take place in terms of possibilities of movement or reaction.

The paraphrase of "path" that one arrives at, is as follows:

A path is that spatial aspect that results from the movement in sociogeographical space of an individual or of any moving phenomenon. It is the sum of all spatial parts that are covered by an agent (or phenomenon) in a concatenation of displacements in sociogeographical space.

Orientation, then, is the specific notion of direction in sociogeographical space that results from the active and deliberate process of the placement of an agent in sociogeographical space. Typically, not only the positions of initial and final states of action are represented, but also several other spatially relevant aspects of the environment in which the agent performs.

232. Navigating

Navigation is a specific spatial phenomenon: it involves the displacement by individuals of themselves (and eventually of the foods that have to be transported) over distances, all the while referring to a complex and highly elaborate multidimensional representation in a symbolic device, a number of geosos. Different types of compasses, charts, and specific flight or sail routes can be used during navigation. Peoples of different parts of the world are known to have developed often sophisticated devices for these purposes. Probably one of the best known is the representational "basket" that is used by Puluwatans (e.g., Gladwin, 1973, p. 133) as a map of different seaways that are recognized in connection with different colors of water, different winds, and so on, in order to determine the direction that has to be taken in their incredible canoe voyages across the Pacific Ocean.

The use of the device as an instrument in the acts of navigating is most often the task of a specialist, in the Puluwatan as well as in the Western tradition (the navigator). The complex series of acts involving this combination of observing, instrument usage, and directing one's action is what "navigating" is all about. I thus present the following paraphrase:

Navigating is the specific act of organizing movements of oneself and others (and other goods) by means of a complex representational instrument that maps in a certain sense any information in the environment relevant to the actual displacement of the individual from place y to place y (with x and y at a distance from each other). The nature and the amount of what is considered "relevant" will depend on the cultural knowledge system investigated.

The Cosmological Notions

The cosmological notions in the UFOR, specifically numbers 326 through 331 and 335 and 336 will not be explained here, since they were not used in the Navajo material. They can be consulted in the more elaborate version of the UFOR mentioned earlier (Pinxten, forthcoming).

140. Global Spatial Characteristics

All spaces have some general, formal characteristics bestowed on them. All spatial aspects automatically share these characteristics, since they are conceived of as being made up by space, and the other way around. However, all three magnitudes of space need not have the same features: physical and social space can be believed to be unbounded, while cosmological space is clearly bounded. In every particular cultural knowledge system it remains to be analyzed which conceptualization obtains on this point. Therefore, even the global characteristics must be presented separately for all three spaces.

240 and 340. Global Spatial Characteristics in Sociogeographic and Cosmological Space

Some global characteristics of sociogeographical space might differ from those of the object space in a particular culture: for example, in the Dogon social space, there is believed to be a qualitative difference between wild land and cultivated land, in the sense that different rules hold for each of them (Pinxten, 1975). A similar point can sometimes be made about the character of cosmological space. Thus, before Giordano Bruno the Catholic scholars thought that the universe was finite, but placed in the infinite being (space?) of God. Later, the feature of infiniteness was attributed to all space (Koyré, 1957).

141. Absolute/Relative

The distinction was, in the Western tradition, most dramatically apparent between the views of Newton and Leibniz. It is this same distinction that I wish to introduce for cultural analysis.

The more common view on absolute space is that of a container space: anything in space is located in a definite way with reference to the constant and immovable "container" that delimits space in some conceivable way. Swinburne (1968, p. 50) gives the more elegant and sufficiently general paraphrase: "Absolute Space is thus the Space, the places constituting which are reidentified by the frame of reference which does not really move."

A relativistic view on space was defended by Leibniz. It emphasizes the point that we only know of spatial relationships between things within space, and that space can thus be nothing else but the structural scheme that results thereof. In short, then, a relativistic view on space will stress the lack of any fixed and immovable frame of reference (or will omit reference to it) and will concentrate on the interrelatedness of all elements, units, and things perceived or acted upon.

241 and 341. Absolute/Relative in Sociogeographical and Cosmological Space

The same paraphrases obtain, modified to such an extent that they speak of sociogeographical and cosmological knowledge of the West; the former is still being worked out at a more conscious level in contemporary geography and architecture (cf. for example, Abler, Adams, and Gould's point, 1971, p. 72: "The shift to a relative spatial context is still in progress . . .").

142. Finite/Infinite

Finiteness has been defined in various ways in the history of Western natural philosophy. One of the more sophisticated and highly culture-specific approaches is given in Reichenbach: "Infinity of space to him [= the physicist] means that there are no limits for the laying down of measuring rods and that will not be reached after a finite number of operations" (1958, p. 79). The definition has the advantage of giving a more or less praxiological view on the problem: the definition of what should be done to reach the situation described. On the other hand, it is much too specific to be used in the present UFOR, since only metric approaches are allowed in Reichenbach's position. I propose to stick to the basic idea (the praxiological outlook), and to generalize it.

Space is considered to be finite by any cultural knowledge system if it is conceived of as being such that, any agent, when crossing the space at random in all different directions and in numerous ways, will have to come across the same place or the same spatial unit at least twice within any humanly feasible time.

Space is considered to be infinite provided the agent will never and in no binding sense have to cross the same place or the same spatial unit when crossing the space at random.

242 and 342. Finite/Infinite in Sociogeographical and Cosmological Space

The same paraphrases obtain, being modified in such a way that they speak of sociogeographical and cosmological space.

143. Bounded/Unbounded

The description of notions of bordering has already led to an answer to the present problem. Instead of borders of particular spatial units, however, the boundedness of space itself is dealt with here. Again, Swinburne (1968,

p. 31) points to the possible answer: "[For Greeks] space is of logical necessity surrounded on all sides by other regions of space."

Reinterpreting this information in praxiological terms, I reach the following paraphrase:

Space is considered to be unbounded in a cultural knowledge system, provided that the characteristics of the space allow for any movement by an agent to be performed and continued at will in any random direction, that is, without obliging the agent to alter or reverse the movement at any time.

Space is bounded, provided such criterion does not hold and—in consequence—the agent is obliged to reverse or alter his movement at specific times and places.

243 and 343. Bounded/Unbounded in Sociogeographical and Cosmological Space

The same paraphrases hold, being modified in such a way that they speak of sociogeographical and cosmological space.[16]

144. Continuous/Discontinuous

These features have had tremendous consideration in the last hundred years in natural philosophy, physics, and formal logic. It is impossible and hardly useful for the present purposes to reconsider the literature available. Let us stress the physical continuity of space. Reichenbach (1958, p. 59) offers a topological interpretation of continuity: "neighborhood relations in infinitesimal domains are preserved; no tearing of the surface or shifting of relative positions of points occur[s] at any place." The definition, though general, still abounds in specific elements (such as "neighborhood," "infinitesimal," "point," "place").

Space is continuous provided that an action or movement by a human agent has been proved possible to perform at a particular place (within a particular spatial unit), owing to the spatial characteristics of the agent's in any similar or comparable part of space apart from the one performed in. What will be considered similar or comparable is, of course, again subject to the judgment of the particular cultural community acting.

Space is discontinuous, provided actions cannot be performed in similar ways in parts of space that are judged similar or comparable.

This characteristic is important when dealing with specific types of action. For example, for the Dogon of Mali "space" was considered discontinuous in terms of the strict selection of spatial units for religious or magical purposes: places alike in all other respects were markedly different in that

16. A paraphrase of bordering in cosmological space was already given, in a more specific sense, previously (number 104). Here, the structural aspect is characterized rather than the spatial phenomenon of "borders" themselves.

one was liable to be used for profane purposes and not for sacred practices while another was used exclusively for sacred purposes and forbidden for daily activities.

244 and 344. Continuous/Discontinuous in Sociogeographical and Cosmological Space

The same paraphrases obtain when modified with reference to sociogeographical and cosmological spaces, respectively.

145. Homogeneous/Heterogeneous

Space is considered in any particular cultural knowledge system to be built up according to certain rules and laws. If, for any culturally specific reason, these laws and rules seem to exist in the eyes of the natives for certain parts of space only, and tend to be altered or dropped in other parts, then the global system of space (in the native concept) is heterogeneous. If, on the other hand, any rule and/or law holds true throughout all conceivable parts of space, then this space is considered to be homogeneous.

I can paraphrase this in terms of action.

Space is considered homogeneous by an agent, provided the agent can perform similar actions in random parts of the space, taking into account the rules and laws by which space is built up and to which he has to comply. Nowhere will his actions need total alteration because of the dramatic change of rules in any particular part of space.

Space is considered heterogeneous by an agent if he can perform actions in a certain part of space, taking into account the rules and laws of space in that part, but not in certain other parts that are distinctly different from the former ones.

245 and 345. Homogeneous/Heterogeneous in Sociogeographical and Cosmological Space

The same paraphrases obtain, having been modified to speak of sociogeographical or cosmological spaces.

This ends the presentation of the present format of the UFOR for spatial analysis. Any suggestions and elaborations are welcomed wholeheartedly. Anybody interested in other aspects or in previous or present formats of the UFOR can write the senior author of this book about them.

Bibliography

Navajo Materials

Alexander, Herbert B.
1953   *The World's Rim*. Lincoln: University of Nebraska Press.

Astrow, Margot
1950   "The Concept of Motion as Psychological Leitmotiv in Navajo Life and Literature." In: *Journal of American Folklore*, Vol. 63:45–56.

Farella, John R.
1980   "A Navajo Philosophy." Ph.D. dissertation, Northwestern University.

Franciscan Fathers
1910   *An Ethnologic Dictionary of the Navajo Language*. St. Michaels, Ariz.: The Franciscan Fathers.

Garrison, Edward R.
1974   "Navajo Semantics: 'Classificatory' Verbs." Ph.D. dissertation, Northwestern University.

Haile, Berard
1943   *Soul Concepts of the Navajo*. Annali Lateranensi, Vol. 7. Vatican City.
1947   *Star Lore Among the Navajo*. Chicago and Sante Fe: University of Chicago Press.
1950–51 A Stem Vocabulary of the Navajo Language. St. Michaels, Ariz.: The Franciscan Fathers.

Hoijer, Harry
1945–49 "The Apachaean Verb 1–5." *International Journal of American Linguistics*, Vol. 11:193–203; Vol. 12:1–13, 51–59; Vol. 14:247–259; Vol. 15: 12–22.
1974   *A Navajo Lexicon*. University of California Publications in Linguistics, Vol. 78. Berkeley: University of California Press.

Kluckhohn, Clyde
1964   "Navajo Categories." In: *Culture in History*. Edited by S. Diamond. New York: Columbia University Press.

Landar, Herbert
1967   "Two Athapaskan Verbs of 'Being'." In: *The Verb "To Be" and Its Synonyms*. Edited by John W. M. Verhaar. Foundations of Language, Supplementary Series, Vol. 1. New York: Humanities Press.

McNeley, James K.
1975   "The Navajo Theory of Life and Behavior." Ph.D. dissertation, University of Hawaii.
1981   *Holy Wind in Navajo Philosophy*. Flagstaff: University of Northern Arizona Press.

Minnick, Norris
1975   "Analysis of Navajo Spatial Enclitics." Mimeographed.
Newcomb, Franc; Fishler, Stanley; and Wheelwright, Mary C.
1956   *A Study of Navajo Symbolism*. Peabody Museum of Archaeology and Ethnology, Harvard University, Vol. 32, no. 3. Cambridge, Mass.
Pinxten, Rik
1979b   "Morality and Knowledge. Teachings from a Navajo Experience." *Philosophica*, Vol. 23:177–99.
Reichard, Gladys
1950   *Navajo Religion*. Bollingen Series, Vol. 18. New York: Pantheon.
Reichard, Gladys and Newcomb, Franc
1975   Sandpaintings of the Navajo Shooting Chant. New York: Dover.
Remington, Judith A.
1981   "An Epistemological Study of Navajo Divination and European Science." Ph.D. dissertation, Northwestern University.
Symposium on the Summer Healing Ceremony of Navajo Indians.
1976   Navajo Community College, Tsaile, Ariz.
Underhill, Ruth
1964   *Red Man's Religion*. Norman: University of Oklahoma Press.
Wall, Leon and Morgan, William L.
1968   *Navajo-English Dictionary*. Window Rock, Ariz.: BIA, U.S. Dept. of the Interior.
Werner, Oswald
1968   "Styles of Learning: The Evidence from Navajo Thought." Ms.
Werner, Oswald and Begishe, Kenneth Y.
1970   "A Lexemic Typology of Navajo Anatomical Terms: The Foot." *International Journal of American Linguistics*, Vol. 36:247–65.
Werner, Oswald; Manning, Allan; and Begishe, Kenneth Y.
in press   "A Taxonomic View of the Traditional Navajo Universe." In: *Handbook of North American Indians*. Edited by William Sturtevant. Washington, D.C.: Smithsonian Institution.
Wilson, T., ed.
forthcoming   *Rock Point Community School Curriculum, Navajo Auto Parts*. Chinle, Ariz.: Rock Point School.
Witherspoon, Gary
1971   "Navajo Categories of Objects at Rest." *American Anthropologist*, Vol. 73:110–27.
1977   *Language and Art in the Navajo Universe*. Ann Arbor: University of Michigan Press.
Wyman, Leland C.
1975   *Blessingway*. Tucson: University of Arizona Press.
Young, Robert W. and Morgan, William
1942   *The Navaho Language*. Salt Lake City: U.S. Indian Service.
1980   *The Navaho Language*. Albuquerque: University of New Mexico Press.

Other Materials

Abler, R.; Adams, John; and Gould, Peter
1971   *Spatial Organization; The Geographer's View of the World*. Englewood Cliffs: Prentice-Hall.

Amedeo, Douglas and Colledge, Reginald G.
1975   *An Introduction to Scientific Reasoning in Geography.* New York: John Wiley.
Arnold, B. H.
1962   *Intuitive Concepts in Elementary Topology.* Englewood Cliffs: Prentice-Hall.
Beck, R.
1967   "Spatial Meaning and the Properties of the Environment." In: *Environmental Perception and Behavior.* Edited by David Lowenthal. Department of Geography Research Papers, University of Chicago, Vol. 109. Chicago.
Berlin, Brent and Kay, Paul
1969   *Basic Color Terms: Their Universality and Evolution.* Berkeley: University of California Press.
Boudon, Pierre
1971   *Sur l'espace architectural.* Paris: Dunod.
Bourdieu, Pierre
1972   *Esquisse d'une théorie de la pratique.* Geneva: Droz.
Bourne, Lyle L.
1975   *Psychology of Thinking.* Englewood Cliffs: Prentice-Hall.
Bovet, Magalie
1974   "Cognitive Processes among Illiterate Children and Adults." In: *Culture and Cognition.* Edited by John Berry and Peter Dasen. London: Methuen.
Bruner, Jerome; Goodnow, Jacqueline; and Austin, George A.
1956   *A Study of Thinking.* New York: Science Editions, John Wiley.
Calame-Griaule, Geneviève
1968   Dictionnaire Dogon. Paris: Klincksieck.
Campbell, Donald T.
1964   "Distinguishing Differences of Perception from Failures to Communicate in Cross-Cultural Studies." In: *Crosscultural Understanding.* Edited by F. S. C. Northrop and Helen Livingstone. New York: Harper and Row.
1973   "Ostensive Instances and Entitativity in Language Learning." In: *Unity through Diversity. A Festschrift for Ludwig von Bertalanffy.* Edited by William Gray and Nicholas D. Rizzo. New York: Gordon and Breach.
1977   "Descriptive Epistemology: Psychological, Sociological and Evolutionary." William James Lecture, Harvard University.
1979   In: *On Going Beyond Kinship, Sex and the Tribe. Interviews With Contemporary Anthropologists in the U.S.A.* By Rik Pinxten. Ghent: Story.
Care, Norman and Landesman, Charles
1968   *Theory of Action.* Bloomington: Indiana University Press.
Carnap, Rudolf
1958   *Introduction to Symbolic Logic.* New York: Dover.
Chomsky, Noam
1968   *Language and Mind.* New York: Harcourt Brace.
Cole, Michael
1979   In: *On Going Beyond Kinship, Sex and the Tribe. Interviews With Contemporary Anthropologists in the U.S.A.* By Rik Pinxten. Ghent: Story.
Cole, Michael; Gay, John; Glick, Jay; and Sharp, Donald
1971   *The Cultural Context of Learning and Thinking.* London: Methuen.
Conklin, Harold C.
1972   *Folk Classification.* New Haven: Yale University Press.
1973   "Color Categorization." *American Anthropologist*, Vol. 75:913–42.

Dieterlen, Germaine
1950   "Les correspondances cosmo-biologiques chez les Soudanais." *Journal Psychologique Normale et Pathologique*, Vol. 3:350–66.
Douglas, Mary
1974   *Rules and Meanings*. London: Pelican.
Einstein, Albert
1949   "Einstein's Autobiography." In: *Albert Einstein: Philosopher-Scientist*. Edited by Paul A. Schilpp. London: Cambridge University Press.
Fabian, Johannes
1979   "Rule and Process: Thoughts on Ethnography as Communication." *Philosophy of Social Sciences*, Vol. 9:1–26.
Feather, Norman
1974   *Matter and Motion*. London: Penguin.
Fishman, Joshua
1979   In: *On Going Beyond Kinship, Sex and the Tribe. Interviews With Contemporary Anthropologists in the U.S.A.* By Rik Pinxten. Ghent: Story.
Gibson, James J.
1968   *The Senses Considered as Perceptual Systems*. London: Allen and Unwin.
Gladwin, Thomas
1973   *East is a Big Bird*. Cambridge, Mass.: Harvard University Press.
Goodenough, Ward H.
1970   *Description and Comparison in Cultural Anthropology*. Chicago: Aldine.
Goodman, Nelson
1968/1977   *The Structure of Appearance*. Boston Studies in Philosophy of Science. Dordrecht: Reidel.
Gould, Peter
1972   Mental Maps. In: *Man, Space and Environment*. Edited by Paul English and Robert Mayfield. Oxford: Oxford University Press.
Gould, Peter and White, Rodney
1974   *Mental Maps*. London: Penguin.
Granet, Marcel
1935   *La pensée chinoise*. Paris: A. Michel.
Graumann, Carl F.
1960   *Perspektivität*. Berlin: De Gruyter.
Greimas, Alisdir J.
1974   "Pour une sémiotique topologique." *Notes méthodologiques en architecture et en urbanisme*, Institut de l'Environnement, Vol. 3/4. Paris.
Griaule, Marcel
1938   *Masques Dogous*. Institut d'Ethnographie, Vol. 33. Paris.
Griaule, Marcel and Dieterlen, Germaine
1965   *Le Renard Pâle*. Paris: Institut d'Ethnographie.
Grunbaum, Adolf
1964   *Philosophical Problems of Space and Time*. London: Routledge and Kegan Paul.
Hall, Edward T.
1968   *The Hidden Dimension*. New York: Dell.
Halliday, Michael A. K.
1968   The Users and Uses of Language. In: *Readings in the Sociology of Language*. Edited by Joshua Fishman. The Hague: Mouton.

Hamlyn, David W.
1970   *Theory of Knowledge*. London: Cambridge University Press.
Harris, Marvin
1976   "History and Significance of the Emic/Etic Distinction." *Annual Review of Anthropology*, Vol. 12.
Howard, I. P. and Templeton, W.
1966   *Human Spatial Orientation*. New York: John Wiley.
Inhelder, Bärbel and Piaget, Jean
1966   *The Growth of Logical Thinking*. London: Routledge and Kegan Paul.
Ittelson, William H.
1968   *The Ames Demonstrations in Perception*. New York: Holt, Rinehart and Winston.
Kagame, Alexis
1956   *La philosophie bantoue-rwandaise de l'être*. Koninklÿke Academie van Koloniale Wetenschappen, Vol. 12. Brussels.
Katz, Jerrold J.
1972   *Semantic Theory*. New York: Harper and Row.
Kay, Paul
1979   In: *On Going Beyond Kinship, Sex and the Tribe. Interviews With Contemporary Anthropologists in the U.S.A.* By Rik Pinxten. Ghent: Story.
Kay, Paul and McDaniel, Chad
1978   "The Linguistic Significance of the Meaning of Basic Color Terms." *Language*, Vol. 54:610–46.
Kotarbinski, Tadeus
1964   *Leçons sur l'histoire de la logique*. Paris: PUF.
Kourilsky, Raoul and Grapin, Pierre
1968   *Main droite et main gauche. Norme et lateralité*. Paris: PUF.
Koyré, Alexandre
1957   *From the Closed World to the Infinite Universe*. London: Johns Hopkins University Press.
Kuhn, Thomas
1962   *The Structure of Scientific Revolutions*. Chicago: University of Chicago Press.
Lloyd, Barbara
1972   *Perception and Cognition. A Cross Cultural Perspective*. London: Penguin.
Long, Charles H.
1969   *Alpha. The Myths of Creation*. New York: Collier.
Lowenthal, David
1972   "Geography, Experience and Imagination: Towards a Geographical Epistemology." In: *Man, Space and Environment*. Edited by Paul English and Robert Mayfield. Oxford: Oxford University Press.
Lynch, Kevin
1960   *The Image of the City*. Cambridge, Mass.: MIT Press.
Minnaert, Marcel
1968   *De natuurkunde van het vrije veld*. Zutphen, Holland: Thieme.
Needham, Joseph
1956   *Science and Civilization in China*. London: Cambridge University Press.
Needham, Rodney
1974   *Right and Left*. Chicago: University of Chicago Press.
Newman, Stanley, ed.
1960   *The World of Mathematics*. New York: Simon and Schuster.

Panofsky, Erwin
1960   "Dürer as a Mathematician." In: *The World of Mathematics*. Edited by Stanley Newman. New York: Simon and Schuster.
Piaget, Jean and Inhelder, Bärbel
1947, 1972   *La construction de l'espace chez l'enfant*. Paris: PUF.
Pinxten, Rik
1972   "The Concept of 'Concept' in Cognitive Psychology." *Philosophica*, Vol. 9:15–33.
1975   "Bijdrage tot een studie van het wereldbeeld van de mens." Ph.D. dissertation, Rijksuniversiteit-Gent, Ghent, Belgium.
1976a   "Epistemic Universals: A Contribution to Cognitive Anthropology." In: *Universalism versus Relativism in Language and Thought*. Edited by Rik Pinxten. The Hague: Mouton.
1976b   *Universalism versus Relativism in Language and Thought*. The Hague: Mouton.
1977   "Descriptive Semantics and Cognitive Anthropology: In Search for a New Model." In: "Semantics." Edited by Fernand Vandamme and Rik Pinxten. *Communication and Cognition*, Vol. 10:89–106. Ghent.
1979a   *On Going Beyond Kinship, Sex and the Tribe. Interviews with Contemporary Anthropologists in the U.S.A*. Ghent: Story.
forthcoming   *Space in Social Sciences. The Universal Frame of Reference for Spatial Analysis*. Ghent: Communication and Cognition Books, Publishers.
Pinxten, Rik and Bernabé, Jean, eds.
1974   "Diversification within Cognitive Anthropology." *Communication and Cognition*, Vol. 7:289–478. Ghent.
Plato   *The State*. Encyclopedia Britannica Philosophical Library.
Pribram, Karl
1971   *Languages of the Brain; Experimental Paradoxes and Principles in Neuropsychology*. Englewood Cliffs: Prentice-Hall.
Quine, Willard V. O.
1960   *Word and Object*. Cambridge, Mass.: MIT Press.
1969   *Ontological Relativity and Other Essays*. New York: Columbia University Press.
Radin, Paul
1957   *Primitive Man as Philosopher*. New York: Dover.
Raven, Peter H.; Breedlove, Donald; and Berlin, Brent
1971   "The Origins of Taxonomy." *Science*, Vol. 171:1210–13.
Reichenbach, Hans
1958   *The Philosophy of Space and Time*. New York: Dover.
Rosh, Ruth
1974   "Spatial Analysis." In: *Cognition and the Symbolic Processes*. Edited by Walter Weimer and David Palermo. Hillsdale, N.J.: LEA Press.
Rucker, R. V. B.
1977   *Geometry, Relativity and the Fourth Dimension*. New York: Dover.
Russell, Bertrand
1914   *Our Knowledge of the External World*. London: Allen and Unwin.
1921   *The Analysis of Mind*. London: Allen and Unwin.
Schaff, Adam
1976   "Generative Grammar and the Concept of Innate Ideas." In: *Universalism ver-*

sus Relativism in Language and Thought. Edited by Rik Pinxten. The Hague: Mouton.

Sauvy, J. and Sauvy, S.
1972   *L'enfant à la découverte de l'espace*. Paris: Casterman.

Segall, Marshal; Campbell, Donald; and Herskovits, Melvin
1966   *The Influence of Culture on Visual Perception: An Advanced Study in Psychology and Anthropology*. Indianapolis: Bobbs-Merrill.

Smart, John J.
1964   *Problems in Space and Time*. New York: Macmillan.

Speiregen, Peter
1965   *Urban Design*. New York: McGraw-Hill.

Stea, David
1970   "Space, Territory and Human Movements." In: *Environmental Psychology: Man in His Physical Setting*. Edited by Harold Proshansky, William Ittelson, and Leanne Rivlin. New York: Holt, Rinehart and Winston.

Swinburne, Richard.
1968   *Space and Time*. New York: Macmillan.

Tan, R. Y. D.
1967   "The Domestic Architecture of South Bali." *Bijdragen tot Land-, Taal- en Volkenkunde*, Vol. 123:442–75.

Tarski, Alfred
1956   "Foundations of the Geometry of Solids." In: *Logic, Semantics and Metamathematics*. By Alfred Tarski. Oxford: Clarendon.

Thom, René
1977   *Stabilité structurelle et morphogénèse*. Paris: Interéditions.

Vandamme, Fernand
1977   "Register Semantics." In: "Semantics." Edited by Fernand Vandamme and Rik Pinxten. *Communication and Cognition*, Vol. 10:1–221. Ghent.

Vandamme, Fernand and Pinxten, Rik, eds.
1977   "Semantics." *Communication and Cognition*, Vol. 10:1–221. Ghent.

Vernon, M. D.
1970   *A Further Study of Visual Perception*. Cambridge, England: Cambridge University Press.

von Senden, M.
1960   *Space and Sight*. London: Methuen.

von Wright, Heinrich
1963   "The Logic of Action. A Sketch." In: *Topics in Philosophical Logic*. Edited by Nicolas Rescher. Dordrecht: Reidel.

Waddington, Conrad H.
1977   *Tools for Thought*. St. Albans, England: Paladin.

Weimer, Walter and Palermo, David, eds.
1974   *Cognition and the Symbolic Processes*. Hillsdale, N.J.: LEA Press.

Werner, Oswald
1974   "Intermediate Memory: A Central Explanatory Concept for Ethnoscience." In: "Diversification within Cognitive Anthropology." Edited by Rik Pinxten and Jean Bernabé. *Communication and Cognition*, Vol. 7:281–314. Ghent.
1977   "The Synthetic Informant Model: On the Simulation of Large Lexical/ Semantic Fields." In: *Language and Thought*. Edited by William McCormack and Stephen Wurm. Anthropological Issues. The Hague: Mouton.

1979   In: *On Going Beyond Kinship, Sex and the Tribe. Interviews with Contemporary Anthropologists in the U.S.A.* By Rik Pinxten. Ghent: Story.

Werner, Oswald and Fenton, Joan
1973   "Method and Theory in Ethnoscience." In: *Handbook of Method in Cultural Anthropology.* Edited by Raoul Naroll and Ronald Cohen. New York: Columbia University Press.

Werner, Oswald; Hagedorn, W.; Roth, G.; Schepers, E.; and Uriarte, L.
1974   "Some New Developments in Ethnosemantics and the Theory and Practice of Lexical/Semantic Fields." In: *Current Trends in Linguistics*, Vol. 12. Edited by Thomas A. Sebeok. The Hague: Mouton.

Whitehead, Alfred North
1919   *An Enquiry Concerning the Principles of Natural Knowledge.* Cambridge, England: Cambridge University Press.
1920   *The Concept of Nature.* Cambridge, England: Cambridge University Press.
1953   "On Mathematical Concepts of the Material World." In: *Alfred N. Whitehead; An Anthology.* Edited by F. S. C. Northrop and Hyman Gross. Cambridge, England: Cambridge University Press.

Whorf, Benjamin Lee
1950   "An American Indian Model of the Universe." *International Journal of American Linguistics*, Vol. 16:67–72. Also in: *Language, Thought, and Reality. Selected Writings of Benjamin Lee Whorf.* Edited by John B. Carroll. Cambridge: MIT Press, 1956.
1956   *Language, Thought, and Reality. Selected Writings of Benjamin Lee Whorf.* Edited by John B. Carroll. Cambridge, Mass.: MIT Press.

Zusne, Leonard
1970   *Visual Perception of Form.* New York: Academic Press.

Index of Names

Subject Index